The Rev. S.C. Malan, D.D.

The Book of Adam and Eve

The Rev. S.C. Malan, D.D.

The Book of Adam and Eve

ISBN/EAN: 9783741133671

Manufactured in Europe, USA, Canada, Australia, Japa

Cover: Foto ©Andreas Hilbeck / pixelio.de

Manufactured and distributed by brebook publishing software (www.brebook.com)

The Rev. S.C. Malan, D.D.

The Book of Adam and Eve

THE BOOK OF ADAM AND EVE,

ALSO CALLED

THE CONFLICT OF ADAM AND EVE WITH SATAN,

A Book of the early Eastern Church,
Translated from the Ethiopic,

WITH NOTES FROM THE KUFALE, TALMUD, MIDRASHIM, AND OTHER EASTERN WORKS,

BY

THE REV. S. C. MALAN, D.D.,
VICAR OF BROADWINDSOR.

WILLIAMS AND NORGATE,
14, HENRIETTA STREET, COVENT GARDEN, LONDON;
AND 20, SOUTH FREDERICK STREET, EDINBURGH.

1882.

To

THE REV. DR. ERNEST TRUMPP,

REGIUS PROFESSOR OF ORIENTAL LANGUAGES AND LITERATURE IN THE
UNIVERSITY OF MUNICH, AND ORDINARY MEMBER OF THE ROYAL
BAVARIAN ACADEMY OF SCIENCES,

In token of respect for his accurate and profound Oriental scholarship,

from the Translator.

PREFACE.

In the Sixth Book of the Apostolic Constitutions,* we find a severe censure of certain early works, among which are reckoned βιβλία ἀπόκρυφα Μωσέως καὶ Ἐνὼχ, καὶ Ἀδὰμ, Ἡσαίου τε καὶ Δαβίδ κ. τ. λ. "The apocryphal Books of Moses, of Enoch, of Adam, as well as those of Isaiah and David," etc. Those works, however, do not deserve all that the Apostles are made to say of them.

The apocryphal "Book of Moses," there alluded to, is probably the λεπτὴ Γένεσις or "lesser Genesis," known as having existed of old in Greek, under that name; and also under that of Ἀποκάλυψις M., or τὰ Ἰουβηλαῖα "the Apocalypse of Moses," or "the Book of Jubilees," quoted by S. Epiphanius,† Geo. Syncellus,‡ Geo. Cedrenus,§ and others. Of those three titles, τὰ Ἰουβηλαῖα remained little understood, until Dr. Dillmann published in 1859, the Ethiopic *Kufale*, or "Liber Jubilæorum;" so named by him, because throughout the book, said to have been revealed to Moses by "the Angel of the Face," or Michael—the division of periods of time is by jubilees of forty-nine—fifty years. The Kufale is often quoted in the notes to this book.

* Ch. xvi, ed. Cotel.   † *Hæres.*, xxxix, 6.
‡ *Chronogr.*, vol. i, p. 7, ed. D.   § *Hist. Comp.*, vol. i, p. 9.

As to the "Book of Enoch," it was known only through a quotation from it by S. Jude v. 14, 15; and after him, from allusions to it by S. Hilarius, S. Clement of Alexandria, Origen, Geo. Syncellus, and others—until it was discovered in Abyssinia by Bruce, who brought several Ethiopic copies of it from thence to Europe; one of which is now in the Bodleian Library. This was published and also translated by Archbishop Lawrence, in 1838. A later and more accurate edition of it was issued by Dr. Dillmann at Leipzig, in 1851, from several MSS. brought from Abyssinia since the days of Bruce; and it has been translated more than once within the last few years. It is highly interesting, as a work of the probable date of its composition—not long before or after the coming of Christ. It is often quoted in the following pages.

As to the "Book of Adam," mentioned in the passage above given from the Apostolic Constitutions, if it is not the *Sidra l'Adam*, also called "the Book of Adam," of the Mandæans, it may be Βίος 'Αδάμ, "the Life of Adam," alluded to by Geo. Syncellus,* as distinct from the λεπτὴ Γένεσις. It is also said to exist in Syriac and in Arabic, in the Vatican Library; and "Vita Adæ et Evæ" has lately been worked out of the 'Αποκάλυψις 'Αδάμ, and of other documents in Latin, by Dr. W. Meyer, of the Academy of Munich, and published there in 1879.

Lastly, by the apocryphal "Book of Isaiah," is probably meant his "Ascension," only known in Ethiopic; and published in Ethiopic and in English, by Archbishop Lawrence, at Oxford, in 1819. It dates, probably, from the early days of the Church, and is mentioned by Origen and by S. Epiphanius,† as τὸ ἀναβατικὸν 'Ησαίου. It alludes, among other things, to the martyrdom of Isaiah, who was sawn asunder by order of Manasseh.

The present interesting work, however, has little in common with those apocrypha; among which it has no right to take

---

* *Chron.*, vol. i, p. 7.   † *Hæres.*, xl, 2; lxvii, 3.

place. Whereas they all are apparently of Jewish origin, this "Conflict of Adam" is altogether a Christian work, and of a later date than those writings. It is probably the work of some pious and orthodox Egyptian of the fifth or sixth century, who tells his story, or stories—some of which are also found in the Talmud and thence in the Coran and elsewhere—as they were then believed; adding here and there a good deal of his own. Yet all is told in the simple—to Western taste, perhaps, childish—style of pious Eastern writers of those days. The author's devout faith runs throughout his narrative; he seems willing and ready to believe much rather than to doubt; to take things for granted, rather than to question the truth of them.

His object then, is to connect the first Adam with the coming of the second, Christ; five thousand five hundred years* after Adam's fall in Eden, and in fulfilment of the promise then made him of a Saviour. In our author's words, Adam holds frequent intercourse with "the Word of God," who tells him of His coming in the flesh in order to save him; a promise Adam charges his children to remember and to hand down to their own children. Then, when dead, his body is embalmed, and laid in the Cave of Treasures, where he and Eve had spent their life; it is thence taken by Noah, with the gold, the incense and the myrrh brought from Eden, and laid in the ark; whence it is taken out by Melchizedec after the Flood; and brought by him, together with Shem and an angel sent to show them the way, to "the Middle of the Earth;" ὀμφαλὸς τῆς γῆς, to the hill "Cranium," or Golgotha. There, the rock opens of its own accord to receive the body of Adam, and then closes in again. It is the very spot on which the Saviour's cross was raised, when He was crucified.

This book, now first translated into English, and that tells much that will be new to most readers—was probably written in Arabic in Egypt; whence it was taken farther south, and

* According to the LXX.

translated into Ethiopic. At all events no Greek or Egyptian original of it, is, as yet, known to exist; neither does it betray the least vestige of Hellenism. There is, indeed, a Syriac work of the early Church, called *M'ārath gāze*, "the Cave of Treasures" mentioned by Asseman,* and ascribed to S. Ephrem by the presbyter Simeon,† who lived in the thirteenth century. Judging from its title, it may have much in common with the present work; yet in the absence of all knowledge of that Syriac MS., one can, for the present, only look upon the Arabic copy, written in Egypt, as the probable original. For the Ethiopic version, although written in good style, bears unmistakable marks of an Arabic origin.

It is, of course, as yet impossible to fix with certainty the date of either the Arabic original, or of the Ethiopic translation. Dr. Dillmann, in the preface to his German translation, seems to think this "Conflict of Adam" may date from the fifth or sixth century; and there does not seem to be any good reason for thinking otherwise. It is, however, certain that it must have been written before the ninth century; judging from the numerous extracts from it, given word for word, by Saîd Ibn-Batrik, or Eutychus, physician, and also Melkite Patriarch, who lived in the ninth century; when he wrote his *Nazam al-jawāhir*, or "String of Gems" as he called his "Annals of the World," from the creation to his own time. It is a work of merit; although, perhaps, too full of stories that cannot be received as authentic.

The present translation was made on the accurate and scholarly Ethiopic edition lately published by the great orientalist Dr. E. Trumpp, Professor at the University of Munich. He had the advantage of the Arabic original which he frequently quotes in his valuable notes, of which I have often availed myself; an advantage the "magnus Apollo," in Ethiopic lore, Dr. Dillmann, does not seem to have had,

---

* *Bibl. Or.*, vol. iii, p. 281, and vol. ii, p. 498.
† *Ib.*, vol. iii, p. 563

PREFACE. vii

for comparison with the more or less imperfect MSS. on which he made his German translation in 1853.

As the Ethiopic text is irregularly divided in sections,—some of great length, owing to the subject in hand,—I thought more convenient to divide my translation into Books, and chapters, some of which have the same headings as those given in the text.

Book I—takes in the whole life of Adam and Eve, from the day they left Eden; their dwelling in the Cave of Treasures; their trials and temptations; Satan's manifold apparitions to them, and the Word of God coming to comfort and help them. Then the birth of Cain, of Abel, and of their twin sisters; Cain's love for his own twin sister, Luluwa, whom Adam and Eve wished to join to Abel; hence Cain's hatred and murder of his brother; and Adam's sorrow and death.

Book II—gives the history of the patriarchs who lived before the Flood; the dwelling of the children of Seth on the Holy Mountain—Mount Hermon—until they were lured by Genun and by the daughters of Cain, to come down from the mountain; and as "fallen angels," to lose God's love for them. Then Cain's death, when slain by Lamech the blind; and the lives of the other patriarchs, until the birth of Noah.

Book III—gives the history of the building of the ark; of the Flood, of the settlement of Noah and his family; and of the carrying of the body of Adam to " the Middle of the Earth ;" the growth of idolatry under Nimrud; the destruction of idols; and the call of Abraham.

Book IV—gives a short history of the patriarchs, judges and kings, from Abraham to the coming of Christ.

The first three Books are by far the most interesting.

The fourth professes to give genealogies that were irretrievably lost; yet somehow, discovered and given in detail by the author. Most of the names are of pure Ethiopic origin, and others are so disfigured as not to be recognized. I have, therefore, given them unaltered; as they cannot be of any great moment.

I have only to add that although frequently obliged to translate freely sundry passages unfit for a more accurate rendering, I have yet kept as much as I could to the style of the original, as best in a work of this kind. I have also added a few notes from the Talmud, Midrashim and other Eastern writings, placed at the end of the volume, and numbered, to which reference is made in the text—in order either to illustrate the matter in hand, or to supply details of particular interest.

S. C. MALAN.

THE VICARAGE, BROADWINDSOR,
  July 12*th*, 1882.

THE BOOK OF ADAM AND EVE,

ALSO CALLED

THE CONFLICT OF ADAM AND EVE WITH SATAN.

BOOK I.

In the name of the Father, and of the Son, and of the Holy Ghost: One God.

We begin, with the help of God, to whom be glory, the writing of the Conflict of Adam and Eve, that befell them after they had come out of the garden, and while they dwelt in the Cave of Treasures, by command of God the Creator.*

CHAPTER I.

On the third day,† God planted¹ the garden² in the east of the earth, on the border of the world³ eastward, beyond which, towards the sun-rising, one finds nothing but water, that encompasses the whole world, and reaches unto the borders of heaven.⁴‡

And to the north [of the garden] there is a sea of water, clear and pure to the taste, like unto nothing else; so that,

---

* The Ethiopic translator adds here—" their Creator and Ruler, to Him by name, the living God, endowed with reason and speech, Creator of all creatures —be glory."

† Of the week, *Beresh. Rab.*, sect. i, fol. 18.

‡ For the most learned work as yet published on the probable site of Eden, see *Wo lag das Paradies?* of Dr. F. Delitzsch, 1881.

through the clearness thereof, one may look into the depths of the earth.* And when a man washes himself in it, he becomes clean of the cleanness thereof, and white of its whiteness—even if he were dark.†

And God created that sea of His own good pleasure,‡ for He knew what would come of the man He should make; so that after he had left the garden, on account of his transgression,[5] men should be born in the earth, from among whom righteous ones should die, whose souls God would raise at the last day; when they should return to their flesh; should bathe in the water of that sea, and all of them repent of [their] sins.

But when God made Adam go out of the garden,[6] He did not place him on the border of it northward, lest he should draw near to the sea of water, and he and Eve wash themselves in it, be cleansed from their sins, forget the transgression they had committed, and be no longer reminded of it in the thought§ of their punishment.

Then, again, as to the southern side [of the garden], God was not pleased to let Adam dwell there; because, when the wind blew from the north, it would bring him, on that southern side, the delicious smell of the trees of the garden. Wherefore God did not put Adam there, lest he should smell the sweet smell of [those] trees,[7] forget his transgression, and find consolation for what he had done, take delight in the smell of the trees, and not be cleansed from his transgression.[8]

Again, also, because God is merciful and of great pity, and governs all things in a way He alone knows—He made our father Adam dwell in the western border of the garden, because on that side the earth is very broad.[9] And God commanded him to dwell there in a cave in a rock—the Cave of Treasures below the garden.[10]

---

* Lit. world.   † Or, black.
‡ Or, "with a deliberate plan or purpose of His own." Arab.
§ Lit. sound or echo.

CHAPTER II.

But when our father Adam, and Eve, went out of the garden,[11] they trod [the ground] on their feet, not knowing they were treading.

And when they came to the opening of the gate of the garden, and saw the broad earth spread before them, [covered] with stones large and small, and with sand, they feared and trembled, and fell on their faces, from the fear that came upon them; and they were as dead.

Because—whereas they had hitherto been in the garden-land, beautiful [ly planted] with all manner of trees—they now saw themselves, in a strange land, which they knew not, and had never seen.[12]

[And] because at that time they were filled with the grace of a bright nature,[13] and they had not hearts [turned] towards earth [ly things].

Therefore had God pity on them; and when He saw them fallen before the gate of the garden, He sent His Word* unto father Adam and Eve, and raised them from their fallen state.†

CHAPTER III.

Concerning the promise‡ of the great five days and a half.

God said to Adam, "I have ordained on this earth days and years, and thou and thy seed shall dwell and walk in it, until the days and years are fulfilled; when I shall send the Word that created thee, and against which thou hast transgressed,

---

* By "the Word of God" throughout this book, is to be understood in general, the second person of the most Holy Trinity, ὁ λόγος (S. John i.) מימרא דיי or מימרא of the Targums and Talmuds also; as abundantly shown in the book *Yezirah* (ed. Amst. 1642, p. 84, 89).

† Lit. their fall. ‡ Or, covenant.

the Word that made thee come out of the garden, and that raised thee when thou wast fallen. Yea, the Word that will again save thee when the five days and a half are fulfilled."*

But when Adam heard these words from God, and [of] the great five days and a half, he did not understand the meaning of them.

For Adam was thinking that there would be but five days and a half for him, to the end of the world.

And Adam wept, and prayed God to explain it to him.

Then God in His mercy for Adam [who was made after] His own image and similitude, explained to him, that these were 5000 and 500 years; and how One would then come and save him and his seed.[14]

But God had before that made this covenant with our father,† Adam, in the same terms, ere he came out of the garden, [when he was] by the tree whereof Eve took [the fruit] and gave it him to eat.

Inasmuch as, when our father Adam came out of the garden, he passed by‡ that tree, and saw how God had then changed the appearance of it into another form, and how it withered.

And as Adam went to it he feared, trembled and fell down; but God in His mercy lifted him up, and then made this covenant with him.§

And, again, when Adam was by the gate of the garden, and saw the cherub with a sword of flashing fire in his hand, and the cherub grew angry and frowned at him, both Adam and Eve became afraid of him, and thought he meant to put them to death. So they fell on their faces, and trembled with fear.

But he had pity on them, and showed them mercy; and turning [from them] went up to heaven, and prayed unto the Lord, and said:—

---

* According to *Cod. Nasar. III*, p. 69, this world is to last from the creation of Adam, 480,000 years. † Or, made this promise to.
‡ Or, went away from. § Or, made him this promise.

"Lord, Thou didst send me to watch at the gate of the garden, with a sword of fire.

"But when Thy servants, Adam and Eve, saw me, they fell on their faces, and were as dead. O my Lord, what shall we do to Thy servants?"

Then God had pity on them, and showed them mercy, and sent His Angel to keep the garden.

And the Word of the Lord came unto Adam and Eve, and raised them up.

And the Lord said to Adam, "I told thee that at the end of five days and a half, I will send my Word and save thee.

"Strengthen thy heart, therefore, and abide in the Cave of Treasures, of which I have before spoken to thee."

And when Adam heard this Word from God, he was comforted with that which God had told him. For He had told him how He would save him.

CHAPTER IV.

But Adam and Eve wept for having come out of the garden, their first abode.

And, indeed, when Adam looked at his flesh,* that was altered, he wept bitterly, he and Eve, over what they had done. And they walked and went gently down into the Cave of Treasures.

And as they came to it Adam wept over himself and said to Eve, "Look at this cave that is to be our prison in this world, and a place of punishment!

"What is it compared with the garden? What is its narrowness compared with the space† of the other?

"What is this rock, by the side of those groves? What is the gloom of this cavern, compared with the light of the garden?

* Or, body, and so throughout.   † Or, room, breadth.

"What is this overhanging ledge of rock to shelter us, compared with the mercy of the Lord that overshadowed us ?

"What is the soil of this cave compared with the garden-land ? This earth, strewed with stones; and that, planted with delicious fruit-trees ?"

And Adam said to Eve, "Look at thine eyes, and at mine, which afore beheld angels in heaven, praising; and they, too, without ceasing.

"But now we do not see as we did : our eyes have become of flesh ; they cannot see in like manner as they saw before."

Adam said again to Eve, "What is our body to-day, [compared] to what it was in former days, when we dwelt in the garden ?"

After this Adam did not like to enter the cave, under the overhanging rock; nor would he ever have entered it.

But he bowed to God's orders; and said to himself, "unless I enter the cave, I shall again be a transgressor."

CHAPTER V.

Then Adam and Eve entered the cave, and stood praying,[15] in their own tongue, unknown to us, but which they knew well.

And as they prayed, Adam raised his eyes, and saw the rock and the roof of the cave that covered [him] overhead, so that he could see neither heaven, nor God's creatures. So he wept and smote heavily upon his breast, until he dropped, and was as dead.

And Eve sat weeping; for she believed he was dead.

Then she arose, spread her hands towards God, suing Him for mercy and pity, and said, "O God, forgive me my sin, [the sin] which I committed, and remember it not against me.

"For I alone[16] caused Thy servant to fall from the garden into this lost estate;* from light into this darkness; and from the abode of joy into this prison.

"O God, look upon this Thy servant thus fallen,† and raise him from his death, that he may weep and repent of his transgression which he committed through me.

"Take not away his soul this once; but let him [live] that he may stand after the measure of his repentance, and do Thy will, as before his death.

"But if Thou do not raise him up, then, O God, take away my own soul, [that I be] like him; and leave me not in this dungeon, one and alone; for I could not stand alone in this world, but with him [only].

"For Thou, O God, didst cause a slumber to come upon him, and didst take a bone from his side,[17] and didst restore the flesh in the place of it, by Thy divine power.

"And Thou didst take me, the bone, and make me a woman, bright like him, with heart, reason, and speech;‡ and in flesh, like unto his own; and Thou didst make me after the likeness of his countenance, by Thy mercy and power.

"O Lord, I and he are one, and Thou, O God, art our Creator, Thou art [He] who made us both in one day.[18]

"Therefore, O God, give him life, that he may be with me in this strange land, while we dwell in it on account of our trangression.

"But if Thou wilt not give him life, then take me, even me, like him; that we both may die the same day."§

And Eve wept bitterly, and fell upon our father Adam; from her great sorrow.

CHAPTER VI.

But God looked upon them; for they had killed themselves through great grief.

---

* Lit. extinction, destruction. † Or, cast down.
‡ *Kufale*, p. 11, 12. § Lit. with a fervent heart.

But He would raise them and comfort them.

He, therefore, sent His Word unto them; that they should stand and be raised forthwith.

And the Lord said unto Adam and Eve, "You transgressed of your own free will, until you came out of the garden in which I had placed you. Of your own free will have you transgressed[19] through your desire for divinity, greatness, and an exalted state, such as I have; so that I deprived you of the bright nature in which you then were, and I made you come out of the garden to this land, rough and full of trouble.

"If only you had not transgressed My commandment and had kept My law, and had not eaten of the [fruit of the] tree, near which I told you not to come! And there were fruit trees in the garden better than that one.

"But the wicked Satan[20] who continued not in his first estate, nor kept his faith; in whom was no good [intent] towards Me, [and who] though I had created him, yet set Me at naught, and sought the Godhead, so that I hurled him down from heaven,—he it is who made the tree* appear pleasant in your eyes, until you ate of it, by hearkening to him.[21]

"Thus have you transgressed My commandment, and therefore have I brought upon you all these sorrows.[22]

"For I am God the Creator, who, when I created My creatures, did not intend to destroy them. But after they had sorely roused My anger, I punished them with grievous plagues, until they repent.

"But, if on the contrary, they still continue hardened in their transgression,† they shall be under a curse for ever."

CHAPTER VII.

When Adam and Eve heard these words from God, they wept and sobbed yet more; but they strengthened their hearts

---

* Whose fruit was either grapes, apple of Paradise, or figs. *Beresh. Rab.*, sect, xiv, fol. 18.

† Lit. are in debt of it.

in God, because they now felt that the Lord was to them like a father and a mother; and for this very reason, they wept before Him, and sought mercy from Him.

Then God had pity on them, and said: "O Adam, I have made My covenant with thee,* and I will not turn from it; neither will I let thee return to the garden, until My covenant of the great five days and a half is fulfilled."

Then Adam said unto God, "O Lord, Thou didst create us, and make us [fit] to be in the garden; and before I transgressed, Thou madest all beasts come to me, that I should name them.

"Thy grace was then on me; and I named every one according to Thy mind; and Thou madest them all subject unto me.[23]

"But now, O Lord God, that I have transgressed Thy commandment, all beasts will rise against me and will devour me, and Eve Thy handmaid; and will cut off our life from the face of the earth.

"I therefore beseech Thee, O God, that, since Thou hast made us come out of the garden, and hast made us be in a strange land, Thou wilt not let the beasts hurt us."

When the Lord heard these words from Adam, He had pity on him, and felt that he had truly said that the beasts [of the field] would rise and devour him and Eve, because He, the Lord, was angry with them [two] on account of their transgression.

Then God commanded the beasts, and the birds, and all that moves upon the earth, to come to Adam and to be familiar with him,† and not to trouble him and Eve; nor yet any of the good and righteous among their posterity.

Then the beasts did obeisance to Adam, according to the commandment of God; except the serpent, against which God was wroth. It did not come to Adam, with the beasts.‡

* Or, I made thee a promise.
† Or, do obeisance to him; or to submit to him.
‡ Another reading is that God did not bring the serpent, or forbade it to come, with the other beasts, because He was angry with it.

CHAPTER VIII.

Then Adam wept and said, "[O] God, when we dwelt in the garden, and our hearts were lifted up, we saw the angels that sang praises in heaven, but now we do not see as we were used to do;[24] nay, when we entered the cave, all creation became hidden from us."

Then God the Lord said unto Adam, "When thou wast under subjection [to Me], thou hadst a bright nature within thee,[25] and for that reason couldst thou see things afar off. But after thy transgression thy bright nature was withdrawn from thee; and it was not left to thee to see things afar off, but only near at hand; after the ability of the flesh; for it is brutish."

When Adam and Eve had heard these words from God, they went their way; praising and worshipping Him with a sorrowful heart.

And God ceased to commune with them.

CHAPTER IX.

Then Adam and Eve came out of the Cave of Treasures, and drew near to the garden gate, and there they stood to look at it, and wept for having come away from it. And Adam and Eve went from before the gate of the garden to the southern side of it, and found there the water that watered the garden, from the root of the Tree of Life, and that parted itself from thence into four rivers over the earth.*

Then they came and drew near to that water, and looked at it; and saw† that it was the water that came forth from under the root of the Tree of Life in the garden. And Adam wept and wailed, and smote upon his breast, for being severed from the garden; and said to Eve:—

---

* *Beresh. Rab.*, sect. xvi, fol. 18, 19; and *More Nevukim*, sect. ii, ch. 30.
† Lit. knew.

"Why hast thou brought upon me, upon thyself, and upon our seed, so [many] of [these] plagues and punishments?"

And Eve said unto him, "What is it thou hast seen, to weep and to speak to me in this wise?"

And he said to Eve, "Seest thou not this water that was with us in the garden, that watered the trees of the garden, and flowed out [thence]?

"And we, when we were in the garden, did not care about it;* but since we came to this strange land, we love it, and turn it to use for our body."

But when Eve heard these words from him, she wept; and from the soreness of their weeping, they fell into that water; and would have put an end to themselves in it, so as never again to return and behold the creation; for when they looked upon the work of creation, they [felt they must] put an end to themselves.†

CHAPTER X.

Then God, merciful and gracious, looked upon them thus lying in the water, and nigh unto death, and sent an angel, who brought them out of the water, and laid them on the sea-shore as dead.

Then the angel went up to God, was welcome, and said, "[O] God, Thy creatures have breathed their last."

Then God sent His Word unto Adam and Eve, who raised them from [their] death.

And Adam said, after he was raised, "O God, while we were in the garden we did not [require, or] care for this water;‡ but since we came to this land we cannot do without it.

---

* It is said that " he that increaseth knowledge increaseth sorrow " (Eccl. i. 18). So did Adam increase his sorrow when he increased his knowledge. *Bereah. Rab.*, sect. xix, fol. 20.

† *i.e.*, from sorrow at having left the garden so much more heavenly and more beautiful.

‡ The Ethiopic translator added : " For Thy mercy was with us; we needed not this water."

Then God said to Adam, "While thou wast under My command and wast a bright angel, thou knewest not this water.*

"But after that thou hast transgressed My commandment, thou canst not do without water, wherein to wash thy body and make it grow; for it is now like [that of] beasts, and is in want of water."

When Adam and Eve heard these words from God, they wept a bitter cry; and Adam entreated God to let him return into the garden, and look at it a second time.

But God said unto Adam, "I have made thee a promise;† when that promise is fulfilled, I will bring thee back into the garden, thee and thy righteous seed."

And God ceased to commune with Adam.

CHAPTER XI.

Then Adam and Eve felt themselves burning with thirst, and heat, and sorrow.

And Adam said to Eve, "We shall not drink of this water, even if we were to die. O Eve, when this water comes into our inner parts, it will increase our punishments and that of our children, that shall come after us."

Both Adam and Eve then withdrew from the water, and drank none of it at all; but came and entered the Cave of Treasures.

But [when in it] Adam could not see Eve; he only heard the noise she made. Neither could she see Adam, but heard the noise he made.

---

* Διετέλουν ὡς ἄσαρκοι, σαρκικῆς διαθέσεως οὔπω καιρὸν ἔχοντες. Cedren. H. Comp., p. 14.

† Also: "I have bound thee to Me in a covenant; when that covenant is fulfilled—."

Then Adam wept, in deep affliction, and smote upon his breast; and he arose and said to Eve, "Where art thou?"

And she said unto him, "Lo, I am standing in this darkness."

He then said to her, "Remember the bright nature in which we lived, while we abode in the garden!"

"O Eve! remember the glory* that rested on us in the garden.[26] O Eve! remember the trees that overshadowed us in the garden while we [moved] among them.

"O Eve! remember that while we were in the garden, we knew neither night nor day. Think of the Tree of Life,† from below which flowed the water, and that shed lustre over us! Remember, O Eve, the garden-land, and the brightness thereof!

"Think, oh think of that garden in which was no darkness, while we dwelt therein.

"Whereas no sooner did we come into this Cave of Treasures than darkness compassed us round about; until we can no longer see each other; and all the pleasure of this life has come to an end."

CHAPTER XII.

Then Adam smote upon his breast, he and Eve, and they mourned the whole night until dawn drew near, and they sighed over the length of the night in Miyazia.‡

And Adam beat himself, and threw himself on the ground in the cave, from bitter grief, and because of the darkness, and lay there as dead.

But Eve heard the noise he made in falling upon the earth. And she felt about for him with her hands, and found him like a corpse.

Then she was afraid, speechless, and remained by him.

---

* Or, grace, favour. Arab.

† "Whose height was מהלך חמש מאה שנין a walk of 500 years."— *Targ. Jonathan*, in Gen. iii.

‡ May.

But the merciful Lord looked on the death of Adam, and on Eve's silence from fear of the darkness.

And the Word of God came unto Adam and raised him from his death, and opened Eve's mouth that she might speak.

Then Adam arose in the cave and said, "O God, wherefore has light departed from us, and darkness come over us? Wherefore dost Thou leave us in [this] long darkness? Why wilt Thou plague us thus?

"And this darkness, O Lord, where was it ere it came upon us? It is such, that we cannot see each other.

"For, so long as we were in the garden, we neither saw nor even knew [what] darkness [is]. I was not hidden from Eve, neither was she [hidden] from me, until [now that] she cannot see me; and no darkness came upon us, to separate us from each other.

"But she and I were both in one bright light. I saw her and she saw me. Yet now since we came into this cave, darkness has come upon us, and parted us asunder, so that I do not see her, and she does not see me.

"O Lord,* wilt Thou then plague us with this darkness?"

CHAPTER XIII.

Then when God, who is merciful and full of pity, heard Adam's voice, He said unto him:—

"O Adam, so long as the good angel was obedient to Me, a bright light rested on him and on his hosts.

"But when he transgressed My commandment, I deprived him of that bright nature, and he became dark.

"And when he was in the heavens, in the realms of light, he knew naught of darkness.

---

* Arab. adds: "but now be gracious unto us."

"But he transgressed, and I made him fall from heaven upon the earth; and it was this darkness that came upon him.*

"And on thee, O Adam, while in My garden and obedient to Me, did that bright light rest also.

"But when I heard of thy transgression,† I deprived thee of that bright light. Yet, of My mercy, I did not turn thee into darkness, but I made thee thy body of flesh, over which I spread this skin, in order that it may bear cold and heat.‡

"If I had let My wrath fall heavily upon thee, I should have destroyed thee; and had I turned thee into darkness, it would have been as if I killed thee.

"But in My mercy, I have made thee as thou art; when thou didst transgress My commandment, O Adam, I drove thee from the garden, and made thee come forth into this land; and commanded thee to dwell in this cave; and darkness came upon thee, as it did upon him who transgressed My commandment.

"Thus, O Adam, has this night deceived thee. It is not to last for ever; but is only of twelve hours; when it is over, daylight will return.

"Sigh not, therefore, neither be moved; and say not in thy heart that this darkness is long and drags on wearily; and say not in thy heart that I plague thee with it.

"Strengthen thy heart, and be not afraid. This darkness is not a punishment. But, O Adam, I have made the day, and have placed the sun in it to give light; in order that thou and thy children should do your work.

"For I knew thou shouldest sin and transgress, and come out into this land. Yet would I not [force thee, nor] be hard upon thee, nor shut thee up; nor doom thee through thy fall;§

---

* Arab. "upon them all together," *i.e.*, Satan and his hosts.
† Arab. reads: "but when thou didst transgress against me," omitting "I heard."
‡ Arab. "to keep off heat and cold from thee."
§ Dr. Trumpp translates this: "Yet thou wast not forced (or obliged) to transgress; neither did I fasten thee down (seal thee) nor doom thee to the fall."

nor through thy coming out from light into darkness; nor yet [through thy coming] from the garden into this land.

"For I made thee of the light; and I willed to bring out children of light from thee, and like unto thee.

"But thou didst not keep one day My commandment; until I had finished the creation and blessed everything in it.

"Then I commanded thee concerning the tree, that thou eat not thereof. Yet I knew that Satan, who deceived himself, would also deceive thee.

"So I made known to thee by means of the tree, not to come near him.* And I told thee not to eat of the fruit thereof, nor to taste of it, nor yet to sit under it,† nor to yield to it.

"Had I not been and spoken to thee, O Adam, concerning the tree, and had I left thee without a commandment, and thou hadst sinned—it would have been an offence on My part, for not having given [thee] any order; thou wouldst turn round and blame Me [for it].

"But I commanded thee, and warned thee, and thou didst fall. So that My creatures‡ cannot blame me; but the blame rests on them alone.

"And, O Adam, I have made the day for thee and for thy children after thee, for them to work, and toil therein. And I have made the night for them to rest in it from their work; and for the beasts [of the field] to go forth by night and seek their food.

"But little of darkness now remains, O Adam; and daylight will soon appear."

CHAPTER XIV.

Then Adam said unto God: "O Lord, take Thou my soul, and let me not see this gloom any more; or remove me to some place where there is no darkness.

---

* *i.e.*, Satan.   † Or, haunt it.   ‡ Or works.

But God the Lord said to Adam, "Verily I say unto thee, this darkness will pass from thee, every day I have determined for thee, until the fulfilment of My covenant; when I will save thee and bring thee back again into the garden, into the abode of light thou longest for, wherein is no darkness. I will bring thee to it—in the kingdom of heaven."

Again said God unto Adam, "All this misery that thou hast been made to take upon thee because of thy transgression, will not free thee from the hand of Satan, and will not save thee."

"But I [will]. When I shall come down from heaven, and shall become flesh of thy seed, and take upon Me the infirmity from which thou sufferest, then the darkness that came upon thee in this cave shall come upon Me in the grave, when I am in the flesh of thy seed.

"And I, who am without years, shall be subject to the reckoning of years, of times, of months, and of days, and I shall be reckoned as one of the sons of men, in order to save thee."

And God ceased to commune with Adam.*

CHAPTER XV.

Then Adam and Eve wept and sorrowed by reason of God's word to them, that they should not return to the garden until the fulfilment of the days decreed upon them; but mostly because God had told them that He should suffer for their salvation.

CHAPTER XVI.

After this Adam and Eve ceased not to stand in the cave, praying and weeping, until the morning dawned upon them.

* Lit. and God withdrew His Word from Adam.

And when they saw the light returned to them, they restrained from fear, and strengthened their hearts.

Then Adam began to come out of the cave. And when he came to the mouth of it, and stood and turned his face towards the east, and saw the sun rise in glowing rays, and felt the heat thereof on his body, he was afraid of it, and thought in his heart that this flame came forth to plague him.

He wept then, and smote upon his breast, and fell upon the earth on his face, and made his request, saying :—

"O Lord, plague me not, neither consume me, nor yet take away my life from the earth."

For he thought the sun was God.

Inasmuch as while he was in the garden and heard the voice of God and the sound He made in the garden, and feared Him, Adam never saw the brilliant light of the sun, neither did the flaming heat thereof touch his body.

Therefore was he afraid of the sun when flaming rays of it reached him. He thought God meant to plague him therewith all the days He had decreed for him.

For Adam also said in his thoughts, As God did not plague us with darkness, behold, He has caused [this sun] to rise and to plague us with burning heat.

But while he was thus thinking in his heart, the Word of God came [unto him and said] :—

"O Adam, arise and stand up. This sun is not God; but it has been created to give light by day, of which I spake unto thee in the cave [saying], 'that the dawn would break forth, and there would be light by day.'

"But I am God who comforted thee in the night."

And God ceased to commune with Adam.

CHAPTER XVII.

Then Adam and Eve came out at the mouth of the cave, and went towards the garden.

But as they drew near to it, before the western gate, from which Satan came when he deceived Adam and Eve, they found the serpent that became Satan coming at the gate, and sorrowfully licking the dust, and wriggling on its breast on the ground, by reason of the curse that fell upon it from God.[27]

And whereas aforetime [the serpent] was the most exalted of all beasts,[28] now it was changed and become slippery, and the meanest of them all, and it crept on its breast and went on its belly.[29]

And whereas it was the fairest of all beasts, it had been changed, and was become the ugliest of them all. Instead of feeding on the best food, now it turned to eat the dust. Instead of dwelling, as before, in the best places, now it lived in the dust.

And, whereas it had been the most beautiful of all beasts, all of which stood dumb at its beauty, it was now abhorred of them.

And, again, whereas it dwelt in one beautiful abode, to which all other animals came from elsewhere; [and] where it drank, they drank also of the same; now, after it had become venomous, by reason of God's curse, all beasts fled from its abode, and would not drink of the water it drank; but fled from it.

CHAPTER XVIII.

When the accursed serpent saw Adam and Eve, it swelled its head, stood on its tail, and with eyes blood-red, did as if it would kill them.

It made straight for Eve, and ran after her; while Adam standing by, wept because he had no stick in his hand[30] wherewith to smite the serpent, and knew not how to put [it] to death.

But with a heart burning for Eve, Adam approached the

serpent, and held it by the tail; when it turned towards him and said unto him:—

"O Adam, because of thee and of Eve, I am slippery, and go upon my belly." Then by reason of its great strength, it threw down Adam and Eve and pressed upon them, as if it would kill them.

But God sent an angel who threw the serpent away from them, and raised them up.

Then the Word of God came to the serpent, and said unto it, "In the first instance I made thee glib, and made thee to go upon thy belly; but I did not deprive thee of speech.

"Now, however, be thou dumb; and speak no more, thou and thy race;[31] because in the first place, has the ruin My creatures happened through thee, and now thou wishest to kill them."*

Then the serpent was struck dumb, and spake no more.

And a wind came to blow from heaven by command of God, that carried away the serpent from Adam and Eve, threw it on the sea shore, and it landed in India.

CHAPTER XIX.

But Adam and Eve wept before God. And Adam said unto Him:—

"O Lord, when I was in the cave, I said this to Thee, my Lord, that the beasts [of the field] would rise and devour me, and cut off my life from the earth." Then Adam, by reason of what had befallen him, smote upon his breast, and fell upon the earth like a corpse; then came to him the Word of God, who raised him, and said unto him, "O Adam, not one of these beasts will be able to hurt thee; because when I made the beasts and other moving things come to thee in the cave, I did not let the serpent come with them, lest it should rise against you, make you tremble; and the fear of it should fall

* Καὶ ἰὸν ἐντίθησιν ὑπὸ τὴν γλῶτταν αὐτοῦ, Jos. Ant. Jud. Lib. i, c. i, 4.

into your hearts. For I knew that that accursed one is wicked; therefore would I not let it come near you with the [other] beasts.

"But now strengthen thy heart and fear not. I am with thee unto the end of the days I have determined on thee."

CHAPTER XX.

Then Adam wept and said, "O God, remove us to some other place, that the serpent may not come again near us, and rise against us. Lest it find Thy handmaid Eve alone and kill her; for its eyes are hideous [and] evil."

But God said to Adam and Eve, "Henceforth fear not, I will not let it come near you; I have driven it away from you, from this mountain; neither will I leave in it aught to hurt you."

Then Adam and Eve worshipped before God and gave Him thanks, and praised Him for having delivered them from death.

CHAPTER XXI.

Then Adam and Eve went in search of the garden.

And the heat beat like a flame on their faces; and they sweated from the heat, and wept before the Lord.

But the place where they wept was nigh unto a high mountain, facing the western gate of the garden.

Then Adam threw himself down from the top of that mountain; his face was torn and his flesh was flayed; much blood flowed from him, and he was nigh unto death.

Meanwhile Eve remained standing on the mountain weeping over him, thus lying.

And she said, "I wish not to live after him; for all that he did to himself was through me."

Then she threw herself after him; and was torn and scotched by stones; and remained lying as dead.

But the merciful God, who looks upon His creatures, looked upon Adam and Eve as they lay dead, and He sent His Word unto them, and raised them.

And said to Adam, "O Adam, all this misery which thou hast wrought upon thyself, will not avail against [My] rule, neither will it alter the covenant of the 5500 years."

CHAPTER XXII.

Then Adam said to God, "I wither in the heat; I am faint from walking, and am loth of this world. And I know not when Thou wilt bring me out of it, to rest."

Then the Lord God said unto him, "O Adam, it cannot be at present, [not] until thou hast ended* thy days. Then shall I bring thee out of this wretched land."

And Adam said to God, "While I was in the garden I knew neither heat, nor languor, neither moving about, nor trembling, nor fear; but now, since I came to this land, all this affliction has come upon me."

Then God said to Adam, "So long as thou wast keeping My commandment, My light and My grace rested on thee. But when thou didst transgress My commandment, sorrow and misery befell thee in this land."

And Adam wept and said, "O Lord, do not cut me off for this, neither smite me with heavy plagues, nor yet repay me according to my sin; For we, of our own will, did transgress Thy commandment, and forsook Thy law, and sought to become gods like unto Thee, when Satan the enemy† deceived us."

Then God said again unto Adam, "Because thou hast borne fear and trembling in this land, languor and suffering, treading

* Lit. paid, redeemed.   † Lit. hater.

and walking about,* going upon this mountain, and dying [from it], I will take all this upon Myself in order to save thee."

CHAPTER XXIII.

First offering made by Adam.

Then Adam wept more and said, "O God, have mercy on me, so far as to take upon Thee, that which I will do."

But God took His Word from Adam and Eve.

Then Adam and Eve stood on their feet; and Adam said to Eve, "Gird thyself,† and I also will gird myself." And she girded herself, as Adam told her. Then Adam and Eve took stones and placed them in the shape of an altar;‡ and they took leaves from the trees outside the garden, with which they wiped, from the face of the rock, the blood they had spilled. But that which had dropped on the sand, they took together with the dust [wherewith it was mingled] and offered it upon the altar as an offering unto God.

Then Adam and Eve stood under the altar§ and wept, thus entreating God, "Forgive us our trespass and our sin, and look upon us with Thine eye of mercy. For when we were in the garden our praises and our hymns went up before Thee without ceasing.

"But when we came into this strange land, pure praise was no longer ours, nor righteous prayer, nor understanding hearts, nor sweet thoughts, nor just counsels, nor long discernment, nor upright feelings, neither is our bright nature left us. But our body is changed from the similitude in which it was at first, when we were created.

---

* Arab. ' toil, labour.'

† This is the literal rendering in Ethiopic of the Arabic word that means also "brace, or strengthen thyself."

‡ Lit. of an ark, the middle part of a church in Abyssinia.

§ Lit. the sanctuary or temple; literal rendering of the probable Arabic original. It is a canopy over the Holy Table, on which the *tābūt*, or ark, is placed.

"Yet now look upon our blood which is offered upon these stones, and accept it at our hands, like the praises we used to sing unto Thee at first, when in the garden."

And Adam began to make more requests unto God.

CHAPTER XXIV.

Then the merciful God, good and lover of men, looked upon Adam and Eve, and upon their blood, which they had held up as an offering unto Him; without an order from Him [for so doing]. But He wondered at them; and accepted their offerings.

And God sent from His presence a bright fire, that consumed their offering.

He smelt the sweet savour of their offering, and showed them mercy.

Then came the Word of God to Adam, and said unto him, " O Adam, as thou hast shed thy blood, so will I shed My own blood when I become flesh of thy seed; and as thou didst die, O Adam, so also will I die. And as thou didst build an altar, so also will I make for thee an altar on the earth; and as thou didst offer thy blood upon it, so also will I offer My blood upon an altar on the earth."

" And as thou didst sue for forgiveness through that blood, so also will I make My blood forgiveness of sins, and blot out transgressions in it.

"And now, behold, I have accepted thy offering, O Adam, but the days of the covenant, wherein I have bound thee, are not fulfilled. When they are fulfilled, then will I bring thee back into the garden.

" Now, therefore, strengthen thy heart; and when sorrow comes upon thee, make Me an offering, and I will be favourable to thee."

CHAPTER XXV.

But God knew that Adam had in his thoughts, that he should often kill himself and make an offering to Him of his blood.

Therefore did He say unto him, "O Adam, do not again kill thyself as thou didst, by throwing thyself down from that mountain."

But Adam said unto God, "It was in my mind to put an end to myself at once, for having transgressed Thy commandments, and for my having come out of the beautiful garden; and for the bright light of which Thou hast deprived me; and for the praises which poured forth from my mouth without ceasing, and for the light that covered me.

"Yet of Thy goodness, O God, do not away with me altogether; but be favourable to me every time I die, and bring me to life.

"And thereby it will be made known that Thou art a merciful God, who willest not that one should perish; who lovest not that one should fall; and who dost not condemn any one cruelly, badly, and by whole destruction."

Then Adam remained silent.

And the Word of God came unto him, and blessed him, and comforted him, and covenanted with him, that He would save him at the end of the days determined upon him.

This, then, was the first offering Adam made unto God; and so it became his custom to do.

CHAPTER XXVI.

Then Adam took Eve, and they began to return to the Cave of Treasures where they dwelt. But when they neared it and saw it from afar, heavy sorrow fell upon Adam and Eve when they looked at it.

Then Adam said to Eve, "When we were on the mountain we were comforted by the Word of God that conversed with us; and the light that came from the east, shone over us.

"But now the Word of God is hidden from us; and the light that shone over us is so changed as to disappear, and [let] darkness and sorrow come upon us.

"And we are forced to enter this cave [which is] like a prison, wherein darkness covers us, so that we are parted from each other; and thou canst not see me, neither can I see thee."

When Adam had said these words, they wept and spread their hands before God; for they were full of sorrow.

And they entreated God to bring the sun to them, to shine on them, so that darkness return not upon them, and they come not again under this covering of rock. And they wished to die rather than see the darkness.

Then God looked upon Adam and Eve and upon their great sorrow, and upon all they had done with a fervent heart, on account of all the [trouble] they were in, instead of their former well-being, and on account of all the misery that came upon them in a strange land.

Therefore God was not wroth with them; nor impatient with them; but He was long-suffering and forbearing towards them, as [towards] the children He had created.

Then came the Word of God to Adam, and said unto him, "Adam, as for the sun, if I were to take it [and bring it to thee],* days, hours, years and months would all come to naught, and the covenant I have made with thee, would never be fulfilled.

"But thou shouldest then be turned and left in a long plague, and no salvation would be left to thee for ever.

"Yea, rather, bear long and calm thy soul while thou abidest night and day; until the fulfilment of the days, and the time of My covenant is come.

* Also—" to withhold it, days," &c.

"Then shall I come and save thee, O Adam, for I do not wish that thou be afflicted.

"And when I look at all the good things in which thou didst live, and why thou camest out of them, then would I willingly show thee mercy.

"But I cannot alter the covenant that has gone out of My mouth; else would I have brought thee back into the garden.

"When, however, the covenant is fulfilled, then shall I show thee and thy seed mercy, and bring thee into a land of gladness, where there is neither sorrow nor suffering; but abiding joy and gladness, and light that never fails, and praises that never cease; and a beautiful garden that shall never pass away."

And God said again unto Adam, "Be long suffering and enter the cave, for the darkness of which thou wast afraid, shall only be twelve hours long; and when ended, light shall arise."

Then when Adam heard these words from God, he and Eve worshipped before Him, and their hearts were comforted. They returned into the cave after their custom, while tears flowed from their eyes, sorrow and wailing came from their hearts, and they wished their soul would leave their body.

And Adam and Eve stood praying, until the darkness of night came upon them, and Adam was hid from Eve, and she from him.

And they remained standing in prayer.

CHAPTER XXVII.

First apparition of Satan to Adam.

When Satan, the hater of all good, saw how they continued in prayer, and how God communed with them, and comforted them, and [how He had] accepted their offering—Satan made an apparition. He began with transforming his hosts; in his hands was a flashing fire, and they were in a great light.

He then placed his throne near the mouth of the cave because he could not enter into it by reason of their prayers. And he shed light into the cave, until the cave glistened over Adam and Eve; while his hosts began to sing praises.

And Satan did this, in order that when Adam saw the light, he should think within himself that it was a heavenly light, and that [Satan's] hosts were angels; and that God had sent them to watch at the cave, and to give him light in the darkness.

So that when Adam came out of the cave and saw them, and Adam and Eve bowed to Satan, then he would overcome* Adam thereby, and a second time humble him before God.

When, therefore, Adam and Eve saw the light, fancying it was real, they strengthened their hearts; yet, as they were trembling, Adam said to Eve :—

"Look at that great light, and at those many songs of praise, and at that host standing outside that do not come in to us, do not tell us what they say, or whence they come, or what is the meaning of this light; what those praises are; wherefore they have been sent hither, and why they do not come in.

"If they were from God, they would come to us in the cave, and would tell us their errand."

Then Adam stood up and prayed unto God with a fervent heart, and said:—

"O Lord, is there in the world another god than Thou, who created angels and filled them with light, and sent them to keep us, who would come with them?

"But, lo we see these hosts that stand at the mouth of the cave; they are in a great light; they sing loud praises. If

* Or, away.

they are of some other god than Thou, tell me; and if they are sent by Thee, inform me of the reason for which Thou hast sent them."

No sooner had Adam said this, than an angel from God appeared unto him in the cave, who said unto him, "O Adam, fear not. This is Satan and his hosts; he wishes to deceive you as he deceived you at first. For the first time, he was hidden in the serpent; but this time he is come to you in the similitude of an angel of light; in order that, when you worshipped him, he might enthrall you, in the very presence of God."

Then the angel went from Adam, and seized Satan at the opening of the cave, and stripped him of the feint he had assumed, and brought him in his own hideous form to Adam and Eve; who were afraid of him when they saw him.

And the angel said to Adam, "This hideous form has been his ever since God made him fall [from heaven]. He could not have come near you in it; therefore did he transform himself into an angel of light."

Then the angel drove away Satan and his hosts from Adam and Eve, and said unto them, "Fear not; God who created you, will strengthen you."

And the angel went from them.

But Adam and Eve remained standing in the cave; no consolation came to them; they were divided [in their thoughts].

And when it was morning they prayed; and then went out to seek the garden. For their hearts were towards it, and they could get no consolation for having left it.

CHAPTER XXVIII.

Second apparition of Satan to Adam and Eve.

But when the wily Satan saw them, that they were going to

the garden, he gathered together his host, and came in appearance upon a cloud, intent on deceiving them.

But when Adam and Eve saw him thus in a vision, they thought they were angels of God come to comfort them about their having left the garden, or to bring them back again into it.

And Adam spread his hands unto God, beseeching Him to make him understand what they were.

Then Satan, the hater of all good, said unto Adam, "O Adam, I am an angel of the great God; and, behold the hosts that surround me.

"God has sent me and them to take thee and bring thee to the border of the garden northwards; to the shore of the clear sea, and bathe thee and Eve in it, and raise you to your former gladness, that ye return again to the garden."

These words sank into the heart of Adam and Eve.

Yet God withheld His Word from Adam, and did not make him understand at once, but waited to see his strength; whether he would be overcome as Eve was when in the garden, or whether he would prevail.

Then Satan called to Adam and Eve, and said, "Behold, we go to the sea of water," and they began to go.

And Adam and Eve followed them at some little distance.

But when they came to the mountain to the north of the garden, a very high mountain, without any steps to the top of it, the Devil* drew near to Adam and Eve, and made them go up to the top in reality, and not in a vision; wishing, as he did, to throw them down and kill them, and to wipe off their name from the earth; so that this earth should remain to him and his hosts alone.

CHAPTER XXIX.

But when the merciful God saw that Satan wished to kill

* Lit. Diabolos.

Adam with his manifold devices, and saw that Adam was meek and without guile, God spake unto Satan in a loud voice, and cursed him.

Then he and his hosts fled, and Adam and Eve remained standing on the top of the mountain, whence they saw below them the wide world, high above which they were. But they saw none of the host which anon were by them.

They wept, both Adam and Eve, before God, and begged for forgiveness of Him.

Then came the Word from God to Adam, and said unto him, "Know thou and understand concerning this Satan, that he seeks to deceive thee and thy seed after thee."

And Adam wept before the Lord God, and begged and entreated Him to give him something from the garden, as a token to him, wherein to be comforted.[32]

And God looked upon Adam's thought, and sent the angel Michael as far as the sea that reaches unto India, to take from thence golden rods and bring them to Adam.

This did God in His wisdom, in order that these golden rods, being with Adam in the cave, should shine forth with light in the night around him, and put an end to his fear of the darkness.

Then the angel Michael went down by God's order, took golden rods, as God had commanded him, and brought them to God.

CHAPTER XXX.

After these things, God commanded the angel Gabriel to go down to the garden, and say to the cherub who kept it, "Behold, God has commanded me to come into the garden, and to take thence sweet smelling incense, and give it to Adam."

Then the angel Gabriel went down by God's order to the garden, and told the cherub as God had commanded him.

The cherub then said, "Well." And [Gabriel] went in and took the incense.

Then God commanded His angel Raphael to go down to the garden, and speak to the cherub about some myrrh, to give to Adam.

And the angel Raphael went down and told the cherub as God had commanded him, and the cherub said, "Well." Then [Raphael] went in and took the myrrh.

The golden rods were from the Indian sea, where there are precious stones. The incense was from the eastern border of the garden; and the myrrh from the western border, whence bitterness came upon Adam.

And the angels brought these three things to God, by the Tree of Life, in the garden.

Then God said to the angels, "Dip them in the spring of water; then take them and sprinkle their water over Adam and Eve, that they be a little comforted in their sorrow, and give them to Adam and Eve.

And the angels did as God had commanded them, and they gave all those things to Adam and Eve on the top of the mountain upon which Satan had placed them, when he sought to make an end of them.

And when Adam saw the golden rods, the incense and the myrrh, he was rejoiced and wept because he thought that the gold was a token of the kingdom whence he had come, that the incense was a token of the bright light which had been taken from him, and that the myrrh was a token of the sorrow in which he was.

CHAPTER XXXI.

After these things God said unto Adam, "Thou didst ask of Me something from the garden, to be comforted therewith, and I have given thee these three tokens as a consolation to thee; that thou trust in Me and in My covenant with thee.

THE GOLD, INCENSE AND MYRRH.

"For I will come and save thee; and kings*[33] shall bring me [when] in the flesh, gold, incense and myrrh; gold as a token of My kingdom;† incense as a token of My divinity; and myrrh as a token of My sufferings and of My death.[34]

"But, O Adam, put these by thee in the cave; the gold that it may shed light over thee by night; the incense, that thou smell its sweet savour; and the myrrh, to comfort thee in thy sorrow."

When Adam heard these words from God, he worshipped before Him. He and Eve worshipped Him and gave Him thanks, because He had dealt mercifully with them.

Then God commanded the three angels, Michael, Gabriel and Raphael, each to bring what he had brought, and give it to Adam. And they did so, one by one.

And God commanded Suriyel and Salathiel to bear up Adam and Eve, and bring them down from the top of the high mountain, and to take them to the Cave of Treasures.

There they laid the gold on the south side of the cave, the incense on the eastern side, and the myrrh on the western side. For the mouth of the cave was on the north side.

The angels then comforted Adam and Eve, and departed.

The gold was seventy rods; the incense, twelve pounds; and the myrrh, three pounds.

These remained by Adam in the House‡ of Treasures; therefore was it called "of concealment." But other interpreters say it was called the "Cave of Treasures," by reason of the bodies of righteous men that were in it.

These three things did God give to Adam, on the third day after he had come out of the garden, in token of the three days the Lord should remain in the heart of the earth.

---

* Three magi-kings came to worship Him. Tchamitch. *Hist. Armen.* vol. i, p. 277. See the note at the end of this work.

† *i.e.*, of My being king.

‡ The word *bât*, cave, and *bêt*, house, were probably mistaken the one for the other.

And these three things, as they continued with Adam in the cave, gave him light by night; and by day they gave him a little relief from his sorrow.*

CHAPTER XXXII.

And Adam and Eve remained in the Cave of Treasures until the seventh day; they neither ate of the fruit of the earth, nor drank water.

And when it dawned on the eighth day, Adam said to Eve, "O Eve, we prayed God to give us somewhat from the garden, and He sent His angels who brought us what we had desired.

"But now, arise, let us go to the sea of water we saw at first, and let us stand in it, praying that God will again be favourable to us and take us back to the garden; or give us something; or that He will give us comfort in some other land than this in which we are."

Then Adam and Eve came out of the cave, went and stood on the border of the sea in which they had before thrown themselves, and Adam said to Eve :—

"Come, go down into this place, and come not out of it until the end of thirty days, when I shall come to thee. And pray to God with a fervent heart and a sweet voice, to forgive us.

"And I will go to another place, and go down into it, and do like thee."

Then Eve went down into the water, as Adam had commanded her. Adam also went down into the water; and they stood praying; and besought the Lord to forgive them their offence, and to restore them to their former state.

And they stood thus praying, unto the end of the five-and-thirty days.

* See note 38.

CHAPTER XXXIII.

Third apparition of Satan to Adam and Eve.

But Satan, the hater of all good, sought them in the cave, but found them not, although he searched diligently for them.

But he found them standing in the water praying, and thought within himself, "Adam and Eve are thus standing in that water beseeching God to forgive them their transgression, and to restore them to their former estate, and to take them from under my hand.

"But I will deceive them so that they shall come out of the water, and not fulfil their vow."*

Then the hater of all good, went not to Adam, but he went to Eve, and took the form of an angel of God, praising and rejoicing, and said to her:—

"Peace be unto thee! Be glad and rejoice! God is favourable unto you, and He sent me to Adam. I have brought him the glad tidings of salvation, and of his being filled with bright light as he was at first.

"And Adam, in his joy for his restoration, has sent me to thee, that thou come to me, in order that I crown thee with light like him. And he said to me, 'Speak unto Eve; if she does not come with thee, tell her of the sign when we were on the top of the mountain; how God sent His angels who took us and brought us to the Cave of Treasures; and laid the gold on the southern side; incense, on the eastern side; and myrrh on the western side.' Now come to him."

When Eve heard these words from him, she rejoiced greatly. And thinking that [Satan's] appearance† was real, she came out of the sea.

He went before, and she followed him until they came to Adam. Then Satan hid himself from her, and she saw him no more.

* Or, desire. † Lit. sign.

She then came and stood before Adam, who was standing by the water and rejoicing in God's forgiveness.

And as she called to him, he turned round, found her [there] and wept when he saw her, and smote upon his breast; and from the bitterness* of his grief, he sank into the water.

But God looked upon him and upon his misery, and upon his being about to breathe his last. And the Word of God came from heaven, raised him out of the water, and said unto him, "Go up the high bank to Eve." And when he came up to Eve he said unto her, "Who said to thee 'come hither?'"

Then she told him the discourse of the angel who had appeared unto her and had given her a sign.

But Adam grieved, and gave her to know it was Satan. He then took her and they both returned to the cave.

These things happened to them the second time they went down to the water, seven days after their coming out of the garden.

They fasted in the water thirty-five days; altogether forty-two days since they had left the garden.[35]

CHAPTER XXXIV.

And on the morning of the forty-third day, they came out of the cave, sorrowful and weeping. Their bodies were lean, and they were parched from hunger and thirst, from fasting and praying, and from their heavy sorrow on account of their transgression.

And when they had come out of the cave they went up the mountain to the west of the garden.

There they stood and prayed and besought God to grant them forgiveness of their sins.

And after their prayers Adam began to entreat God, saying, "O my Lord, my God, and my Creator, Thou didst command

* Lit. greatness.

the four elements to be gathered together,* and they were gathered together by Thine order.

"Then Thou spreadest Thy hand and didst create me out of one element, that of dust of the earth; and Thou didst bring me into the garden at the third hour, on a Friday, and didst inform me of it in the cave.

"Then, at first, I knew neither night nor day, for I had a bright nature; neither did the light in which I lived ever leave me to know night or day.

"Then, again, O Lord, in that third hour in which Thou didst create me, Thou broughtest to me all beasts, and lions, and ostriches, and fowls of the air, and all things that move in the earth, which Thou hadst created at the first hour [before me] of the Friday.

"And Thy will was that I should name them all, one by one, with a suitable name. But Thou gavest me understanding and knowledge, and a pure heart and a right mind from Thee, that I should name them after Thine own mind regarding [the naming of them].

"O God, Thou madest them obedient to me, and [didst order] that not one of them break from my sway, according to Thy commandment, and to the dominion which Thou hast given me over them. But now they are all estranged from me.

"Then it was in that third hour of Friday, in which Thou didst create me, and didst command me concerning the tree, to which I was neither to draw near, nor to eat thereof; for Thou saidst to me in the garden, 'When thou eatest of it, of death thou shalt die.'

"And if Thou hadst punished† me as Thou saidst, with death, I should have died that very moment.‡

"Moreover, when Thou commandedst me regarding the tree, I was neither to approach nor to eat thereof, Eve was not with me; Thou hadst not yet created her, neither hadst Thou yet

---

* See note 8.   † Lit. judged, sentenced.
‡ Lit. in my hour, or time.

taken her out of my side; nor had she yet heard this order from Thee.

"Then, at the end of the third hour of that Friday, O Lord, Thou didst cause a slumber and a sleep to come over me, and I slept, and was overwhelmed in sleep.

"Then Thou didst draw a rib out of my side, and created it after my own similitude and image. Then I awoke; and when I saw her and knew who she was, I said, 'This is bone of my bones, and flesh of my flesh; henceforth she shall be called woman.'

"It was of Thy good will, O God, that Thou broughtest a slumber and a sleep over me, and [that Thou] didst forthwith bring Eve out of my side, until she was out, so that I did not see how she was made; neither could I witness, O my Lord, how awful and great are Thy goodness and glory.

"And of Thy goodwill, O Lord, Thou madest us both with bodies of a bright nature, and Thou madest us two, one; and Thou gavest us Thy grace, and didst fill* us with praises of the Holy Spirit; that we should be neither hungry nor thirsty, nor know what sorrow is, nor [yet] faintness of heart; neither suffering, fasting, nor weariness.

"But now, O God, since we transgressed Thy commandment and broke Thy law, Thou hast brought us out into a strange land, and has caused suffering, and faintness, hunger and thirst to come upon us.

"Now, therefore, O God, we pray Thee, give us something to eat from the garden,[36] to satisfy our hunger with it; and something wherewith to quench our thirst.

"For, behold, many days, O God, we have tasted nothing and drunk nothing, and our flesh is dried up, and our strength is wasted, and sleep is gone from our eyes from faintness and weeping.

"Then, O God, we dare not gather aught of the fruit of

---

* Lit. satisfy.

trees, from fear of Thee. For when we transgressed at first Thou didst spare us, and didst not make us die.

"But now, we thought in our hearts, if we eat of the fruit of trees, without God's order, He will destroy us this time, and will wipe us off from the face of the earth.

"And if we drink of this water, without God's order, He will make an end of us, and root us up at once.

"Now, therefore, O God, that I am come to this place with Eve, we beg Thou wilt give us of the fruit of the garden, that we may be satisfied with it.

"For we desire the fruit that is on the earth, and all [else] that we lack in it."

CHAPTER XXXV.

Then God looked again upon Adam and his weeping and groaning, and the Word of God came to him, and said unto him:—

"O Adam, when thou wast in My garden, thou knewest neither eating nor drinking; neither faintness nor suffering; neither leanness of flesh, nor change; neither did sleep depart from thine eyes. But since thou transgressedst, and camest into this strange land, all these trials are come upon thee.

CHAPTER XXXVI.

Then God commanded the cherub, who kept the gate of the garden with a sword of fire in his hand, to take some of the fruit of the fig-tree, and to give it to Adam.

The cherub obeyed the command of the Lord God, and went into the garden and brought two figs on* two twigs, each fig hanging to its leaf; they were from two of the trees among which Adam and Eve hid themselves when God went to walk

* Lit. and.

in the garden, and the Word of God came to Adam and Eve and said unto them, "Adam, Adam, where art thou?" And Adam answered, "O God, here am I. I hid myself among fig-trees; and when I heard the sound of Thee and Thy voice, I hid myself, because I am naked."

Then the cherub took two figs and brought them to Adam and to Eve. But he threw them to them from afar; for they might not come near the cherub by reason of their flesh, that could not come near the fire.

At first, angels trembled at the presence of Adam and were afraid of him.* But now Adam trembled before the angels and was afraid of them.

Then Adam drew near and took one fig, and Eve also came in turn and took the other.

And as they took them up in their hands, they looked at them, and knew they were from the trees among which they had hidden themselves.

And Adam and Eve wept sore.

CHAPTER XXXVII.

Then Adam said to Eve, "Seest thou not these figs and their leaves, with which we covered ourselves when we were stripped of our bright nature? But now, we know not what misery and suffering may come upon us from eating them.

"Now, therefore, O Eve, let us restrain ourselves and not eat of them, thou and I; and let us ask God to give us of the fruit of the Tree of Life."

Thus did Adam and Eve restrain themselves, and did not eat of those figs.

But Adam began to pray to God and to beseech Him to give him of the fruit of the Tree of Life, saying thus: "O God, when we transgressed Thy commandment at the sixth

* See note 24.

hour of Friday, we were stripped of the bright nature we had,[37] and did not continue in the garden after our transgression, more than three hours.

"But on the evening Thou madest us come out of it. O God, we transgressed against Thee one hour, and all these trials and sorrows have come upon us until this day.

"And those days together with this the forty-third day, do not redeem* that one hour in which we transgressed!

"O God, look upon us with an eye of pity, and do not requite us according to our transgression of Thy commandment, in presence of Thee.

"O God, give us of the fruit of the Tree of Life, that we may eat of it, and live, and turn not to see sufferings and other [trouble], in this earth; for Thou art God.

"When we transgressed Thy commandment, Thou madest us come out of the garden, and didst send a cherub to keep the Tree of Life, lest we should eat thereof, and live; and know nothing of faintness after we transgressed.

"But now, O Lord, behold, we have endured all these days, and have borne sufferings. Make these forty-three days an equivalent† for the one hour in which we transgressed.

CHAPTER XXXVIII.

After these things the Word of God came to Adam, and said unto him :—

"O Adam, as to the fruit of the Tree of Life, for which thou askest, I will not give it thee now, but when the 5500 years are fulfilled. Then will I give thee of the fruit of the Tree of Life, and thou shalt eat, and live for ever, thou, and Eve, and thy righteous seed.

* Or, make up for.   † Even with.

"But these forty-three days cannot make amends* for the hour in which thou didst transgress My commandment.

"O Adam, I gave thee to eat of the fig-tree in which thou didst hide thyself. Go and eat of it, thou and Eve.

"I will not deny† thy request, neither will I disappoint thy hope; therefore, bear up unto the fulfilment of the covenant I made with thee."

And God withdrew His Word from Adam.

CHAPTER XXXIX.

Then Adam returned to Eve, and said to her, "Arise, and take a fig for thyself, and I will take another; and let us go to our cave."

Then Adam and Eve took [each a fig] and went towards the cave; the time was about the setting of the sun; and their thoughts made them long to eat of the fruit.

But Adam said to Eve, "I am afraid to eat of this fig. I know not what may come upon me from it."

So Adam wept, and stood praying before God, saying, "Satisfy my hunger, without my having to eat this fig; for after I have eaten it, what will it profit me? And what shall I desire and ask of Thee, O God, when it is gone?"

And he said again, "I am afraid to eat of it; for I know not what will befall me through it."

CHAPTER XL.

Then the Word of God came to Adam, and said unto him, "O Adam, why hadst thou not this dread, neither this fasting, nor this care ere this? And why hadst thou not this fear before thou didst transgress?

---

* Or, redeem.   † Or, reject, turn back.

"But when thou camest to dwell in this strange land, thy animal body could not be on earth without earthly food, to strengthen it and to restore its powers."

And God withdrew His Word from Adam.

CHAPTER XLI.

Then Adam took the fig, and laid it on the golden rods. Eve also took [her] fig, and put it upon the incense.[36]

And the weight of each fig was that of a water-melon; for the fruit of the garden was much larger than the fruit of this land.

But Adam and Eve remained standing and fasting the whole of that night, until the morning dawned.

When the sun rose they were at their prayers, and Adam said to Eve, after they had done praying:—

"O Eve, come, let us go to the border of the garden looking south; to the place whence the river flows, and is parted into four heads.* There we will pray to God, and ask Him to give us to drink of the Water of Life.

"For God has not fed us with the Tree of Life, in order that we may not live. We will, therefore, ask Him to give us of the Water of Life, and to quench our thirst with it, rather than with a drink of water of this land."†

When Eve heard these words from Adam, she agreed; and they both arose and came to the southern border of the garden, upon the brink of the river of water at some little distance from the garden.

And they stood and prayed before the Lord, and asked Him to look upon them this once, to forgive them, and to grant them their request.

---

* Or, streams.

† As read by Dillmann, it may also mean, that we may do without the water of this land—or, of this earth.

After this prayer from both of them, Adam began [to pray] with [his] voice before God, and said:—

" O Lord, when I was in the garden and saw the water that flowed from under the Tree of Life, my heart did not desire, neither did my body require to drink of it; neither did I know thirst, for I was living; and above that which I am now.

" So that in order to live I did not require any Food of Life, neither did I drink of the Water of Life.

"But now, O God, I am dead; my flesh is parched with thirst. Give me of the Water of Life that I may drink of it and live.

" Of Thy mercy, O God, save me from these plagues and trials, and bring me into another land different from this, if Thou wilt not let me dwell in Thy garden."

CHAPTER XLII.

Then came the Word of God to Adam, and said unto him:—

" O Adam, as to what thou sayest, 'Bring me into a land where there is rest,' it is not another land than this, but it is the kingdom of heaven where [alone] there is rest.

" But thou canst not make thy entrance into it at present; but [only] after thy judgment* is past and fulfilled.

" Then will I make thee go up into the kingdom of heaven, thee and thy righteous seed; and I will give thee and them the rest thou askest for at present.

" And if thou saidst, 'Give me of the Water of Life that I may drink and live'—it cannot be this day, but on the day that I shall descend into hell, and break the gates of brass, and bruise in pieces the kingdoms of iron.

" Then will I in mercy save thy soul and the souls of the righteous, [to give them] rest in My garden. And that shall be when the end of the world is come.

* *i.e.,* thy sentence—or, punishment.

"And, again, as regards the Water of Life thou seekest, it will not be granted thee this day; but on the day that I shall shed My blood upon thy head in the land of Golgotha.

" For My blood shall be the Water of Life unto thee, at that time, and not to thee alone, but unto all those of thy seed who shall believe in Me; that it be unto them for rest for ever."

The Lord said again unto Adam, " O Adam, when thou wast in the garden, these trials did not come to thee.

"But since thou didst transgress My commandment, all these sufferings have come upon thee.

"Now, also, does thy flesh require food and drink; drink [then] of that water that flows by thee on the face of the earth."

Then God withdrew His Word from Adam.

And Adam and Eve worshipped the Lord, and returned from the river of water to the cave. It was noon-day; and when they drew near to the cave, they saw a large fire by it.

CHAPTER XLIII.

Fourth apparition of Satan to Adam and Eve.

Then Adam and Eve were afraid, and stood still. And Adam said to Eve, " What is that fire by our cave ? We do nothing in it to bring about this fire.

" We neither have bread to bake therein, nor broth* to cook there. As to this fire, we know not the like, neither do we know what to call it.

" But ever since God sent the cherub with a sword of fire that flashed and lightened in his hand, from fear of which we fell down and were like corpses [have we not seen the like].

" But now, O Eve, behold, this is the same fire that was in

* Or, soup, mess, cooking.

the cherub's hand, which God has sent to keep the cave in which we dwell.

"O Eve, [it is] because God is angry with us, and will drive us from it.

"O Eve, we have again transgressed [His] commandment in that cave, so that He has sent this fire to [burn] around it, and to prevent us from going into it.*

"If this be really so, O Eve, where shall we dwell? and whither shall we flee from before the face of the Lord? Since, as regards the garden, He will not let us abide in it, and He has deprived us of the good things thereof; but He has placed us in this cave, in which we have borne darkness, trials and hardships, until [at last] we found comfort therein.

"But now that He has brought us out into another land, who knows what may happen in it? And who knows but that the darkness of that land may be far greater than the darkness of this land?

"Who knows what may happen in that land by day or by night? And who knows whether it will be far or near, O Eve? Where it will please God to put us, [may be] far from the garden, O Eve! or where God will prevent us from beholding Him, because we have transgressed His commandment, and because we have made requests unto Him at all times?

"O Eve, if God will bring us into a strange land other than this, in which we find consolation, it must be to put our souls† to death, and blot out our name from the face of the earth.

"O Eve, if we are farther estranged from the garden and from God, where shall we find Him again, and ask Him to give us gold, incense, myrrh, and some fruit of the fig-tree?

"Where shall we find Him, to comfort us a second time? Where shall we find Him, that He may think of us, as regards the covenant He has made on our behalf?" ‡

---

* Or, and He will not let us enter into it.
† Or, "us."   ‡ Or, "the promise He has made us."

Then Adam said no more. And they kept looking, he and Eve, towards the cave, and at the fire that flared up around it.

But that fire was from Satan. For he had gathered trees and dry grasses, and had carried and brought them to the cave, and had set fire to them, in order to consume the cave and what was in it.

So that Adam and Eve should be left in sorrow, and he should cut off their trust in God, and make them deny Him.

But by the mercy of God he could not burn the cave,* for God sent His angel round the cave to guard it from such a fire, until it went out.

And this fire lasted from noon-day until the break of day. That was the forty-fifth day.

CHAPTER XLIV.

Yet Adam and Eve were standing and looking at the fire, and unable to come near the cave from their dread of the fire.

And Satan kept on bringing trees and throwing them into the fire, until the flame thereof rose up on high, and covered the whole cave, thinking, as he did in his own mind, to consume the cave with much fire. But the angel of the Lord was guarding it.

And yet he could not curse Satan, nor injure him by word, because he had no authority over him, neither did he take to doing so with words from his mouth.

Therefore did the angel bear with him, without saying one bad word, until the Word of God came who said to Satan, "Go hence; once before didst thou deceive My servants, and this time thou seekest to destroy them.

"Were it not for My mercy I would have destroyed thee

---

* The Arabic here adds, "for God defeated the thoughts of that deceiver, so that the fire did not hurt the cave; but the angel," &c.

and thy hosts from off the earth. But I have had patience with thee,* unto the end of the world."

Then Satan fled from before the Lord. But the fire went on burning around the cave like a coal-fire the whole day; which was the forty-sixth day Adam and Eve had spent since they came out of the garden.

And when Adam and Eve saw that the heat of the fire had somewhat cooled down, they began to walk towards the cave to get into it as they were wont; but they could not, by reason of the heat of the fire.

Then they both took to weeping because of the fire that made separation between them and the cave, and that drew towards them, burning. And they were afraid.

Then Adam said to Eve, "See this fire of which we have a portion in us: which formerly yielded to us, but no longer does so, now that we have transgressed the limit of creation, and changed our condition, and our nature is altered. But the fire is not changed in its nature, nor altered from its creation. Therefore has it now power over us; and when we come near it, it scorches our flesh."

CHAPTER XLV.

Then Adam rose and prayed unto God, saying, "See, this fire has made separation between us and the cave in which Thou hast commanded us to dwell; but now, behold, we cannot go into it."

Then God heard Adam, and sent him His Word, that said:—

"O Adam, see this fire! how [different] the flame and heat thereof are from the garden of delights and the good things in it!

"When thou wast under My control, all creatures yielded to

* Or, "respited thee."

thee; but after thou hast transgressed My commandment, they all rise over thee."

Again said God unto him, "See, O Adam, how Satan has exalted thee! He has deprived thee of the Godhead, and of an exalted state like unto Me, and has not kept his word to thee; but, after all, is become thy foe. It is he who made this fire in which he meant to burn thee and Eve.

"Why, O Adam, has he not kept his agreement with thee, not even one day; but has deprived thee of the glory that was on thee—when thou didst yield to his command?

"Thinkest thou, Adam, that he loved thee when he made this agreement with thee? Or, that he loved thee and wished to raise thee on high?

"But no, Adam, he did not do all that out of love to thee; but he wished to make thee come out of light into darkness; and from an exalted state to degradation; from glory to abasement; from joy to sorrow; and from rest to fasting and fainting."

God said also to Adam, "See this fire kindled by Satan around thy cave; see this wonder that surrounds thee; and know that it will encompass about both thee and thy seed, when ye hearken to his behest; that he will plague you with fire; and that ye shall go down into hell after ye are dead.

"Then shall ye see the burning of his fire, that will thus be burning around you and your seed. There shall be no deliverance from it for you, but at My coming; in like manner as thou canst not now go into thy cave, by reason of the great fire [around it]; [not] until My Word shall come that will make a way for thee on the day My covenant is fulfilled.

"There is no way for thee at present to come from hence to rest, not until My Word comes, who is My Word.* Then will He make a way for thee, and thou shalt have rest." Then God called with His Word to that fire that burned around the

---

* The Arabic original here reads more definitely: "not until My voice comes, which is My Word," i.e., God speaking to us through His Son.

cave, that it part itself asunder, until Adam had gone through it. Then the fire parted itself by God's order, and a way was made for Adam.

And God withdrew His Word from Adam.

CHAPTER XLVI.

Then Adam and Eve began again to come into the cave.

And when they came to the way between the fire, Satan blew into the fire like a whirlwind, and made on Adam and and Eve a burning coal-fire; so that their bodies were singed; and the coal-fire scorched them.

And from the burning of the fire Adam and Eve cried aloud, and said, "O Lord, save us! Leave us not to be consumed and plagued by this burning fire; neither requite us for having transgressed Thy commandment."

Then God looked upon their bodies, on which Satan had caused fire to burn, and God sent His angel that stayed the burning fire. But the wounds remained on their bodies.

And God said unto Adam, "See Satan's love for thee, who pretended to give thee the Godhead and greatness; and, behold, he burns thee with fire, and seeks to destroy thee from off the earth.

"Then look at Me, O Adam; I created thee, and how many times have I delivered thee out of his hand? If not, would he not have destroyed thee?

God said again to Eve, "What is that he promised thee in the garden, saying, 'At the time ye shall eat of the tree, your eyes will be opened, and you shall become like gods, knowing good and evil.' But lo! he has burnt your bodies with fire, and has made you taste the taste of fire, for the taste of the garden; and has made you see the burning of fire, and the evil thereof, and the power it has over you.

"Your eyes have seen the good he has taken from you, and in truth he has opened your eyes; and you have seen the garden in which ye were with Me, and ye have also seen the evil that has come upon you from Satan. But as to the Godhead he cannot give it you, neither fulfil his speech to you. Nay, he was bitter against you and your seed, that will come after you."

And God withdrew His Word from them.

CHAPTER XLVII.

Then Adam and Eve came into the cave, yet trembling at the fire that had scorched their bodies. So Adam said to Eve:—

"Lo, the fire has burnt our flesh in this world; but how will it be when we are dead, and Satan shall punish* our souls? Is not our deliverance long and far off, unless God come, and in mercy to us fulfil His promise?"

Then Adam and Eve passed into the cave, blessing themselves for coming into it once more. For it was in their thoughts, that they never should enter it, when they saw the fire around it.

But as the sun was setting the fire was [still] burning and nearing Adam and Eve in the cave, so that they could not sleep in it. After the sun had set, they went out of it. This was the forty-seventh day after they came out of the garden.

Adam and Eve then came under the top of hill by† the garden to sleep, as they were wont.

And they stood and prayed God to forgive them their sins, and then fell asleep under the summit of the mountain.

But Satan, the hater of all good, thought within himself: Whereas God has promised salvation to Adam by covenant, and that He would deliver him out of all the hardships that

---

* Lit. judge, or sentence. † Lit. of.

have befallen him—but has not promised me by covenant, and will not deliver me out of [my] hardships; nay, since He has promised him that He should make him and his seed dwell in the kingdom in which I [once] was—I will kill Adam. The earth shall be rid of him; and shall be left to me alone; so that when he is dead he may not have any seed left to inherit the kingdom that shall remain my own realm; God will then be in want of me, and He will restore me to it with my hosts.

CHAPTER XLVIII.

Fifth apparition of Satan to Adam and Eve.

After this Satan called to his hosts, all of which came to him, and said unto him:—

"O, our Lord, what wilt thou do?"

He then said unto them, "Ye know that this Adam, whom God created out of the dust, is he who has taken our kingdom. Come, let us gather together and kill him; or hurl a rock at him and at Eve, and crush them under it."

When Satan's hosts heard these words, they came to the part of the mountain where Adam and Eve were asleep.

Then Satan and his hosts took a huge rock, broad and even, and without blemish, thinking within himself, "If there should be a hole in the rock, when it fell on them, the hole in the rock might come upon them, and so they would escape and not die."

He then said to his hosts, "Take up this stone, and throw it flat upon them, so that it roll not from them to somewhere else. And when ye have hurled it, flee and tarry not." And they did as he bid them. But as the rock fell down from the mountain upon Adam and Eve, God commanded it to become a kind of shed over them, that did them no harm. And so it was by God's order.

But when the rock fell, the whole earth quaked with it, and was shaken from the size of the rock.

And as it quaked and shook, Adam and Eve awoke from sleep, and found themselves under a rock like a shed.* But they knew not how it was; for [when they fell asleep] they were under the sky, and not under a shed; and when they saw it, they were afraid.

Then Adam said to Eve, "Wherefore has the mountain bent [itself], and the earth quaked and shaken on our account? And why has this rock spread itself over us like a tent?

"Does God intend to plague us and to shut us up in this prison? Or will He close the earth upon us?

"He is angry with us for our having come out of the cave, without His order; and for our having done so of our own accord, without consulting Him, when we left the cave and came to this place."

Then Eve said, "If, indeed, the earth quaked for our sake, and this rock forms a tent over us because of our transgression, then woe be to us, O Adam, for our punishment will be long.

"But arise and pray to God to let us know concerning this, and what this rock is, that is spread over us like a tent."

Then Adam stood up and prayed before the Lord, to let him know about this strait. And Adam thus stood praying until the morning.

CHAPTER XLIX.

Then the Word of God came and said:—

"O Adam, who counselled thee, when thou camest out of the cave, to come† to this place?"

And Adam said unto God, "O Lord, we came to this place

---

* Tent or awning. † Lit. and camest.

because of the heat of the fire, that came upon us inside the cave."

Then the Lord God said unto Adam, "O Adam, thou dreadest the heat of fire for one night, but how will it be when thou dwellest in hell?*

"Yet, O Adam, fear not, neither say in thy heart that I have spread this rock as an awning over thee, to plague thee therewith.

"It came from Satan, who had promised thee the Godhead and majesty. It is he who threw down this rock to kill thee under it, and Eve with thee, and thus to prevent you from living upon the earth.

"But, in mercy for you, just as that rock was falling down upon you, I commanded it to form an awning over you; and the rock under you, to lower itself.

"And this sign, O Adam, will happen to Me at My coming upon earth: Satan will raise the people of the Jews to put Me to death; and they will lay Me in a rock, and seal a large stone upon Me, and I shall remain within that rock three days and three nights.

"But on the third day I shall rise again, and it shall be salvation to thee, O Adam, and to thy seed, to believe in Me. But, O Adam, I will not bring thee from under this rock until three days and three nights are passed."

And God withdrew His Word from Adam.

But Adam and Eve abode under the rock three days and three nights, as God had told them.

And God did so to them because they had left their cave and had come to this same place without God's order.

But, after three days and three nights, God opened the rock and brought them out from under it. Their flesh was dried up, and their eyes and their hearts were troubled from weeping and sorrow.

---

* Also Arab.: how would it be if thou wert dwelling or abiding in hell?

CHAPTER L.

Then Adam and Eve went forth and came into the Cave of Treasures, and they stood praying in it the whole of that day, until the evening.

And this took place at the end of fifty days after they had left the garden.

But Adam and Eve rose again and prayed to God in the cave the whole of that night, and begged for mercy from Him.

And when the day dawned, Adam said unto Eve, "Come! let us go and do some work for our bodies."

So they went out of the cave, and came to the northern border of the garden, and they sought something to cover their bodies withal. But they found nothing, and knew not how to do the work. Yet their bodies were stained,* and they were speechless from cold and heat.

Then Adam stood and asked God to show him something wherewith to cover their bodies.

Then came the Word of God and said unto him, "O Adam, take Eve and come to the sea-shore, where ye fasted before. There ye shall find skins of sheep, whose flesh was devoured by lions, and whose skins were left. Take them and make raiment for yourselves, and clothe yourselves withal.

CHAPTER LI.

When Adam heard these words from God, he took Eve and removed from the northern end of the garden to the south of it, by the river of water, where they [once] fasted.

But as they were going in the way, and before they reached that place, Satan the wicked one, had heard the Word of God communing with Adam respecting his covering.

* Lit. dyed.

It grieved him, and he hastened to the place where the sheep-skins were, with the intention of taking them and throwing them into the sea, or of burning them with fire, that Adam and Eve should not find them.

But as he was about to take them, the Word of God came from heaven, and bound him by the side of those skins until Adam and Eve came near him. But as they neared him they were afraid of him, and of his hideous look.

Then came the Word of God to Adam and Eve, and said to them, "This is he who was hidden in the serpent, and who deceived you, and stripped you of the garment of light and glory in which you were.

"This is he who promised you majesty and divinity. Where, then, is the beauty that was on him? Where is his divinity? Where is his light? Where is the glory that rested on him?

"Now his figure is hideous; he is become abominable among angels; and he has come to be called Satan.

"O Adam, he wished to take from you this earthly garment of sheepskins, and to destroy it, and not let you be covered with it.

"What, then, is his beauty that you should have followed him? And what have you gained by hearkening to him? See his evil works and then look at Me; at Me, your Creator, and at the good deeds I do you.

"See, I bound him until you came and saw him and beheld his weakness, that no power is left with him."

And God released him from his bonds.

CHAPTER LII.

After this Adam and Eve said no more, but wept before God on account of their creation, and of their bodies that required an earthly covering.

Then Adam said unto Eve, "O Eve, this [is the] skin of beasts with which we shall be covered. But when we have put it on, behold, a token of death shall have come upon us, inasmuch as the owners of these skins have died, and have wasted away. So also shall we die, and pass away."

Then Adam and Eve took the skins, and went back to the Cave of Treasures; and when in it, they stood and prayed as they were wont.

And they thought how they could make garments of those skins; for they had no skill for it.

Then God sent to them His angel to show them how to work it out. And the angel said to Adam, "Go forth, and bring some palm-thorns." Then Adam went out, and brought some, as the angel had commanded him.

Then the angel began before them to work out the skins, after the manner of one who prepares a shirt. And he took the thorns and stuck them into the skins, before their eyes.

Then the angel again stood up and prayed God that the thorns in those skins should be hidden, so as to be, as it were, sewn with one thread.

And so it was, by God's order; they became garments for Adam and Eve, and He clothed them withal.[39]

From that time the nakedness of their bodies was covered from the sight of each other's eyes.

And this happened at the end of the fifty-first day.

Then when Adam and Eve's bodies were covered, they stood and prayed, and sought mercy of the Lord, and forgiveness, and gave Him thanks for that He had had mercy on them, and had covered their nakedness. And they ceased* not from prayer the whole of that night.

Then when the morn dawned at the rising of the sun, they said† their prayers after their custom; and then went out of the cave.

* Lit. moved. † Lit. prayed.

And Adam said unto Eve, "Since we know not what there is to the westward of this cave, let us go forth and see it to-day." Then they came forth and went towards the western border.

CHAPTER LIII.

Sixth apparition of Satan to Adam and Eve.

They were not very far from the cave, when Satan came towards them, and hid himself* between them and the cave, under the form of two ravenous lions three days [without food], that came towards Adam and Eve, as if to break them in pieces and devour them.

Then Adam and Eve wept, and prayed God to deliver them from their paws.

Then the Word of God came to them, and drove away [the lions] from them.

And God said unto Adam, "O Adam, what seekest thou on the western border? And why hast thou left of thine own accord the eastern border, in which was thy dwelling-place?

"Now, then, turn back to thy cave, and remain in it, that Satan do not deceive thee, nor work his purpose† upon thee.

"For in this western border, O Adam, there will go from thee a seed, that shall replenish it; and that will defile themselves with their sins, and with their yielding to the behests of Satan, and by following his works.

"Therefore will I bring upon them the waters of a flood, and overwhelm them all. But I will deliver what is left of the righteous among them; and I will bring them to a distant land, and the land in which thou dwellest now shall remain desolate and without one inhabitant in it."

After God had thus discoursed to them, they went back to

---

* Arab. " he stepped, or placed himself."   † Or, counsel.

the Cave of Treasures. But their flesh was dried up, and their strength failed from fasting and praying, and from the sorrow they felt at having trespassed against God.

CHAPTER LIV.

Then Adam and Eve stood up in the cave and prayed the whole of that night until the morning dawned. And when the sun was risen they both went out of the cave; their heads wandering from heaviness of sorrow, and they not knowing whither they went.

And they walked thus unto the southern border of the garden. And they began to go up that border until they came to the eastern border [beyond] which there was no [farther] space.

And the cherub who guarded the garden was standing at the western gate, and guarding it against Adam and Eve, lest they should suddenly come into the garden. And the cherub turned round, as if to put them to death; according to the commandment God had given him.

When Adam and Eve came to the eastern border of the garden—thinking in their hearts that the cherub was not watching—as they were standing by the gate as if wishing to go in, suddenly came the cherub with a flashing sword of fire in his hand; and when he saw them, he went forth to kill them. For he was afraid lest God should destroy him if they went into the garden without His order.

And the sword of the cherub seemed to flame afar off. But when he raised it over Adam and Eve, the flame thereof did not flash forth. Therefore did the cherub think that God was favourable to them, and was bringing them back into the garden. And the cherub stood wondering.

He could not go up to Heaven to ascertain God's order regarding their getting into the garden; he therefore abode standing by them, unable as he was to part from them; for he was afraid lest they should enter the garden without leave from God, who [then] would destroy him.

When Adam and Eve saw the cherub coming towards them with a flaming sword of fire in his hand, they fell on their faces from fear, and were as dead.

At that time the heavens and the earth shook; and other cherubim came down from heaven to the cherub who guarded the garden, and saw him amazed and silent.

Then, again, other angels came down nigh unto the place where Adam and Eve were. They were divided between joy and sorrow.

They were glad, because they thought that God was favourable to Adam, and wished him to return to the garden; and [wished to] restore him to the gladness he once enjoyed.

But they sorrowed over Adam, because he was fallen like a dead [man], he and Eve; and they said in their thoughts, "Adam has not died in this place; but God has put him to death, for his having come to this place, and wishing to get into the garden without His leave."

CHAPTER LV.

Then came the Word of God to Adam and Eve, and raised them from their dead state, saying unto them, "Why came ye up hither? Do you intend to go into the garden, from which I brought you out? It can not be to-day; but [only] when the covenant I have made with you is fulfilled."

Then Adam, when he heard the Word of God, and the fluttering of the angels whom he did not see, but only hear the sound of them with his ears, he and Eve wept, and said to the angels:—

"O Spirits, who wait upon God, look upon me, and upon my

being unable to see you! For when I was in my former bright nature, then I could see you. I sang praises as you do; and my heart was far above you.

But now, that I have transgressed, that bright nature is gone from me, and I am come to this miserable state.* And now am I come to this, that I cannot see you, and you do not serve me as you were wont. For I am become animal flesh.

"Yet now, O angels of God, ask God with me, to restore me to that wherein I was formerly; to rescue me from this misery, and to remove from me the sentence of death He passed upon me, for having trespassed against Him."

Then, when the angels heard these words, they all grieved over him; and cursed Satan who had beguiled Adam, until he came from the garden to misery; from life to death; from peace to trouble; and from gladness to a strange land.

Then the angels said unto Adam, "Thou didst hearken to Satan, and didst forsake the Word of God who created thee; and thou didst believe that Satan would fulfil all he had promised thee.

"But now, O Adam, we will make known to thee, what came upon us through him, before his fall from heaven.

"He gathered together his hosts, and deceived them, promising them to give them a great kingdom, a divine nature; and other promises he made them.

"His hosts believed that his word was true, so they yielded to him, and renounced the glory of God.

"He then sent for us—according to the orders† in which we were—to come under his command, and to hearken to his vain promise. But we would not, and we took not his advice.

"Then after he had fought with God, and had dealt frowardly with Him, he gathered together his hosts, and made war with us. And if it had not been for God's strength that was with us, we could not have prevailed against him to hurl him from heaven.

* Or, figure. † Ranks, or dignities.

"But when he fell from among us, there was great joy in heaven, because of his going down from us. For had he continued in heaven, nothing, not even one angel would have remained in it.

"But God in His mercy, drove him from among us to this dark earth; for he had become darkness itself and a worker of unrighteousness.

"And he has continued, O Adam, to make war against thee, until he beguiled thee and made thee come out of the garden, to this strange land, where all these trials have come to thee. And death, which God brought upon him he has also brought to thee, O Adam, because thou didst obey him, and didst transgress against God."

Then all the angels rejoiced and praised God, and asked Him not to destroy Adam this time, for his having sought to enter the garden; but to bear with him until the fulfilment of the promise; and to help him in this world until he was free from Satan's hand.

CHAPTER LVI.

Then came the Word of God to Adam, and said unto him:—

"O Adam, look at that garden of joy and at this earth of toil, and behold the angels who are in the garden—that is full of them, and [see] thyself alone on this earth, with Satan whom thou didst obey.

"Yet, if thou hadst submitted, and been obedient to Me, and hadst kept My Word, thou wouldst be with My angels in My garden.

"But when thou didst transgress and hearken to Satan, thou didst become his guest among his angels, that are full of wickedness; and thou camest to this earth, that brings forth to thee thorns and thistles.

"O Adam, ask him who deceived thee, to give thee the divine nature he promised thee, or to make thee a garden as I had made for thee; or to fill thee with that same bright nature with which I had filled thee.

"[Ask him] to make thee a body like the one I made thee, or to give thee a day of rest as I gave thee; or to create within thee a reasonable soul, as I did create for thee; or to remove thee hence to some other earth than this one which I gave thee. But, O Adam, he will not fulfil even one of the things he told thee.

"Acknowledge, then, My favour towards thee, and My mercy on thee, My creature; that I have not requited thee for thy transgression against Me, but in My pity for thee I have promised thee that at the end of the great five days and a half I will come and save thee."

Then God said again to Adam and Eve, "Arise, go down hence, lest the cherub with a sword of fire in his hand destroy you."

But Adam's heart was comforted by God's words to him, and he worshipped before Him.

And God commanded His angels to escort Adam [and Eve] to the cave with joy, instead of the fear that had come upon them.

Then the angels took up Adam and Eve, and brought them down from the mountain by the garden, with songs and psalms, until they brought them to the cave. There the angels began to comfort and to strengthen them, and then departed from them towards heaven, to their Creator, who had sent them.

But, after the angels were gone from Adam and Eve, came Satan, with shamefacedness, and stood at the entrance of the cave in which were Adam and Eve. He then called to Adam, and said, "O Adam, come, let me speak to thee."

Then Adam came out of the cave, thinking he was one of God's angels that was come to give him some good counsel.

CHAPTER LVII.

Seventh apparition of Satan to Adam and Eve.

But when Adam came out and saw his hideous figure, he was afraid of him, and said unto him, "Who art thou?"

Then Satan answered and said unto him, "It is I, who hid myself within the serpent, and who talked to Eve, and beguiled her until she hearkened to my command. I am he who sent her, through the wiles of my speech, to deceive thee, until thou and she ate of the fruit of the tree, and ye came away from under the command of God."

But when Adam heard these words from him, he said unto him, "Canst thou make me a garden as God made for me? Or canst thou clothe me in the same bright nature in which God had clothed me?

"Where is the divine nature thou didst promise to give me? Where is that fair speech of thine, thou didst hold with us at first, when we were in the garden?"

Then Satan said unto Adam, "Thinkest thou, that when I have spoken to one about anything, I shall ever bring it to him or fulfil my word? Not so. For I myself have never even thought of obtaining what I asked.

"Therefore did I fall, and did I make you fall by that for which I myself fell; and [with you] also, whosoever accepts my counsel, falls thereby.

"But now, O Adam, by reason of thy fall thou art under my rule,* and I am king over thee; because thou hast hearkened to me, and hast transgressed against thy God. Neither will there be any deliverance from my hands until the day promised thee by thy God."

Again he said, "Inasmuch as we do not know the day agreed upon with thee by thy God, nor the hour in which thou

---

* Sentence, or judgment.

shalt be delivered, for that reason will we multiply war and murder upon thee and thy seed after thee.

"This is our will and our good pleasure, that we may not leave one of the sons of men to inherit our orders* in heaven.

"For as to our abode, O Adam, it is in burning fire; and we will not cease our evil doing, no, not one day nor one hour. And I, O Adam, shall sow fire upon thee when thou comest into the cave to dwell there."

When Adam heard these words he wept and mourned, and said unto Eve, "Hear what he said; that he will not fulfil aught of what he told thee in the garden. Did he really [then] become king over us?

"But we will ask God, who created us, to deliver us out of his hands."

CHAPTER LVIII.

Then Adam and Eve spread their hands unto God, praying and entreating Him to drive Satan away from them; that he do them no violence, and do not force them to deny God.

Then God sent to them at once His angel, who drove away Satan from them. This happened about sunset, on the fifty-third day† after they had come out of the garden.

Then Adam and Eve went into the cave, and stood up and turned their faces to the earth, to pray to God.

But ere they prayed Adam said unto Eve, "Lo, thou hast seen what temptations‡ have befallen us in this land. Come, let us arise, and ask God to forgive us the sins we have committed; and we will not come out until the end of the day next to the fortieth. And if we die herein, He will save us."

Then Adam and Eve arose, and joined together in entreating God.

---

* Ranks, or stations.   † There is confusion of numbers in the text.   ‡ Or, trials.

They abode thus praying in the cave; neither did they come out of it, by night or by day, until their prayers went up out of their mouths, like a flame of fire.

CHAPTER LIX.

Eighth apparition of Satan to Adam and Eve.

But Satan, the hater of all good, did not allow them to end their prayers. For he called to his hosts, and they came, all of them. He then said to them, "Since Adam and Eve, whom we beguiled, have agreed together to pray to God night and day, and to entreat Him to deliver them, and [since they] will not come out of the cave until the end of the fortieth day.

"And since they will continue their prayers as they have both agreed to do, that He will deliver them out of our hands, and restore them to their [former] state, see what we shall do unto them." And his hosts said unto him, "Power is thine, O our Lord, to do what thou listest."

Then Satan, great in wickedness, took his hosts and came into the cave, in the thirtieth night of the forty days and one; and he smote Adam and Eve, until he left them dead.

Then came the Word of God unto Adam and Eve, who raised them from their suffering, and God said unto Adam, "Be strong, and be not afraid of him who has just come to thee."

But Adam wept and said, "Where wast Thou, O my God, that they should smite me with such blows, and that this suffering should come upon us; upon me and upon Eve, Thy handmaid?"

Then God said unto him, "O Adam, see, he is lord and master* of all thou hast, he who said, he would give thee

---

* Or, steward, trustee, patron, master of all thou hast.

divinity. Where is his love for thee? And where is the gift he promised?

"For once has it pleased him, O Adam, to come to thee, to comfort thee, and to strengthen thee, and to rejoice with thee, and to send his hosts to guard thee; because thou hast hearkened to him, and hast yielded to his counsel; and hast transgressed My commandment but has followed his behest?"

Then Adam wept before the Lord, and said, "O Lord because I transgressed a little, Thou hast sorely plagued me in return for it, I ask Thee to deliver me out of his hands; or else have pity on me, and take my soul out of my body now in this strange land."

Then God said unto Adam, "If only there had been this sighing and praying before, ere thou didst transgress! Then wouldst thou have rest from the trouble in which thou art now."

But God had patience with Adam, and let him and Eve remain in the cave until they had fulfilled the forty days.

But as to Adam and Eve, their strength and flesh withered from fasting and praying, from hunger and thirst; for they had not tasted either food or drink since they left the garden; nor were the functions of their bodies yet settled; and they had no strength left to continue in prayer from hunger, until the end of the next day to the fortieth. They were fallen down in the cave; yet what speech escaped from their mouths, was only in praises.

CHAPTER LX.

Ninth apparition of Satan to Adam and Eve.

Then on the eighty-ninth day, Satan came to the cave, clad in a garment of light,[40] and girt about with a bright girdle.

In his hands was a staff of light, and he looked most awful: but his face was pleasant and his speech was sweet.

He thus transformed himself in order to deceive Adam and Eve, and to make them come out of the cave, ere they had fulfilled the forty days.

For he said within himself, "Now that when they had fulfilled the forty days' fasting and praying, God would restore them to their [former] estate; but if He did not do so, He would still be favourable to them; and even if He had not mercy on them, would He yet give them something from the garden to comfort them; as already twice before."

Then Satan drew near the cave in this fair appearance, and said:—

"O Adam, rise ye, stand up, thou and Eve, and come along with me, to a good land; and fear not. I am flesh and bones like you; and at first I was a creature that God created.

"And it was so, that when He had created me, He placed in a garden in the north,* on the border of the world.

"And He said to me, 'Abide here.' And I abode there according to His Word, neither did I transgress His commandment.

"Then He made a slumber to come over me, and He brought thee, O Adam, out of my side, but did not make thee abide by me.

"But God took thee in His divine hand, and placed thee in a garden to the eastward.

"Then I grieved because of thee, for that while God had taken thee out of my side, He had not let thee abide with me.

"But God said unto me: 'Grieve not because of Adam, whom I brought out of thy side; no harm will come to him.

"'For now I have brought out of his side a help-meet for him; and I have given him joy by so doing.'"

Then Satan said again, "I did not know how it is ye are in

---

* Lit. of the north; *i.e.*, the northern paradise or garden.

this cave, nor anything about this trial that has come upon you —until God said to me, ' Behold, Adam has transgressed, he whom I had taken out of thy side, and Eve also, whom I took out of his side ; and I have driven them out of the garden ; I have made them dwell in a land of sorrow and misery, because they transgressed against Me, and have hearkened to Satan. And lo, they are in suffering unto this day, the eightieth.'

"Then God said unto me, ' Arise, go to them, and make them come to thy place, and suffer not that Satan come near them, and afflict them. For they are now in great misery ; and lie helpless* from hunger.'

"He further said to me, 'When thou hast taken them to thyself, give them to eat of the fruit of the Tree of Life, and give them to drink of the water of peace ; and clothe them in a garment of light, and restore them to their former state of grace, and leave them not in misery, for they came from thee. But grieve not over them, nor repent† of that which has come upon them.'

"But when I heard this, I was sorry; and my heart could not patiently bear it for thy sake, O my child.

"But, O Adam, when I heard the name of Satan, I was afraid, and I said within myself,‡ I will not come out, lest he ensnare me, as he did my children, Adam and Eve.

"And I said, 'O God, when I go to my children, Satan will meet me in the way, and war against me, as he did against them.'

"Then God said unto me, ' Fear not; when thou findest him, smite him with the staff that is in thine hand, and be not afraid of him, for thou art [of] old [standing], and he shall not prevail against thee.'

"Then I said, 'O my Lord, I am old, and cannot go. Send Thy angels to bring them.'

* Or, prostrate. † Or, regret, grieve over.
‡ Lit. my thoughts, or mind.

"But God said unto me, 'Angels, verily, are not like them; and they will not consent to come with them. But I have chosen thee, because they are thy offspring, and like thee, and will hearken to what thou sayest.'

"God said further to me, 'If thou hast not strength to walk, I will send a cloud to carry thee and alight thee at the entrance of their cave; then the cloud will return and leave thee [there].

"'And if they will come with thee, I will send a cloud to carry thee and them.'

"Then He commanded a cloud, and it bare me up and brought me to you; and then went back.

"And now, O my children, Adam and Eve, look at my hoar hairs and at my feeble estate, and at my coming from that distant place. Come, come with me, to a place of rest."

Then he began to weep and to sob before Adam and Eve, and his tears poured upon the earth like water.

And when Adam and Eve raised their eyes and saw his beard, and heard his sweet talk,* their hearts softened towards him; they hearkened unto him, for they believed he was true.

And it seemed to them that they really were his offspring, when they saw that his face was like their own; and they trusted him.

CHAPTER LXI.

Then he took Adam and Eve by the hand, and began to bring them out of the cave.

But when they were come a little way out of it, God knew that Satan had overcome them, and had brought them out ere the forty days were ended, to take them to some distant place, and to destroy them.

Then the Word of the Lord God again came and cursed Satan, and drove him away from them.

* Or, speech.

And God began to speak unto Adam and Eve, saying to them, "What made you come out of the cave, unto this place?"

Then Adam said unto God, "Didst thou create a man before us? For when we were in the cave there suddenly came unto us a good old man who said to us, 'I am a messenger from God unto you, to bring you back to some place of rest.'

"And we did believe, O God, that he was a messenger from Thee; and we came out with him; and knew not whither we should go with him."

Then God said unto Adam, "See, that is the father of evil arts,* who brought thee and Eve out of the Garden of Delights. And now, indeed, when he saw that thou and Eve both joined together in fasting and praying, and that you came not out of the cave before the end of the forty days, he wished to make your purpose vain, to break† your mutual bond; to cut off all hope from you, and to drive you to some place where he might destroy you.

"Because he was unable to do aught to you, unless he showed himself in the likeness of you.

"Therefore did he come to you with a face like your own, and began to give you tokens as if they were all true.‡

"But I in mercy and with the favour I had unto you, did not allow him to destroy you; but I drove him away from you.

"Now, therefore, O Adam, take Eve, and return to your cave, and remain in it until the morrow of the fortieth day.§ And when ye come out, go towards the eastern gate of the garden."

Then Adam and Eve worshipped God, and praised and blessed Him for the deliverance that had come to them from Him. And they returned towards the cave. This happened at eventide of the thirty-ninth day.

---

* Or, wiles.   † Lit. alter.
‡ *i.e.*, to show you tokens that appeared true.
§ The fulfilment of the fortieth day.

Then Adam and Eve stood up [and] with great zeal,* prayed to God, to be brought out of their want† of strength; for their strength had departed from them, through hunger and thirst and prayer. But they watched the whole of that night praying, until morning.

Then Adam said unto Eve, "Arise, let us go towards the eastern gate of the garden as God told us."

And they said their prayers as they were wont to do every day; and they went out of the cave, to go near to the eastern gate of the garden.

Then Adam and Eve stood up and prayed, and besought God to strengthen them, and to send them something to satisfy their hunger.[41]

But when they had ended their prayers, they remained [where they were] by reason of their failing strength.

Then came the Word of God again, and said unto them, "O Adam, arise, go and bring hither two figs."

Then Adam and Eve arose, and went until they drew near to the cave.

CHAPTER LXII.

Tenth apparition of Satan to Adam and Eve, about the figs.

But Satan the wicked, was envious, because of the consolation God had given them.‡

So he prevented them, and went into the cave and took the two figs, and buried them outside the cave, so that Adam and Eve should not find them. He also had in his thoughts to destroy them.

But by God's mercy, as soon as those two figs were in the earth, God defeated Satan's counsel regarding them; and

---

* Lit. labour, fervour, or toil.   † Lack, or poverty.
‡ Or, because God had comforted them.

made them into two fruit-trees, that overshadowed the cave. For Satan had buried them on the eastern side of it.

Then when the two trees were grown, and were covered with fruit, Satan grieved and mourned, and said, "Better were it to have left those figs as they were; for now, behold, they have become two fruit-trees, whereof Adam will eat all the days of his life. Whereas I had in mind, when I buried them, to destroy them entirely, and to hide them for aye.

"But God has overturned my counsel; and would not that this sacred fruit should perish; and He has made plain my intention, and has defeated the counsel I had formed against His servants."

Then Satan went away ashamed, of not having wrought out his design.

CHAPTER LXIII.

But Adam and Eve, as they drew near to the cave, saw two fig-trees, covered with fruit, and overshadowing the cave.

Then Adam said to Eve, "It seems to me we have gone astray. When did these two trees grow here? It seems to me that the enemy wishes to lead us astray. Sayest thou that there is in the earth another cave than this?

"Yet, O Eve, let us go into the cave, and find in it the two figs; for this is our cave, in which we were. But if we should not find the two figs in it, then it cannot be our cave."

They went then into the cave, and looked into the four corners of it, but found not the two figs.

And Adam wept, and said to Eve, "Are we come to a wrong cave, then, O Eve? It seems to me these two fig-trees are the two figs that were in the cave." And Eve said, "I, for my part, do not know."

Then Adam stood up and prayed and said, "O God, Thou

didst command us to come back to the cave, to take the two figs, and then to return to Thee.

"But now, we have not found them. O God, hast Thou taken them, and sown these two trees, or have we gone astray in the earth; or has the enemy deceived us? If it be real, then, O God, reveal to us the secret of these two trees and of the two figs."

Then came the Word of God to Adam, and said unto him, "O Adam, when I sent thee to fetch the figs, Satan went before thee to the cave, took the figs, and buried them outside, eastward of the cave, thinking to destroy them; and not sowing them with good intent.

"Not for his mere sake, then, have these trees grown up at once; but I had mercy on thee and I commanded them to grow. And they grew to be two large trees, that you be overshadowed by their branches, and find rest; and that I make you see My power and My marvellous works.

"And, also, to show you Satan's meanness, and his evil works, for ever since ye came out of the garden, he has not ceased, no, not one day, from doing you some harm. But I have not given him power over you."

And God said, "Henceforth, O Adam, rejoice on account of the trees, thou and Eve; and rest under them when ye feel weary. But eat not of their fruit, nor come near them."

Then Adam wept, and said, "O God, wilt Thou again kill us, or wilt Thou drive us away from before Thy face, and cut our life from off the face of the earth?

"O God, I beseech Thee, if Thou knowest that there be in these trees either death or some other evil, as at the first time,* root them up from near our cave, and wither them; and leave us to die of the heat, of hunger and of thirst.

"For we know Thy marvellous works, O God, that they are great, and that by Thy power Thou canst bring one thing out

---

* In the garden.

of another, without one's wish.* For Thy power can make rocks to become trees, and trees to become rocks."

CHAPTER LXIV.

Then God looked upon Adam and upon his strength of mind, upon his endurance of hunger and thirst, and of the heat. And he changed the two fig-trees into two figs, as they were at first, and then said to Adam and to Eve, "Each of you may take one fig." And they took them, as the Lord commanded them.

And he said to them, " Go ye into the cave, and eat the figs, and satisfy your hunger, lest ye die."

So, as God commanded them, they went into the cave, about the time when the sun was setting. And Adam and Eve stood up and prayed at the time of the setting sun.

Then they sat down to eat the figs ; but they knew not how to eat them ; for they were not accustomed to eat earthly food. They feared also lest, if they ate, their stomach should be burdened and their flesh thickened, and their hearts take to liking earthly food.

But while they were thus seated, God, out of pity for them, sent them His angel, lest they should perish of hunger and thirst.

And the angel said unto Adam and Eve, " God says to you that ye have not strength to fast until death ; eat, therefore, and strengthen your bodies ; for ye are now animal flesh, that cannot subsist without food and drink."

Then Adam and Eve took the figs and began to eat of them. But God had put into them a mixture as of savoury bread and blood.

Then the angel went from Adam and Eve, who ate of the figs until they had satisfied their hunger. Then they put by what remained ; but by the power of God, the figs became full

---

* Lit. my will, or wish.

as before, because God blessed them. After this Adam and Eve arose, and prayed with a joyful heart and renewed strength, and praised and rejoiced abundantly the whole of that night. And this was the end of the eighty-third day.

CHAPTER LXV.

And when it was day, they rose and prayed, after their custom, and then went out of the cave.

But as they felt great trouble from the food they had eaten, and to which they were not used, they went about in the cave saying to each other:—

"What has happened to us through eating, that this pain should have come upon us? Woe be to us, we shall die! Better for us to have died than to have eaten; and to have kept our bodies pure, than to have defiled them [with food]."

Then Adam said to Eve, "This pain did not come to us in the garden, neither did we eat such bad food there. Thinkest thou, O Eve, that God will plague us through the food that is in us, or that our inwards will come out; or that God means to kill us with this pain before He has fulfilled His promise to us?"

Then Adam besought the Lord and said, "O Lord, let us not perish through the food we have eaten. O Lord, smite us not; but deal with us according to Thy great mercy, and forsake us not until the day of the promise Thou hast made us."

Then God looked upon them, and at once fitted them for eating food; as unto this day; so that they should not perish.

Then Adam and Eve came back into the cave sorrowful and weeping because of the alteration in their nature. And they both knew from that hour that they were altered [beings], that their hope of returning to the garden was now cut off; and that they could not enter it.

For that now their bodies had strange functions; and all flesh that requires food and drink for its existence, cannot be in the garden.

Then Adam said to Eve, "Behold, our hope is now cut off; and so is our trust to enter the garden. We no longer belong to the inhabitants of the garden; but henceforth we are earthy and of the dust, and of the inhabitants of the earth. We shall not return to the garden, until the day in which God has promised to save us, and to bring us again into the garden, as He promised us."

Then they prayed to God that He would have mercy on them; after which, their mind was quieted, their hearts were broken, and their longing was cooled down; and they were like strangers on earth. That night Adam and Eve spent in the cave, where they slept heavily by reason of the food they had eaten.

CHAPTER LXVI.

When it was morning, the day after they had eaten food, Adam and Eve prayed in the cave, and Adam said unto Eve, "Lo, we asked for food of God, and He gave it. But now let us also ask Him to give us a drink of water."

Then they arose, and went to the bank of the stream of water, that was on the south border of the garden, in which they had before thrown themselves. And they stood on the bank, and prayed to God that He would command them to drink of the water.

Then the Word of God came to Adam, and said unto him, "O Adam, thy body is become brutish, and requires water to drink. Take ye, and drink, thou and Eve; give thanks and praise."

Adam and Eve then drew near, and drank of it, until their bodies felt refreshed. After having drunk, they praised God, and then returned to their cave, after their former custom. This happened at the end of eighty-three days.

Then on the eighty-fourth day, they took two figs and hung them in the cave, together with the leaves thereof, to be to them a sign and a blessing from God. And they placed them there until there should arise a posterity to them, who should see the wonderful things God had done to them.

Then Adam and Eve again stood outside the cave, and besought God to show them some food wherewith to nourish their bodies.

Then the Word of God came and said unto him, "O Adam, go down to the westward of the cave, as far as a land of dark soil,* and there thou shalt find food."

And Adam hearkened unto the Word of God, took Eve, and went down to a land of dark soil, and found there wheat growing, in the ear and ripe, and figs to eat; and Adam rejoiced over it.

Then the Word of God came again to Adam, and said unto him, "Take of this wheat and make thee bread of it, to nourish thy body withal." And God gave Adam's heart wisdom, to work out the corn until it became bread.

Adam accomplished all that, until he grew very faint and weary. He then returned to the cave; rejoicing at what he had learned of what is done with wheat, until it is made into bread for one's use.

Further details would lengthen too much the description of them; we therefore cut short [our narrative].

CHAPTER LXVII.

First wonder that happened to Adam and Eve with Satan, respecting the wheat.

But when Adam and Eve went down to the land of black

* Or, black mud.

mud, and came near to the wheat God had showed them, and saw it ripe* and ready for reaping, as they had no sickle to reap it withal—they girt themselves, and began to pull up the wheat, until it was all done. Then they made it into a heap; and, faint from heat and from thirst, they went under a shady tree, where the breeze fanned them to sleep.

But Satan saw what Adam and Eve had done. And he called his hosts, and said to them, "Since God has shown to Adam and Eve all about this wheat, wherewith to strengthen their bodies—and, lo, they are come and have made a heap of it, and faint from [the toil] are now asleep—come, let us set fire to [this heap of corn], and burn it, and let us take that bottle of water that is by them, and empty it out, so that they may find nothing to drink, and we kill them with hunger and thirst.

"Then, when they wake up from their sleep, and seek to return to the cave, we will come to them in the way, and will lead them astray; so that they die of hunger and thirst; when they may, perhaps, deny God, and He destroy them. So shall we be rid of them."†

Then Satan and his hosts threw fire upon the wheat and consumed it.

But from the heat of the flame Adam and Eve awoke from their sleep, and saw the wheat burning, and the bucket of water by them, poured out.

Then they wept and went back to the cave.

But as they were going up from below the mountain [where they were], Satan and his hosts met them in the form of angels, praising [God].

Then Satan said to Adam, "O Adam, why art thou so pained with hunger and thirst? It seems to me that Satan has burnt up the wheat." And Adam said to him, "Ay."

Again Satan said to Adam, "Come back with us; we are

---

* Lit. dry.   † Lit. have rest from them.

angels of God. God sent us to thee, to show thee another field of corn, better than that; and beyond it is a fountain of good water, and many trees, where thou shalt dwell near it, and work the corn-field to better [purpose] than that which Satan has consumed."

Adam thought that he was true, and that they were angels who talked with him; and he went back with them.

Then Satan began to lead astray Adam and Eve eight days, until they both fell down as if dead, from hunger, thirst, and faintness. Then he fled with his hosts, and left them.

CHAPTER LXVIII.

Then God looked upon Adam and Eve, and upon what had come upon them from Satan, and how he had made them perish.

God, therefore, sent His Word, and raised up Adam and Eve from their state of death.

Then, Adam, when he was raised, said, "O God, Thou hast burnt [and taken] from us the corn Thou hadst given us, and Thou hast emptied out the bucket of water. And Thou hast sent Thy angels, who have waylaid us from the corn-field. Wilt Thou make us perish? If this be from Thee, O God, then take away our souls; but punish us not."

Then God said to Adam, "I did not burn down the wheat, and I did not pour the water out of the bucket, and I did not send My angels to lead thee astray.

"But it is Satan, thy master [who did it]; he to whom thou hast subjected thyself; My commandment being [meanwhile] set aside. He it is, who burnt down the corn, and poured out the water, and who has led thee astray; and all the promises he has made you, verily are but feint, and deceit, and a lie.

"But now, O Adam, thou shalt acknowledge My good deeds done to thee."

ADAM'S OFFERING OF WHEAT

And God told His angels to take Adam and Eve, and to bear them up to the field of wheat,* which they found as before, with the bucket full of water. There they saw a tree, and found on it solid manna; and wondered at God's power. And the angels commanded them to eat of the manna when they were hungry.

And God adjured Satan with a curse, not to come again, and destroy the field of corn.

Then Adam and Eve took of the corn, and made of it an offering,† and took it and offered it up on the mountain, the place where they had offered up their first offering of blood.

And they offered this oblation again on the altar they had built at first. And they stood up and prayed, and besought the Lord saying, "Thus, O God, when we were in the garden, did our praises go up to Thee, like this offering; and our innocence‡ went up to the like incense. But now, O God, accept this offering from us, and turn us not back, reft§ of Thy mercy.‖

Then God said to Adam and Eve, "Since ye have made this oblation and have offered it to Me, I shall make it My flesh,¶ when I come down upon earth to save you; and I shall cause it to be offered continually upon an altar, for forgiveness and for mercy, unto those who partake of it duly."

And God sent a bright fire upon the offering of Adam and Eve, and filled it with brightness, grace, and light; and the Holy Ghost came down upon that oblation.

Then God commanded an angel to take fire-tongs, like a spoon,** and with it to take an offering and bring it to Adam

---

* Lit. place.

† 'Ο σῖτος δὲ καὶ ὁ οἶνος τῶν ἁγίων μυστηρίων αἰνίγματα. S. Athan., Quæst. lxvii, vol. ii, p. 414.

‡ Or, purity. § Or, bare.

‖ The Arabic adds: And God wondered at Adam's wisdom, and Adam's deed pleased him.

¶ Or, body. ** Used at the Eucharist in the East.

and Eve. And the angel did so, as God had commanded him, and offered it to them.

And the souls of Adam and Eve were brightened, and their hearts were filled with joy and gladness and with the praises of God.

And God said to Adam, "This shall be unto you a custom, to do so, when affliction and sorrow come upon you. But your deliverance and your entrance into the garden, shall not be until the days are fulfilled, as [agreed] between you and Me; were it not so, I would, of My mercy and pity for you, bring you back to My garden and to My favour for the sake of the offering you have just made to My name."

Adam rejoiced at these words which he heard from God; and he and Eve worshipped before the altar, to which they bowed, and then went back to the Cave of Treasures.

And this took place at the end of the twelfth day after the eightieth day, from the time Adam and Eve came out of the garden.

And they stood up the whole night praying until morning; and then went out of the cave.

Then Adam said to Eve, with joy of heart, because of the offering they had made to God, and that had been accepted of Him, "Let us do this three times every week, on the fourth day [Wednesday], on the preparation day [Friday], and on the Sabbath [Sunday], all the days of our life."

And as they agreed to these words between themselves, God was pleased with their thoughts, and with the resolution they had each taken with the other.

After this, came the Word of God to Adam, and said, "O Adam, thou hast determined beforehand the days in which sufferings shall come upon Me, when I am made flesh; for they are the fourth [Wednesday], and the preparation day [Friday].

"But as to the first day, I created in it all things, and I raised the heavens. And, again, through My rising again on this day, will I create joy, and raise them on high, who believe in Me; O Adam, offer this oblation, all the days of thy life."

Then God withdrew His Word from Adam.

But Adam continued to offer this oblation thus, every week three times, until the end of seven weeks. And on the first day, which is the fiftieth, Adam made an offering as he was wont, and he and Eve took it and came to the altar before God, as He had taught them.

CHAPTER LXIX.

Twelfth apparition of Satan to Adam and Eve, while Adam was praying over the offering upon the altar; when Satan smote him.

Then Satan, the hater of all good, envious of Adam and of his offering through which he found favour with God, hastened and took a sharp stone from among sharp iron-stones; appeared in the form of a man, and went and stood by Adam and Eve.

Adam was then offering on the altar, and had begun to pray, with his hands spread unto God.

Then Satan hastened with the sharp iron-stone he had with him, and with it pierced Adam on the right side, whence flowed blood and water, then Adam fell upon the altar like a corpse. And Satan fled.

Then Eve came, and took Adam and placed him below the altar. And there she stayed, weeping over him; while a stream of blood flowed from Adam's side upon his offering.

But God looked upon the death of Adam. He then sent His Word, and raised him up and said unto him, "Fulfil thy offering, for indeed, Adam, it is worth much, and there is no shortcoming* in it."

God said further unto Adam, "Thus will it also happen to

* Also: lack, or imperfection, defect, or deficiency.

Me, on the earth, when I shall be pierced and blood shall flow, blood and water from My side, and run over My body, which is the true offering; and which shall be offered on the altar as a perfect offering."

Then God commanded Adam to finish his offering, and when he had ended it he worshipped before God, and praised Him for the signs He had showed him.

And God healed Adam in one day, which is the end of the seven weeks; and that is the fiftieth day.

Then Adam and Eve returned from the mountain, and went into the Cave of Treasures, as they were used to do. This completed for Adam and Eve, one hundred and forty days since their coming out of the garden.

Then they both stood up that night and prayed to God. And when it was morning, they went out, and went down westward of the cave, to the place where their corn was, and there rested under the shadow of a tree, as they were wont.

But [when there] a multitude of beasts came all round them. It was Satan's doing, in his wickedness; in order to wage war against Adam through marriage.

CHAPTER LXX.

Thirteenth apparition of Satan to Adam and Eve, to make war against him, through his marriage with Eve.

After this Satan, the hater of all good, took the form of an angel, and with him two others, so that they looked like the three angels who had brought to Adam, gold, incense, and myrrh.

They passed before Adam and Eve while they were under the tree, and greeted Adam and Eve with fair words that were full of guile.

But when Adam and Eve saw their comely mien, and [heard]

their sweet speech, Adam rose, welcomed them, and brought them to Eve, and they remained all together; Adam's heart the while, being glad because he thought concerning them, that they were the same angels, who had brought him gold, incense, and myrrh.

Because, when they came to Adam the first time, there came upon him from them, peace and joy, through their bringing him good tokens; so Adam thought that they were come a second time to give him other tokens for him to rejoice withal. For he did not know it was Satan; therefore did he receive them with joy and companied with them.

Then Satan, the tallest of them, said, "Rejoice, O Adam, and be glad. Lo, God has sent us to thee to tell thee something."

And Adam said, "What is it?" Then Satan answered, "It is a light thing, yet it is a word of God, wilt thou hear it from us and do it? But if thou hearest not, we will return to God, and tell Him that thou wouldest not receive His word."

And Satan said again to Adam, "Fear not, neither let a trembling come upon thee; dost not thou know us?"

But Adam said, "I know you not."

Then Satan said to him, "I am the angel who brought thee gold, and took it to the cave; this other one is he who brought thee incense; and that third one, is he who brought thee myrrh [when thou wast] on the top of the mountain, and who carried thee to the cave.

But as to [the other angels] our fellows, who bare you to the cave, God has not sent them with us this time; for He said to us, "You suffice."

So when Adam heard these words he believed them, and said to these angels, "Speak the word of God, that I may receive it."

And Satan said unto him, "Swear, and promise me that thou wilt receive it."

Then Adam said, "I know not how to swear and promise."

And Satan said to him, "Hold out thy hand, and put it inside my hand."

Then Adam held out his hand, and put it into Satan's hand; when Satan said unto him, "Say, now—so true* as God is living, rational, and speaking, who raised the heavens in the space, and established the earth upon the waters, and has created me out of the four elements, and out of the dust of the earth—I will not break† my promise, nor renounce my word." And Adam swore thus.

Then Satan said to him, "Lo, it is now some time since thou camest out of the garden, and thou knowest neither wickedness nor evil. But now God says to thee, to take Eve who came out of thy side, and to wed her, that she bear thee children, to comfort thee, and to drive from thee trouble and sorrow; now this thing is not difficult, neither is there any scandal in it to thee."

CHAPTER LXXI.

But when Adam heard these words from Satan, he sorrowed much, because of his oath and of his promise, and said, "Shall I commit adultery with my [flesh and my] bones, and shall I sin against myself, for God to destroy me, and to blot me out from off the face of the earth?

"Since, when at first, I ate of the tree, He drove me out of the garden into this strange land, and deprived me of [my] bright nature, and brought death upon me. If, then, I should do this, He will cut off my life from the earth, and He will cast me into hell, and will plague me there a long time.

"But God never spoke the words thou hast told me; and ye are not God's angels, nor yet sent from Him. But ye are devils, come to me under the false appearance of angels. Away from me; ye cursed of God!"

* Lit. as indeed.   † Lit. foul.

Then those devils fled from before Adam. And he and Eve arose, and returned to the Cave of Treasures, and went into it.

Then Adam said to Eve, "If thou sawest what I did, tell it not; for I sinned against God in swearing by His great name, and I have placed my hand another time into that of Satan." Eve, then, held her peace, as Adam told her.

Then Adam arose, and spread his hands unto God, beseeching and entreating Him with tears, to forgive him what he had done. And Adam remained thus standing and praying forty days and forty nights. He neither ate nor drank until he dropped down upon the earth from hunger and thirst.

Then God sent His Word unto Adam, who raised him up from where he lay, and said unto him, "O Adam, why hast thou sworn by My name, and why hast thou made agreement with Satan another time?"

But Adam wept, and said, "O God, forgive me, for I did this unwittingly; believing they were God's angels."

And God forgave Adam, saying to him, "Beware of Satan." And He withdrew His Word from Adam.

Then Adam's heart was comforted; and he took Eve, and they went out of the cave, to make some food for their bodies.

But from that day Adam struggled in his mind about his wedding Eve; afraid as he was to do it, lest God should be wroth with him.

Then Adam and Eve went to the river of water, and sat on the bank, as people do when they enjoy themselves.

But Satan was jealous of them; and would destroy them.

CHAPTER LXXII.

Fourteenth apparition of Satan to Adam and Eve; as coming up out of the river, in the similitude of young maidens.

Then Satan, and ten from his hosts, transformed themselves into maidens, unlike any others in the whole world for grace.

They came up out of the river in presence of Adam and Eve, and they said among themselves, "Come, we will look at the faces of Adam and of Eve, who are of the men upon earth. How beautiful they are, and how different is their look from our own faces." Then they came to Adam and Eve, and greeted them; and stood wondering at them.

Adam and Eve looked at them also, and wondered at their beauty, and said, "Is there, then, under us, another world, with such beautiful creatures as these in it?"

And those maidens said to Adam and Eve, "Yes, indeed, we are an abundant creation."

Then Adam said to them, "But how do you multiply?"

And they answered him, "We have husbands who wedded us, and we bear them children, who grow up, and who in their turn wed and are wedded, and also bear children; and thus we increase. And if so be, O Adam, thou wilt not believe us, we will show thee our husbands and our children."

Then they shouted over the river as if to call their husbands and their children, who came up from the river, men and children; and every one came to his wife, his children being with him.

But when Adam and Eve saw them, they stood dumb, and wondered at them.

Then they said to Adam and Eve, "You see our husbands and our children, wed Eve as we wed our wives, and you shall have children the same as we." This was a device of Satan to deceive Adam.

Satan also thought within himself, "God at first commanded Adam concerning the fruit of the tree, saying to him, 'Eat not of it; else of death thou shalt die.' But Adam ate of it, and yet God did not kill him; He only decreed upon him death, and plagues and trials, until the day he shall come out of his body.

"Now, then, if I deceive him to do this thing, and to wed Eve without God's commandment, God will kill him then."

Therefore did Satan work this apparition before Adam and Eve; because he sought to kill him, and to make him disappear from off the face of the earth.

Meanwhile the fire of sin came upon Adam, and he thought of committing sin. But he restrained himself, fearing lest if he followed this advice [of Satan] God would put him to death.

Then Adam and Eve arose, and prayed to God, while Satan and his hosts went down into the river, in presence of Adam and Eve; to let them see that they were going back to their own regions.

Then Adam and Eve went back to the Cave of Treasures, as they were wont; about evening time.

And they both arose and prayed to God that night. Adam remained standing in prayer, yet not knowing how to pray, by reason of the thoughts of his heart regarding his wedding Eve; and he continued so until morning.

And when light arose, Adam said unto Eve, "Arise let us go below the mountain, where they brought us gold, and let us ask the Lord concerning this matter."

Then Eve said, "What is that matter, O Adam?"

And he answered her, "That I may request the Lord to inform me about wedding thee; for I will not do it without His order, lest He make us perish, thee and me. For those devils have set my heart on fire, with thoughts of what they showed us, in their sinful apparitions."

Then Eve said to Adam, "Why need we go below the mountain? Let us rather stand up and pray in our cave to God, to let us know whether this counsel is good or not."

Then Adam rose up in prayer and said, "O God, Thou knowest that we transgressed against Thee, and from the moment we transgressed, we were bereft of our bright nature; and our body became brutish, requiring food and drink; and with animal desires.

"Command us, O God, not to give way to them without Thy

order, lest Thou bring us to nothing. For if Thou give us not the order, we shall be overpowered, and follow that advice [of Satan] ; and Thou wilt again make us perish.

"If not, then take our souls from us; let us be rid of this animal lust. And if Thou give us no order respecting this thing, then sever Eve from me, and me from her; and place us each far away from the other.

"Yet again, O God, when Thou hast put us asunder from each other, the devils will deceive us with their apparitions, and destroy our hearts, and defile our thoughts towards each other. Yet if it is not each of us towards the other, it will, at all events, be through their appearance when they show themselves to us." Here Adam ended his prayer.

CHAPTER LXXIII.

. Then God looked upon the words of Adam that they were true, and that he could long await [His order], respecting the counsel of Satan.

And God approved Adam in what he had thought concerning this, and in the prayer he had offered in His presence; and the Word of God came unto Adam and said to him, "O Adam, if only thou hadst had this caution at first, ere thou camest out of the garden into this land!"

After that, God sent His angel who had brought gold, and the angel who had brought incense, and the angel who had brought myrrh to Adam, that they should inform him respecting his wedding Eve.

Then those angels said to Adam, "Take the gold and give it to Eve as a wedding gift, and betroth her; then give her some incense and myrrh as a present; and be ye, thou and she, one flesh."

Adam hearkened to the angels, and took the gold and put

it into Eve's bosom in her garment; and bethrothed her with his hand.

Then the angels commanded Adam and Eve, to arise and pray forty days and forty nights; and after that, that Adam should come in to his wife; for then this would be an act pure and undefiled; and he should have children who would multiply, and replenish the face of the earth.

Then both Adam and Eve received the words of the angels; and the angels departed from them.

Then Adam and Eve began to fast and to pray, until the end of the forty days; and then they came together, as the angels had told them. And from the time Adam left the garden until he wedded Eve, were two hundred and twenty-three days, that is seven months and thirteen days.

Thus was Satan's war with Adam defeated.

CHAPTER LXXIV.

And they dwelt on the earth working, in order to continue in the well-being of their bodies; and were so until the nine months of Eve's child-bearing were ended, and the time drew near when she must be delivered.

Then she said unto Adam, "This cave is a pure spot by reason of the signs [wrought in] it since [we left] the garden; and we shall again pray in it. It is not meet, then, that I should bring forth in it; let us rather repair to that of the sheltering rock, which Satan hurled at us, when he wished to kill us with it; but that was held up and spread as an awning over us by the command of God; and formed a cave."

Then Adam removed Eve to that cave; and when the time came that she should bring forth, she travailed much. So was Adam sorry, and his heart suffered for her sake; for she was nigh unto death; that the word of God to her should be fulfilled: "In suffering shalt thou bear a child, and in sorrow shalt thou bring forth thy child."

But when Adam saw the strait in which Eve was, he arose and prayed to God, and said, "O Lord, look upon me with the eye of Thy mercy, and bring her out of her distress."

And God looked at His maid-servant Eve, and delivered her, and she brought forth her first-born son, and with him a daughter. Then Adam rejoiced at Eve's deliverance, and also over the children she had borne him. And Adam ministered unto Eve in the cave, until the end of eight days; when they named the son Cain,* and the daughter Luluwa.†[41]

The meaning of Cain is "hater," because he hated his sister in their mother's womb; ere they came out of it. Therefore did Adam name him Cain.

But Luluwa means "beautiful," because she was more beautiful than her mother.

Then Adam and Eve waited until Cain and his sister were forty days old, when Adam said unto Eve, "We will make an offering and offer it up in behalf of the children."

And Eve said, "We will make one offering for the first-born son; and afterwards we shall make one for the daughter."

CHAPTER LXXV.

Then Adam prepared an offering, and he and Eve offered it up for their children, and brought it to the altar they had built at first.

And Adam offered up the offering, and besought God to accept his offering.

Then God accepted Adam's offering, and sent a light from heaven that shone upon the offering. And Adam and the son drew near to the offering, but Eve and the daughter did not approach unto it.

* Eth. Cail.   † "Luluwa" is the Arabic for "a pearl."

ADAM'S OFFERING FOR HIS CHILDREN.

Then Adam came down from upon the altar, and they were joyful; and Adam and Eve waited until the daughter was eighty days old; then Adam prepared an offering and took it to Eve and to the children; and they went to the altar, where Adam offered it up, as he was wont, asking the Lord to accept his offering.

And the Lord accepted the offering of Adam and Eve. Then Adam, Eve, and the children, drew near together, and came down from the mountain, rejoicing.

But they returned not to the cave in which they were born; but came to the Cave of Treasures, in order that the children should go round it, and be blessed with the tokens [brought] from the garden.

But after they had been blessed with these tokens, they went back to the cave in which they were born.

However, before Eve had offered up the offering, Adam had taken her, and had gone with her to the river of water, in which they threw themselves at first; and there they washed themselves. Adam washed his body and Eve [hers also] clean, after the suffering and distress that had come upon them.

But Adam and Eve, after washing themselves in the river of water, returned every night to the Cave of Treasures, where they prayed and were blessed; and then went back to their cave, where the children were born.

So did Adam and Eve until the children had done sucking. Then, when they were weaned, Adam made an offering for the souls of his children; other than the three times he made an offering for them, every week.

When the days of nursing the children were ended, Eve again conceived, and when her days were accomplished she brought forth another son and daughter; and they named the son Abel, and the daughter Aklemia.

Then at the end of forty days, Adam made an offering for the son, and at the end of eighty days he made another offering for the daughter, and did by them, as he had done before by Cain and his sister Luluwa.

He brought them to the Cave of Treasures, where they received a blessing, and then returned to the cave where they were born. After the birth of these, Eve ceased from child-bearing.

CHAPTER LXXVI.

And the children began to wax stronger, and to grow in stature; but Cain was hard-hearted, and ruled over his younger brother.

And oftentimes when his father made an offering, he would remain [behind] and not go with them, to offer up.

But, as to Abel, he had a meek heart, and was obedient to his father and mother, whom he often moved to make an offering, because he loved it; and prayed and fasted much.

Then came this sign to Abel. As he was coming into the Cave of Treasures, and saw the golden rods, the incense and the myrrh, he inquired of his parents Adam and Eve concerning them, and said unto them, "How did you come by these?"

Then Adam told him all that had befallen them. And Abel felt deeply about what his father told him.

Furthermore his father Adam told him of the works of God, and of the garden; and after that, he remained behind his father the whole of that night in the Cave of Treasures.

And that night, while he was praying, Satan appeared unto him under the figure of a man, who said to him, "Thou hast oftentimes moved thy father to make an offering, to fast and to pray, therefore I will kill thee, and make thee perish from this world."

But as for Abel, he prayed to God, and drove away [Satan] from him; and believed not the words of the devil. Then when it was day, an angel of God appeared unto him, who said to him, "Shorten neither fasting, prayer, nor offering up an oblation unto thy God. For, lo, the Lord has accepted thy prayer. Be not afraid of the figure which appeared unto thee in the night, and who cursed thee unto death." And the angel departed from him.

Then when it was day, Abel came to Adam and Eve, and told them of the vision he had seen. But when they heard it, they grieved much over it, yet said nothing to him [about it]; they only comforted him.

But as to hard-hearted Cain, Satan came to him by night, showed himself and said unto him, "Since Adam and Eve love thy brother Abel much more than they love thee, and wish to join him in marriage to thy beautiful sister, because they love him; but wish to join thee in marriage to his ill-favoured sister, because they hate thee;

"Now, therefore, I counsel thee, when they do that, to kill thy brother; then thy sister will be left for thee; and his sister will be cast away."

And Satan departed from him. But the wicked One remained [behind] in the heart of Cain, who sought many a time, to kill his brother.

CHAPTER LXXVII.

But when Adam saw that the elder brother hated the younger, he endeavoured to soften their hearts, and said unto Cain, "Take, O my son, of the fruits of thy sowing, and make an offering unto God, that He may forgive thee thy wickedness and thy sin."

He said also to Abel, "Take thou of thy sowing* and make an offering and bring it to God, that He may forgive thy wickedness and thy sin."

* Different from Gen. iv, 4.

Then Abel hearkened unto his father's voice, and took of his sowing, and made a good offering, and said to his father, Adam, "Come with me, to show me how to offer it up."

And they went, Adam and Eve with him, and showed him how to offer up his gift upon the altar. Then after that, they stood up and prayed that God would accept Abel's offering.

Then God looked upon Abel and accepted his offering. And God was more pleased with Abel than with his offering, because of his good heart and pure body. There was no trace of guile in him.

Then they came down from the altar, and went to the cave in which they dwelt. But Abel, by reason of his joy at having made his offering, repeated it three times a week, after the example of his father Adam.

But as to Cain, he took no pleasure in offering; but after much anger on his father's part, he offered up his gift once; and when he did offer up, his eye was on the offering he made,[42] and he took the smallest of his sheep for an offering, and his eye was again on it.

Therefore God did not accept his offering, because his heart was full of murderous* thoughts.

And they all thus lived together in the cave in which Eve had brought forth, until Cain was fifteen years old, and Abel twelve years old.†

CHAPTER LXXVIII.

Then Adam said to Eve, "Behold the children are grown up; we must think of finding wives for them."

Then Eve answered, "How can we do it ?"

---

* Lit. destruction.

† *Midr. Tankhuma* (fol. 5), however, says that Cain and Abel were then about forty years old.

Then Adam said to her, "We will join Abel's sister in marriage to Cain,* and Cain's sister to Abel."

Then said Eve to Adam, "I do not like Cain because he is hard-hearted; but let them bide until we offer up unto the Lord in their behalf."

And Adam said no more.

Meanwhile Satan came to Cain in the figure of a man of the field, and said to him, "Behold Adam and Eve have taken counsel together about the marriage of you two; and they have agreed to marry Abel's sister to thee, and thy sister to him.

"But if it was not that I love thee, I would not have told thee this thing. Yet if thou wilt take my advice, and hearken to me, I will bring thee on thy wedding day beautiful robes, gold and silver in plenty, and my relations will attend† thee."

Then Cain said with joy, "Where are thy relations?"

And Satan answered, "My relations are in a garden in the north, whither I once meant to bring thy father Adam; but he would not accept my offer.

"But thou, if thou wilt receive my [words] and if thou wilt come unto me after thy wedding, thou shalt rest from the misery in which thou art; and thou shalt rest and be better off than thy father Adam."

At these words of Satan Cain opened his ears, and leant towards his speech.

And he did not remain in the field, but he went to Eve, his mother, and beat her, and cursed her, and said to her, "Why are ye about taking my sister to wed her to my brother? Am I dead?"

His mother, however, quieted‡ him, and sent him to the field where he had been.

---

* Adam did so, in order to avoid marrying the brother to his sister of the same birth, and thus to prevent, as far as possible, consanguinity. Masudi., ch. iii, p. 63.

† Lit. assist or help.

‡ Or, beguiled.

Then when Adam came, she told him of what Cain had done.

But Adam grieved and held his peace, and said not a word.

Then on the morrow Adam said unto Cain his son, "Take of thy sheep, young and good,[43] and offer them up unto thy God; and I will speak to thy brother, to make unto his God an offering of corn."

They both hearkened to their father Adam, and they took their offerings, and offered them up on the mountain by the altar.

But Cain behaved haughtily towards his brother, and thrust him from the altar, and would not let him offer up his gift upon the altar; but he offered his own upon it, with a proud heart, full of guile, and fraud.

But as for Abel, he set up stones [that were] near at hand, and upon that, he offered up his gift with a heart humble and free from guile.

Cain was then standing by the altar on which he had offered up his gift; and he cried unto God to accept his offering; but God did not accept it from him; neither did a divine fire come down to consume his offering.

But he remained standing over against the altar, out of humour and wroth, looking towards his brother Abel, to see if God would accept his offering or not.

And Abel prayed unto God to accept his offering. Then a divine fire came down and consumed his offering. And God smelled the sweet savour of his offering; because Abel loved Him and rejoiced in Him.

And because God was well pleased with him He sent him an angel of light in the figure of man who had partaken of his offering, because He had smelled the sweet savour of his offering, and they comforted Abel and strengthened his heart.

But Cain was looking on all that took place at his brother's offering, and was wroth on account of it.

Then he opened his mouth and blasphemed God, because He had not accepted his offering.

But God said unto Cain, "Wherefore is thy countenance sad?⁴⁴ Be righteous, that I may accept thy offering. Not against Me hast thou murmured, but against thyself."

And God said this to Cain in rebuke, and because He abhorred him and his offering.

And Cain came down from the altar, his colour changed and of a woeful countenance, and came to his father and mother and told them all that had befallen him. And Adam grieved much because God had not accepted Cain's offering.

But Abel came down rejoicing, and with a gladsome heart, and told his father and mother how God had accepted his offering. And they rejoiced at it and kissed his face.

And Abel said to his father, "Because Cain thrust me from the altar, and would not allow me to offer my gift upon it, I made an altar for myself and offered [my] gift upon it."

But when Adam heard this he was very sorry, because it was the altar he had built at first, and upon which he had offered his own gifts.

As to Cain, he was so sullen and so angry that he went into the field, where Satan came to him and said to him, "Since thy brother Abel has taken refuge with thy father Adam, because thou didst thrust him from the altar, they have kissed his face, and they rejoice over him, far more than over thee."

When Cain heard these words of Satan, he was filled with rage; and he let no one know. But he was laying wait to kill his brother, until he brought him into the cave, and then said to him:—*

"O brother, the country is so beautiful, and there are such beautiful and pleasurable trees in it, and charming to look at! But brother, thou hast never been one day in the field to take thy pleasure therein.

---

* Lit. field.

"To-day, O, my brother, I very much wish thou wouldest come with me into the field,[45] to enjoy thyself and to bless our fields and our flocks, for thou art righteous, and I love thee much, O, my brother! but thou hast estranged thyself from me."

Then Abel consented to go with his brother Cain into the field.

But before going out, Cain said to Abel, "Wait for me, until I fetch a staff, because of wild beasts."

Then Abel stood [waiting] in his innocence. But Cain, the froward, fetched a staff and went out.

And they began, Cain and his brother Abel, to walk in the way; Cain talking to him, and comforting him, to make him forget everything.

CHAPTER LXXIX.

Murder of Abel the Just, whom his brother, Cain the Infidel, did kill.

And so they went on, until they came to a lonely place, where there were no sheep; then Abel said to Cain, "Behold, my brother, we are weary of walking; for we see none of the trees, nor of the fruits, nor of the verdure, nor of the sheep, nor any one of the things of which thou didst tell me. Where are those sheep of thine thou didst tell me to bless?"

Then Cain said to him, "Come on, and presently thou shalt see many beautiful things, but go before me, until I come up to thee."

Then went Abel forward, but Cain remained behind him.

And Abel was walking in his innocence, without guile; not believing his brother would kill him.

Then Cain, when he came up to him, comforted him with

[his] talk, walking a little behind him; then he hastened, and smote him with the staff, blow upon blow, until he was stunned.

But when Abel fell down upon the ground, seeing that his brother meant to kill him, he said to Cain, " O, my brother, have pity on me. By the breasts we have sucked, smite me not! By the womb that bare us and that brought us into the world, smite me not unto death with that staff! If thou wilt kill me, take one of these large stones, and kill me outright."

Then Cain, the hard-hearted, and cruel murderer, took a large stone, and smote his brother with it upon the head,[46] until his brains oozed out, and he weltered in his blood, before him. And Cain repented not of what he had done.

But the earth, when the blood of righteous Abel fell upon it, trembled, as it drank his blood, and would have brought Cain to naught [for it].

And the blood of Abel cried mysteriously to God, to avenge him of his murderer.

Then Cain began at once to dig the earth [wherein to lay] his brother;[47] for he was trembling from the fear that came upon him, when he saw the earth tremble on his account.

He then cast his brother into the pit [he made], and covered him with dust.[48] But the earth would not receive him; but it threw him up at once.

Again did Cain dig the earth and hid his brother in it; but again did the earth throw him up on itself; until three times did the earth thus throw up on itself the body of Abel. The muddy earth threw him up the first time, because he was not the first creation; and it threw him up the second time and would not receive him, because he was righteous and good, and was killed without a cause; and the earth threw him up the third time and would not receive him, that there might remain before his brother a witness against him.

And so did the earth mock Cain, until the Word of God, came to him concerning his brother.

Then was God angry, and much displeased* at Abel's death; and He thundered from heaven, and lightnings went before Him, and the Word of the Lord God came from heaven to Cain, and said unto him, " Where is Abel thy brother ?"

Then Cain answered with a proud heart and a gruff voice, " How, O God ? am I my brother's keeper ?"

Then God said unto Cain, " Cursed be the earth that has drunk the blood of Abel thy brother; and thou, be thou trembling and shaking; and this will be a sign unto thee, that whosoever finds thee, shall kill thee."

But Cain wept because God had said those words to him; and Cain said unto Him, " O God, whosoever finds me shall kill me, and I shall be blotted out from the face of the earth."

Then God said unto Cain, " Whosoever shall find thee shall not kill thee ;" because before this, God had been saying to Cain, " I shall forego seven punishments on him who kills Cain." For as to the word of God to Cain, " Where is thy brother ?" God said it in mercy for him, to try and make him repent.

For if Cain had repented at that time, and had said, " O God, forgive me my sin, and the murder of my brother," God would then have forgiven him his sin.

And as to God saying to Cain, " Cursed be the ground that has drunk the blood of thy brother "[49] that also, was God's mercy on Cain. For God did not curse him, but He cursed the ground ; although it was not the ground that had killed Abel, and had committed iniquity.

For it was meet that the curse should fall upon the murderer; yet in mercy did God so manage His thoughts as that no one should know it, and turn away from Cain.

And He said to him, " Where is thy brother ?" To which he answered and said, " I know not." Then the Creator said to him, " Be trembling and quaking."

---

* Lit. sighed over, was grieved.

Then Cain trembled and became terrified; and through this sign did God make him an example*[50] before all the creation, as the murderer of his brother. Also did God bring trembling and terror upon him, that he might see the peace in which he was at first, and see also the trembling and terror he endured at the last; so that he might humble himself before God, and repent of his sin, and seek the peace he enjoyed at first.

And [in] the word of God that said, "I will forego seven punishments on whomsoever kills Cain," God was not seeking to kill Cain with the sword, but He sought to make him die of fasting, and praying and weeping by hard rule, until the time that he was delivered from his sin.

And the seven punishments are the seven generations during which God awaited Cain for the murder of his brother.

But as to Cain, ever since he had killed his brother, he could find no rest in any place; but went back to Adam and Eve, trembling, terrified, and defiled with blood.

When they saw him they grieved and wept, not knowing whence came his trembling and terror, and the blood with which he was bespattered.

Cain, then, came running to his sister that was born with him. But when she saw him, she was affrighted, and said unto him, "O, my brother, wherefore art thou come thus trembling?" And he said to her, "I have killed my brother Abel in a certain place."

* Or, notorious.

BOOK II.

CHAPTER I.

WHEN Luluwa heard Cain's words, she wept and went to call her father and mother, and told them how that Cain had killed his brother Abel.

Then they all cried aloud and lifted up their voices, and slapped their faces, and threw dust upon their heads, and rent asunder their garments, and went out and came to the place where Abel was killed.

And they found him lying on the earth, killed, and beasts around him; while they wept and cried because of this just one. From his body, by reason of its purity, went forth a smell of sweet spices. And Adam carried him, his tears streaming down his face; and went to the Cave of Treasures, where he laid him, and wound him up with sweet spices and myrrh.

And Adam and Eve continued by the burial of him in great grief a hundred and forty days. Abel was fifteen and a half years old, and Cain seventeen years and a half.[1]

As for Cain, when the mourning for his brother was ended, he took his sister Luluwa[2] and married her, without leave from his father and mother; for they could not keep him from her, by reason of their heavy heart.

He then went down to the bottom of the mountain, away from the garden, near to the place where he had killed his brother.

BIRTH OF SETH.

And in that place were many [fruit] trees and forest trees. His sister bare him children, who [in their turn] began to multiply by degrees until they filled that place.

But as for Adam and Eve, they came not together after Abel's funeral, for seven years. After this, however, Eve conceived; and while she was with child, Adam said to her, "Come, let us take an offering and offer it up unto God, and ask Him to give us a fair child, in whom we may find comfort, and whom we may join in marriage to Abel's sister.

Then they prepared an offering and brought it up to the altar, and offered it before the Lord, and began to entreat Him to accept their offering, and to give them a good offspring.

And God heard Adam and accepted his offering. Then, they worshipped, Adam, Eve, and their daughter, and came down to the Cave of Treasures and placed a lamp in it, to burn by night and by day, before the body of Abel.

Then Adam and Even continued fasting and praying until Eve's time came that she should be delivered, when she said to Adam, "I wish to go to the cave in the rock, to bring forth in it."

And he said, "Go, and take with thee thy daughter to wait on thee; but I will remain in this Cave of Treasures before the body of my son Abel."

Then Eve hearkened to Adam, and went, she and her daughter. But Adam remained by himself in the Cave of Treasures.

CHAPTER II.

And Eve brought forth a son perfectly beautiful in figure and in countenance. His beauty was like that of his father Adam, yet more beautiful.[3]

Then Eve was comforted when she saw him, and remained

eight days in the cave; then she sent her daughter unto Adam [to tell him] to come and see the child and name him. But the daughter stayed in his place by the body of her brother, until Adam returned. So did she.

But when Adam came and saw the child's good looks, his beauty, and his perfect figure, he rejoiced over him, and was comforted for Abel. Then he named the child Seth,* that means, "that God has heard my prayer, and has delivered me out of my affliction." But it means also "power and strength."

Then after Adam had named the child, he returned to the Cave of Treasures; and his daughter went back to her mother.

But Eve continued in her cave, until forty days were fulfilled, when she came to Adam, and brought with her the child and her daughter.

And they came to a river of water, where Adam and his daughter washed themselves, because of their sorrow for Abel; but Eve and the babe washed for purification.

Then they returned, and took an offering, and went to the mountain and offered it up, for the babe; and God accepted their offering, and sent His blessing upon them, and upon their son Seth; and they came back to the Cave of Treasures.

As for Adam, he knew not again his wife Eve, all the days of his life; neither was any more offspring born of them; but only those five, Cain, Luluwa, Abel, Aklia,* and Seth† alone.‡

But Seth waxed in stature and in strength; and began to fast and pray, fervently.§

CHAPTER III.

Fifteenth apparition of Satan to Adam and Eve, above the roof of the cave.

As for our father Adam, at the end of seven years from the day he had been severed from his wife Eve, Satan envied him,

* Or, Aclemia.
† This does not agree with other accounts. See Fabric. *Cod. Apoc. V. T.*, vol. i.
‡ *i.e.*, without a twin sister. § Lit. with hard labour.

when he saw him thus separated from her; and strove to make him live with her again.⁵

Then Adam arose and went up above the Cave of Treasures; and continued to sleep there night by night. But as soon as it was light every day he came down to the cave, to pray there and to receive a blessing from it.

But when it was evening he went up on the roof of the cave, where he slept by himself, fearing lest Satan should overcome him. And he continued thus apart thirty-nine days.

Then Satan, the hater of all good, when he saw Adam thus alone, fasting and praying, appeared unto him in the form of a beautiful woman, who came and stood before him in the night of the fortieth day, and said unto him:—

"O Adam, from the time ye have dwelt in this cave, we have experienced great peace from you, and your prayers have reached us, and we have been comforted about you.

"But now, O Adam, that thou hast gone up over the roof of the cave to sleep, we have had doubts about thee, and a great sorrow has come upon us because of thy separation from Eve. Then again, when thou art on the roof of this cave, thy prayer is poured out, and thy heart wanders from side to side.

"But when thou wast in the cave thy prayer was like fire gathered together; it came down to us, and thou didst find rest.

"Then I also grieved over thy children who are severed from thee; and my sorrow is great about the murder of thy son Abel; for he was righteous; and over a righteous man every one will grieve.

"But I rejoiced over the birth of thy son Seth; yet after a little while I sorrowed greatly over Eve, because she is my sister. For when God sent a deep sleep over thee, and drew her out of thy side, He brought me out also with her. But He raised her by placing her with thee, while He lowered me.

"I rejoiced over my sister for her being with thee. But God had made me a promise before, and said, 'Grieve not; when

Adam has gone up on the roof of the Cave of Treasures, and is separated from Eve his wife, I will send thee to him, thou shalt join thyself to him in marriage, and bear him five children, as Eve did bear him five.'

"And now, lo! God's promise to me is fulfilled; for it is He who has sent me to thee for the wedding; because if thou wed me, I shall bear thee finer and better children than those of Eve.

"Then again, thou art as yet but a youth; end not thy youth in this world in sorrow; but spend the days of thy youth in mirth and pleasure. For thy days are few and thy trial is great. Be strong; end thy days in this world in rejoicing. I shall take pleasure in thee, and thou shalt rejoice with me in this wise, and without fear.

"Up, then, and fulfil the command of thy God," she then drew near to Adam, and embraced him.

But when Adam saw that he should be overcome by her, he prayed to God with a fervent heart to deliver him from her.

Then God sent His Word unto Adam, saying, "O Adam, that figure is the one that promised thee the Godhead, and majesty; he is not favourably disposed towards thee; but shows himself to thee at one time in the form of a woman; another moment, in the likeness of an angel; on another occasion, in the similitude of a serpent; and at another time, in the semblance of a god; but he does all that only to destroy thy soul.

"Now, therefore, O Adam, understanding thy heart, I have delivered thee many a time from his hands; in order to show thee that I am a merciful God; and that I wish thy good, and that I do not wish thy ruin."

CHAPTER IV.

Then God ordered Satan to show himself to Adam plainly, in his own hideous form.

But when Adam saw him, he feared, and trembled at the sight of him.

And God said to Adam, "Look at this devil,* and at his hideous look, and know that he it is who made thee fall from brightness into darkness, from peace and rest to toil and misery. And look, O Adam, at him, who said of himself that he is God! Can God be black? Would God take the form of a woman? Is there any one stronger than God? And can He be overpowered?

"See, then, O Adam, and behold him bound in thy presence, in the air, unable to flee away! Therefore, I say unto thee, be not afraid of him; henceforth take care, and beware of him, in whatever he may do to thee."

Then God drove Satan away from before Adam, whom He strengthened, and whose heart He comforted, saying to him, "Go down to the Cave of Treasures, and separate not thyself from Eve; I will quell in you all animal lust. From that hour it left Adam and Eve, and they enjoyed rest by the commandment of God. But God did not the like to any one of Adam's seed; but only to Adam and Eve.

Then Adam worshipped before the Lord, for having delivered him, and for having layed his passions. And he came down from above the cave, and dwelt with Eve as aforetime. This ended the forty days of his separation from Eve.

CHAPTER V.

As for Seth, when he was seven years old, he knew good and evil, and was consistent in fasting and praying, and spent all his nights in entreating God for mercy and forgiveness.

He also fasted when bringing up his offering every day, more than his father did; for he was of a fair countenance, like unto an angel of God. He also had a good heart,

* Lit. Diabolos.

preserved the finest qualities of his soul; and for this reason he brought up his offering every day.

And God was pleased with his offering; but He was also pleased with his purity.* And he continued thus in [doing] the will of God, and of his father and mother, until he was seven years old.

After that, as he was coming down from the altar, having ended his offering, Satan appeared unto him in the form of a beautiful angel, brilliant with light; with a staff of light in his hand, himself girt about with a girdle of light.

He greeted Seth with a beautiful smile, and began to beguile him with fair words, saying to him, " O Seth, why abidest thou in this mountain? For it is rough, full of stones and of sand, and of trees with no good fruit on them; a wilderness without habitations and without towns; no good place to dwell in. But all is heat, weariness, and trouble."

He said further, "But we dwell in beautiful places, in another world than this earth. Our world is one of light and our condition is† of the best; our women are handsomer than any others; and I wish thee, O Seth, to wed one of them; because I see that thou art fair to look upon, and in this land there is not one woman good enough for thee. Besides, all those who live in this world, are only five souls.

"But in our world there are very many men and many maidens, all more beautiful one than another. I wish, therefore, to remove thee hence, that thou mayest see my relations and be wedded to which ever thou likest.

"Thou shalt then abide by me and be at peace; thou shalt be filled with splendour and light, as we are.

"Thou shalt remain in our world, and rest from this world and the misery of it; thou shalt never again feel faint and weary; thou shalt never bring up an offering, nor sue for mercy; for thou shalt commit no more sin, nor be swayed by passions.

* Or, innocence. † Lit. conditions are.

"And if thou wilt hearken to what I say, thou shalt wed one of my daughters; for with us it is no sin so to do; neither is it reckoned animal lust.

"For in our world we have no God; but we all are gods; we all are of the light, heavenly, powerful, strong and glorious."

CHAPTER VI.

When Seth heard these words he was amazed, and inclined his heart to Satan's treacherous speech, and said to him, "Saidst thou there is another world created than this; and other creatures more beautiful than the creatures that are in this world?"

And Satan said, "Yes; behold thou hast heard me; but I will yet praise them and their ways, in thy hearing."

But Seth said to him, "Thy speech has amazed me; and thy beautiful description [of it all].

"Yet I cannot go with thee to-day; not until I have gone to my father Adam and to my mother Eve, and told them all thou hast said to me. Then if they give me leave to go with thee, I will come."

Again Seth said, "I am afraid of doing any thing without my father's and mother's leave, lest I perish like my brother Cain, and like my father Adam, who transgressed the commandment of God. But, behold, thou knowest this place; come, and meet me here to-morrow."

When Satan heard this, he said to Seth, "If thou tellest thy father Adam what I have told thee, he will not let thee come with me. But hearken to me; do not tell thy father and mother what I have said to thee; but come with me to-day, to our world; where thou shalt see beautiful things and enjoy thyself there, and revel this day among my children, beholding them and taking thy fill of mirth; and rejoice evermore. Then I shall bring thee back to this place to-morrow; but if thou wouldest rather abide with me, so be it."

Then Seth answered, "The spirit of my father and of my mother, hangs on me; and if I hide from them one day, they will die, and God will hold me guilty of sinning against them.*

"And except that they know I am come to this place to bring up to it [my] offering, they would not be separated from me one hour; neither should I go to any other place, unless they let me. But they treat me most kindly, because I come back to them quickly."

Then Satan said to him, "What will happen to thee if thou hide thyself from them one night, and return to them at break of day?"

But Seth, when he saw how he kept on talking, and that he would not leave him—ran, and went up to the altar, and spread his hands unto God, and sought deliverance from Him.

Then God sent His Word, and cursed Satan, who fled from Him.

But as for Seth, he had gone up to the altar, saying thus in his heart, "The altar is the place of offering, and God is there; a divine fire shall consume it; so shall Satan be unable to hurt me, and shall not take me away thence."

Then Seth came down from the altar and went to his father and mother, whom he found in the way, longing to hear his voice; for he had tarried a while.

He then began to tell them what had befallen him from Satan, under the form of an angel.

But when Adam heard his account, he kissed his face, and warned him against that angel, telling him it was Satan who thus appeared to him. Then Adam took Seth, and they went to the Cave of Treasures, and rejoiced therein.

But from that day forth Adam and Eve never parted from

---

* Lit. of their sin.

him, to whatever place he might go, whether for his offering or for any thing else.

This sign happened to Seth, when he was nine years old.

CHAPTER VII.

When our father Adam saw that Seth was of a perfect heart, he wished him to marry; lest the enemy should appear to him another time, and overcome him.

So Adam said to his son Seth, "I wish, O my son, that thou wed thy sister Aklia, Abel's sister, that she may bear thee children, who shall replenish the earth, according to God's promise to us.

"Be not afraid, O my son; there is no disgrace in it. I wish thee to marry, from fear lest the enemy overcome thee."

Seth, however, did not wish to marry; but in obedience to his father and mother, he said not a word.

So Adam married him to Aklia.* And he was fifteen years old.

But when he was twenty years of age,† he begat a son, whom he called Enos;‡ and then begat other children than him.

Then Enos grew up, married, and begat Cainan.

Cainan also grew up, married, and begat Mahalaleel.

Those fathers were born during Adam's life-time, and dwelt by the Cave of Treasures.

Then were the days of Adam nine hundred and thirty years, and those of Mahalaleel one hundred. But Mahalaleel, when he was grown up, loved fasting, praying, and with hard labour,§ until the end of our father Adam's days drew near.

* Called 'Ωραία by the Sethians. S. Epiph. *Hœres.* xxxix, c. 5. Adam gave to Seth, Owain, Abel's sister, in marriage. Eutych. *Nasam al-jaw.*, p. 18, see note p. 106.

† A hundred and five years old. Eutych. *Nasam al-jaw.*, p. 18.

‡ Τὴν ἰδίαν ἀδελφὴν 'Ασσουὰμ καλουμένην γήμας, ἐγέννησε τὸν 'Ενώς. Cedren. i, *Hist. Comp.*, p. 17.

§ *i.e.*, continually and earnestly.

CHAPTER VIII.

When our father Adam saw that his end was near,[6] he called his son Seth, who came to him in the Cave of Treasures, and he said unto him:—

"O Seth, my son, bring me thy children and thy children's children, that I may shed my blessing on them ere I die."

When Seth heard these words from his father Adam, he went from him, shed a flood of tears over his face,[*] and gathered together his children and his children's children, and brought them to his father Adam.

But when our father Adam saw them around him, he wept at having to be separated from them.

And when they saw him weeping, they all wept together, and fell upon his face saying, "How shalt thou be severed from us, O our father? And how shall the earth receive thee and hide thee from our eyes?" Thus did they lament much, and in like words.[†]

Then our father Adam blessed them all, and said to Seth, after he had blessed them:—

"O Seth, my son, thou knowest this world—that it is full of sorrow, and of weariness; and thou knowest all that has come upon us, from our trials in it. I therefore now command thee in these words: to keep innocency, to be pure and just, and trusting in God; and lean not to the discourses of Satan, nor to the apparitions in which he will show himself to thee. But keep the commandments that I give thee this day; then give the same to thy son Enos; and let Enos give it to his son Cainan; and Cainan to his son Mahalaleel; so that this commandment abide firm among all your children.[7]

"O Seth, my son, the moment I am dead take ye my body and wind it up with myrrh, aloes, and cassia, and leave me here

---

[*] Lit. down his cheeks. [†] Or, strains.

in this Cave of Treasures in which are all these tokens which God gave us from the garden.

"O my son, hereafter shall a flood come[6] and overwhelm all creatures, and leave out only eight souls.

"But, O my son, let those whom it will leave out from among your children at that time, take my body with them out of this cave; and when they have taken it with them, let the oldest among them command his children to lay my body in a ship until the flood has been assuaged, and they come out of the ship. Then they shall take my body and lay it in the middle of the earth, shortly after they have been saved from the waters of the flood.

"For the place where my body shall be laid, is the middle of the earth; God shall come from thence and shall save all our kindred.

"But now, O Seth, my son, place thyself at the head of thy people; tend them and watch over them in the fear of God; and lead them in the good way. Command them to fast unto God; and make them understand they ought not to hearken to Satan, lest he destroy them.

"'Then, again, sever thy children and thy children's children from Cain's children; do not let them ever mix with those, nor come near them either in their words or in their deeds."

Then Adam let his blessing descend upon Seth, and upon his children, and upon all his children's children.

He then turned to his son Seth, and to Eve his wife, and said to them, "Preserve this gold, this incense, and this myrrh, that God has given us for a sign; for in days that are coming, a flood will overwhelm the whole creation. But those who shall go into the ark shall take with them the gold, the incense, and the myrrh, together with my body; and will lay the gold, the incense, and the myrrh, with my body in the midst of the earth.

"Then, after a long time, the city in which the gold, the incense, and the myrrh are found with my body, shall be plundered. But when it is spoiled, the gold, the incense, and the myrrh shall be taken care of with the spoil that is kept; and naught of them shall perish, until the Word of God, made man shall come; when kings shall take them,* and shall offer to Him, gold in token of His being King; incense, in token of His being God of heaven and earth; and myrrh, in token of His passion.

"Gold also, as a token of His overcoming Satan, and all our foes; incense as a token that He will rise from the dead, and be exalted above things in heaven and things in the earth; and myrrh, in token that He will drink bitter gall; and [feel] the pains of hell from Satan.

"And now, O Seth, my son, behold I have revealed unto thee hidden mysteries, which God had revealed unto me. Keep my commandment, for thyself, and for thy people."

CHAPTER IX.

When Adam had ended his commandment to Seth, his limbs were loosened, his hands and feet lost all power, his mouth became dumb, and his tongue ceased altogether to speak. He closed his eyes and gave up the ghost.[9]

But when his children saw that he was dead, they threw themselves over him, men and women, old and young, weeping.

The death of Adam took place at the end of nine hundred and thirty years that he lived upon the earth; on the fifteenth day of Barmudeh, after the reckoning of an epact of the sun, at the ninth hour. It was on a Friday,[10] the very day on which he was created, and on which he rested; and the hour at which he died, was the same as that at which he came out of the garden.

Then Seth wound him up well, and embalmed him with plenty of sweet spices, from sacred trees and from the Holy

---

* *i.e.*, the gold, the incense, and the myrrh.

Mountain; and he laid his body on the eastern side of the inside of the cave, the side of the incense; and placed in front of him a lamp-stand kept burning.

Then his children stood before him weeping and wailing over him the whole night until break of day.

Then Seth and his son Enos, and Cainan, the son of Enos, went out and took good offerings to present unto the Lord, and they came to the altar upon which Adam offered gifts to God, when he did offer.

But Eve said to them, "Wait until we have first asked God to accept our offering, and to keep by Him the soul of Adam His servant, and to take it up to rest."

And they all stood up and prayed.[11]

CHAPTER X.

And when they had ended their prayer, the Word of God came and comforted them concerning their father Adam.

After this, they offered their gifts for themselves and for their father.

And when they had ended their offering, the Word of God came to Seth, the eldest among them, saying unto him, "O Seth, Seth, Seth, three times. As I was with thy father, so also shall I be with thee, until the fulfilment of the promise I made him—thy father [saying], I will send My Word and save thee and thy seed.

"But as to thy father Adam, keep thou the commandment he gave thee; and sever thy seed from that of Cain thy brother."

And God withdrew His Word from Seth.

Then Seth, Eve, and their children, came down from the mountain to the Cave of Treasures.

But Adam was the first whose soul died in the land of

Eden,* in the Cave of Treasures; for no one died before him, but his son Abel, who died murdered.

Then all the children of Adam rose up, and wept over their father Adam, and made offerings to him, one hundred and forty days.

CHAPTER XI.

After the death of Adam and of Eve,[12] Seth severed his children, and his children's children, from Cain's children. Cain and his seed went down and dwelt westward, below the place where he had killed his brother Abel.[13]

But Seth and his children, dwelt northwards upon the mountain of the Cave of Treasures, in order to be near to their father Adam. And Seth the elder, tall and good, with a fine soul, and of a strong mind, stood at the head of his people; and tended them in innocence, penitence, and meekness, and did not allow one of them to go down to Cain's children. But because of their own purity, they were named "Children of God," and they were with God, instead of the hosts of angels who fell; for they continued in praises to God, and in singing psalms unto Him, in their cave—the Cave of Treasures.

Then Seth stood before the body of his father Adam, and of his mother Eve, and prayed night and day, and asked for mercy towards himself and his children; and that when he had some difficult dealing with a child, He would give him counsel.

But Seth and his children did not like earthly work, but gave themselves to heavenly things;[14] for they had no other thought than praises, doxologies, and psalms unto God. Therefore did they at all times hear the voices of angels, praising and glorifying God; from within the garden, or when they were sent [by God] on an errand, or when they were going up to heaven.

---

* In the land in which he was created (the land of Eden). Kufale, p. 19.

For Seth and his children, by reason of their own purity, heard and saw those angels. Then, again, the garden was not far above them, but only some fifteen spiritual cubits. Now one spiritual cubit answers to three cubits of man;* altogether forty-five cubits.

Seth and his children dwelt on the mountain below the garden; they sowed not, neither did they reap; they wrought no food for the body, not even wheat; but only offerings. They ate of the fruit and of trees well flavoured [that grew] on the mountain where they dwelt.

Then Seth often fasted every forty days, as did also his eldest children. For the family of Seth smelled the smell of the trees in the garden, when the wind blew [that way]. They were happy, innocent, without sudden fear, there was no jealousy, no evil action, no hatred among them. There was no animal passion; from no mouth among them went forth either foul words or curse; neither evil counsel nor fraud. For the men of that time never swore, but under hard circumstances, when men must swear, they swore by the blood of Abel the just.†

But they constrained their children and their women every day in the cave to fast and pray, and to worship the most High God. They blessed themselves in the body of their father Adam, and anointed themselves with it. And they did so until the end of Seth drew near.

CHAPTER XII.

Then Seth, the just, called his son Enos, and Cainan, son of Enos, and Mahalaleel, son of Cainan, and said unto them:—

"As my end is near, I wish to build a roof over the altar on which gifts are offered."

* Lit. of the arm.
† They dwelt on Mount Hermon leading a life of purity, and abstaining from marriage; wherefore were they called *Watchers* and *Sons of God.* Bar. Hebr. *Dyn.,* p. 4.

They hearkened to his commandment and went out, all of them, both old and young, and worked hard at it, and built a beautiful roof over the altar.

And Seth's thought, in so doing, was that a blessing should come upon his children on the mountain; and that he should present an offering for them before his death.

Then when the building of the roof was completed, he commanded them to make offerings. They worked diligently at these, and brought them to Seth their father, who took them and offered them upon the altar; and prayed God to accept their offerings, to have mercy on the souls of his children, and to keep them from the hand of Satan.

And God accepted his offering, and sent His blessing upon him and upon his children. And then God made a promise to Seth, saying, "At the end of the great five days and a half, concerning which I have made a promise to thee and to thy father, I will send My Word and save thee and thy seed."

Then Seth and his children, and his children's children, met together, and came down from the altar, and went to the Cave of Treasures—where they prayed, and blessed themselves in the body of our father Adam, and anointed themselves with it.

But Seth abode in the Cave of Treasures, a few days, and then suffered—sufferings unto death.

Then Enos, his first-born son, came to him, with Cainan, his son, and Mahalaleel, Cainan's son, and Jared, the son of Mahalaleel, and Enoch, Jared's son, with their wives and children to receive a blessing from Seth.

Then Seth prayed over them, and blessed them, and adjured them by the blood of Abel the just,[15] saying, "I beg of you, my children, not to let one of you go down from this Holy and pure Mountain. Make no fellowship with the children of Cain the murderer and the sinner, who killed his brother; for ye know, O my children, that we flee from him, and from all his sin with all our might because he killed his brother Abel."

After having said this, Seth blessed Enos, his first-born son, and commanded him habitually to minister in purity before the body of our father Adam, all the days of his life; then, also, to go at times to the altar which he [Seth] had built. And he commanded him to feed his people in righteousness, in judgment and purity all the days of his life.

Then the limbs of Seth were loosened; his hands and feet lost all power; his mouth became dumb and unable to speak; and he gave up the ghost and died the day after his nine hundred and twelfth year; on the twenty-seventh day of the month Abib; Enoch being then twenty years old.

Then they wound up carefully the body of Seth, and embalmed him with sweet spices, and laid him in the Cave of Treasures, on the right side of our father Adam's body, and they mourned for him forty days. They offered gifts for him, as they had done for our father Adam.

After the death of Seth, Enos rose at the head of his people, whom he fed in righteousness, and judgment, as his father had commanded him.[16]

But by the time Enos was eight hundred and twenty years old, Cain had a large progeny; for they married frequently, being given to animal lusts; until the land below the mountain, was filled with them.

CHAPTER XIII.

In those days lived Lamech the blind, who was of the sons of Cain. He had a son whose name was Atun,* and they two had much cattle.

But Lamech was in the habit of sending them [to feed] with a young shepherd,† who tended them; and who, when coming

* In Arabic, it means hot, hard, hasty. † Lamech's grandson.

home in the evening wept before his grandfather, and before his father Atun and his mother Hazina, and said to them, "As for me, I cannot feed those cattle alone, lest one rob me of some of them, or kill me for the sake of them." For among the children of Cain, there was much robbery, murder, and sin.

Then Lamech pitied him, and he said, "Truly, he [when alone], might be overpowered by the [men of this place.]"

So Lamech arose, took a bow he had kept ever since he was a youth, ere he became blind, and he took large arrows, and smooth stones, and a sling which he had, and went to the field with the young shepherd, and placed himself behind the cattle; while the young shepherd watched the cattle. Thus did Lamech many days.

Meanwhile Cain, ever since God had cast him off, and had cursed him with trembling and terror, could neither settle nor find rest in any one place; but wandered from place to place.

[In his wanderings] he came to Lamech's wives, and asked them about him. They said to him, "He is in the field with the cattle."

Then Cain went to look for him; and [as] he came into the field, the young shepherd heard the noise he made, and the cattle herding together from before him.

Then said he to Lamech, "O my lord, is that a wild beast or a robber?"

And Lamech said to him, "Make me understand which way he looks, when he comes up."

Then Lamech bent his bow, placed an arrow on it, and fitted a stone in the sling, and when Cain came out from the open country, the shepherd said to Lamech, "Shoot, behold, he is coming."

Then Lamech shot at Cain with his arrow and hit him in his side. And Lamech struck him with a stone from his sling, that fell upon his face, and knocked out both his eyes; then Cain fell at once and died.[17]

Then Lamech and the young shepherd came up to him, and found him lying on the ground. And the young shepherd said to him, "It is Cain our grandfather, whom thou hast killed, O my lord!"

Then was Lamech sorry for it, and from the bitterness of his regret, he clapped his hands together, and struck with his flat palm the head of the youth, who fell as if dead; but Lamech thought it was a feint; so he took up a stone and smote him, and smashed his head until he died.[18]

CHAPTER XIV.

When Enos was nine hundred years old, all the children of Seth, and of Cainan, and his first-born, with their wives and children, gathered around him, asking for a blessing from him.

He then prayed over them and blessed them, and adjured them by the blood of Abel the just, saying to them, "Let not one of your children go down from this Holy Mountain, and let them make no fellowship with the children of Cain the murderer."

Then Enos called his son Cainan and said to him, "See, O my son, and set thy heart on thy people, and establish them in righteousness, and in innocence; and stand ministering before the body of our father Adam, all the days of thy life."

After this Enos entered into rest, aged nine hundred and eighty-five years; and Cainan wound him up, and laid him in the Cave of Treasures on the left of his father Adam; and made offerings for him, after the custom of his fathers.

CHAPTER XV.

After the death of Enos, Cainan stood at the head of his people in righteousness and innocence, as his father had commanded him; he also continued to minister before the body of Adam, inside the Cave of Treasures.[19]

Then when he had lived nine hundred and ten years, suffering and affliction came upon him. And when he was about to enter into rest, all the fathers with their wives and children came to him, and he blessed them, and adjured them by the blood of Abel the just[20] saying to them, " Let not one among you go down from this Holy Mountain; and make no fellowship with the children of Cain the murderer."

Mahalaleel, his first-born son, received this commandment from his father, who blessed him and died.

Then Mahalaleel embalmed him with sweet spices, and laid him in the Cave of Treasures, with his fathers; and they made offerings for him, after the custom of their fathers.*

CHAPTER XVI.

Then Mahalaleel stood over his people, and fed them in righteousness and innocence, and watched them to see they held no intercourse with the children of Cain.

He also continued in the Cave of Treasures praying and ministering before the body of our father Adam, asking God for mercy on himself and on his people; until he was eight hundred and seventy years old, when he fell sick.

Then all his children gathered unto him, to see him, and to ask for his blessing on them all, ere he left this world.

Then Mahalaleel arose and sat on his bed, his tears streaming down his face, and he called his eldest son Jared, who came to him.

He then kissed his face, and said to him, "O Jared, my son, I adjure thee by Him who made heaven and earth,† to

---

* See also Eutych. *Nazam al-j.*, p. 22.

† Mahalaleel adjured his son Jared, by the blood of Abel, not to let one of his children go down from the mountain to the children of Cain the accursed. Eutych. *Nazam al-j.*, p. 22.

watch over thy people, and to feed them in righteousness and in innocence; and not to let one of them go down from this Holy Mountain to the children of Cain, lest he perish with them.

"Hear, O my son, hereafter there shall come a great destruction upon this earth on account of them; God will be angry with the world, and will destroy them with waters.

"But I also know that thy children will not hearken to thee, and that they will go down from this mountain and hold intercourse with the children of Cain, and that they shall perish with them.

"O my son! teach them, and watch over them, that no guilt attach to thee on their account."

Mahalaleel said, moreover, to his son Jared, "When I die, embalm my body and lay it in the Cave of Treasures, by the bodies of my fathers; then stand thou by my body and pray to God; and take care of them, and fulfil thy ministry before them, until thou enterest into rest thyself."

Mahalaleel then blessed all his children; and then lay down on his bed, and entered into rest like his fathers.

But when Jared saw that his father Mahalaleel was dead, he wept, and sorrowed, and embraced and kissed his hands and his feet; and so did all his children.

And his children embalmed him carefully, and laid him by the bodies of his fathers. Then they arose, and mourned for him forty days.

CHAPTER XVII.

Then Jared kept his father's commandment, and arose like a lion over his people. He fed them in righteousness and innocence, and commanded them to do nothing without his counsel. For he was afraid concerning them, lest they should go to the children of Cain.

Wherefore did he give them orders repeatedly; and continued to do so until the end of the four hundred and eighty-fifth year of his life.

At the end of these said years, there came unto him this sign. As Jared was standing like a lion before the bodies of his fathers, praying and warning his people, Satan envied him, and wrought a beautiful apparition, because Jared would not let his children do aught without his counsel.

Satan then appeared to him with thirty men of his hosts, in the form of handsome men; Satan himself being the elder and tallest among them, with a fine beard.

They stood at the mouth of the cave, and called out Jared, from within it.

He came out to them, and found them looking like fine men, full of light, and of great beauty. He wondered at their beauty and [at their] looks; and thought within himself whether they might not be of the children of Cain.

He said also in his heart, "As the children of Cain cannot come up to the height of this mountain, and none of them is so handsome as these appear to be; and among these men there is not one of my kindred—they must be strangers."

Then Jared and they exchanged a greeting, and he said to the elder among them, " O my father, explain to me the wonder that is in thee, and tell me who these are, with thee; for they look to me like strange men."

Then the elder began to weep, and the rest wept with him; and he said to Jared, " I am Adam whom God made first; and this is Abel my son, who was killed by his brother Cain, into whose heart Satan put to murder him.

"Then this is my son Seth, whom I asked of the Lord, who gave him to me, to comfort me instead of Abel.

"Then this one is my son Enos, son of Seth, and that other one is Cainan, son of Enos, and that other one is Mahalaleel, son of Cainan, thy father."

But Jared remained wondering at their appearance, and at the speech of the elder to him.

Then the elder said to him, "Marvel not, O my son; we live in the land north of the garden, which God created before the world. He would not let us live there, but placed us inside the garden, below which ye are now dwelling.

"But, after that I transgressed, He made me come out of it, and I was left to dwell in this cave; great and sore troubles came upon me; and when my death drew near, I commanded my son Seth to tend his people well; and this my commandment is to be handed from one to another, unto the end of the generations to come.

"But, O Jared, my son, we live in beautiful regions, while you live here in misery, as this thy father Mahalaleel informed me; telling me that a great flood will come and overwhelm the whole earth.

"Therefore, O my son, fearing for your sakes, I rose and took my children with me, and came hither for us to visit thee and thy children; but I found thee standing in this cave weeping, and thy children scattered about this mountain, in the heat and in misery.

"But, O my son, as we missed our way, and came as far as this, we found other men below this mountain; who inhabit a beautiful country, full of trees and of fruits, and of all manner of verdure; it is like a garden; so that when we found them we thought they were you; until thy father Mahalaleel told me they were no such thing.

"Now, therefore, O my son, hearken to my counsel, and go down to them, thou and thy children. Ye will rest from all this suffering in which ye are. But if thou wilt not go down to them, then, arise, take thy children, and come with us to our garden; ye shall live in our beautiful land, and ye shall rest from all this trouble, which thou and thy children are now bearing."

But Jared when he heard this discourse from the elder, wondered; and went hither and thither, but at that moment he found not one of his children.

Then he answered and said to the elder, "Why have you hidden yourselves until this day?"

And the elder replied, "If thy father had not told us, we should not have known it."

Then Jared believed his words were true.

So the elder said to Jared, "Wherefore didst thou turn about, so and so?" And he said, "I was seeking one of my children, to tell him about my going with you, and about their coming down to those about whom thou hast spoken to me."

When the elder heard Jared's intention, he said to him, "Let alone that purpose at present, and come with us; thou shalt see our country; if the land in which we dwell pleases thee, we and thou shall return hither and take thy family with us. But if our country does not please thee, thou shalt come back to thine own place."

And the elder urged Jared, to go before one of his children came to counsel him [otherwise].

Jared, then, came out of the cave and went with them, and among them. And they comforted him, until they came to the top of the mountain of the sons of Cain.

Then said the elder to one of his companions, "We have forgotten something by the mouth of the cave, and that is, the chosen garment we had brought to clothe Jared withal."

He then said to one of them, "Go back, thou, some one; and we will wait for thee here, until thou come back. Then will we clothe Jared, and he shall be like us, good, handsome, and fit to come with us into our country."

Then that one went back.

But when he was a short distance off, the elder called to him and said to him, "Tarry thou, until I come up and speak to thee."

Then he stood still, and the elder went up to him and said to him, "One thing we forgot at the cave, it is this—to put out the lamp that burns inside it, above the bodies that are therein. Then come back to us, quick."

That one went, and the elder came back to his fellows and to Jared. And they came down from the mountain, and Jared with them; and they stayed by a fountain of water, near the houses of the children of Cain, and waited for their companion until he brought the garment [for Jared].

He, then, who went back [to the cave], put out the lamp, and came to them and brought a phantom with him and showed it them. And when Jared saw it he wondered at the beauty and grace thereof, and rejoiced in his heart, believing it was all true.

But while they were staying there, three of them went into houses of the sons of Cain, and said to them, "Bring us to-day some food by the fountain of water, for us and our companions to eat."

But when the sons of Cain saw them, they wondered at them and thought:* "These are beautiful to look at, and such as we never saw before." So they rose and came with them to the fountain of water, to see their companions.

They found them so very handsome, that they cried aloud about their places for others to gather together and come and look at these beautiful beings. Then they gathered around them both men and women.

Then the elder said to them, "We are strangers in your land, bring us some good food and drink, you and your women, to refresh ourselves with you."

When those men heard these words of the elder, every one of Cain's sons brought his wife, and another brought his daughter, and so, many women came to them; every one addressing Jared either for himself or for his wife; all alike.

But when Jared saw what they did, his very soul wrenched itself from them; neither would he taste of their food or of their drink.

The elder saw him as he wrenched himself† from them, and

---

* Lit. said in their thoughts.
† Or, his soul wrenched itself from them.

said to him, "Be not sad; I am the great elder, as thou shalt see me do, do thyself in like manner."

Then he spread his hands and took one of the women, and five of his companions did the same before Jared, that he should do as they did.

But when Jared saw them working infamy he wept, and said in his mind,*—My fathers never did the like.

He then spread his hands and prayed with a fervent heart, and with much weeping, and entreated God to deliver him from their hands.

No sooner did Jared begin to pray than the elder fled with his companions; for they could not abide in a place of prayer.

Then Jared turned round but could not see them, but found himself standing in the midst of the children of Cain.

He then wept and said, "O God, destroy me not with this race, concerning which my fathers have warned me; for now, O my Lord God, I was thinking that those who appeared unto me were my fathers; but I have found them out to be devils, who allured me by this beautiful apparition, until I believed them.

"But now I ask Thee, O God, to deliver me from this race, among whom I am now staying, as Thou didst deliver me from those devils. Send Thy angel to draw me out of the midst of them; for I have not myself power to escape from among them."

When Jared had ended his prayer, God sent His angel in the midst of them, who [took Jared] and set him upon the mountain, and showed him the way, gave him counsel, and then departed from him.

CHAPTER XVIII.

The children of Jared were in the habit of visiting him hour after hour, to receive his blessing and to ask his advice for

* Lit. thought.

every thing they did; and when he had a work to do, they did it for him.

But this time when they went into the cave they found not Jared, but they found the lamp put out, and the bodies of the fathers thrown about, and voices came from them by the power of God, that said, "Satan in an apparition has deceived our son, wishing to destroy him, as he destroyed our son Cain."

They said also, "Lord God of heaven and earth, deliver our son from the hand of Satan, who wrought a great and false apparition before him." They also spake of other matters, by the power of God.

But when the children of Jared heard these voices they feared, and stood weeping for their father; for they knew not what had befallen him.

And they wept for him that day until the setting of the sun.

Then came Jared with a woeful countenance, wretched in mind and body, and sorrowful at having been separated from the bodies of his fathers.

But as he was drawing near to the cave, his children saw him, and hastened to the cave, and hung upon his neck, crying, and saying to him, "O father, where hast thou been, and [why hast thou] left us, as thou wast not wont to do?" And again, "O father, when thou didst disappear, the lamp over the bodies of our fathers went out, the bodies were thrown about, and voices came from them."

When Jared heard this he was sorry, and went into the cave; and there found the bodies thrown about, the lamp put out, and the fathers themselves praying for his deliverance from the hand of Satan.

Then Jared fell upon the bodies and embraced them, and said, "O my fathers, through your intercession, let God deliver me from the hand of Satan! And I beg you will ask God to keep me and to hide me from him unto the day of my death."

Then all the voices ceased save the voice of our father Adam, who spake to Jared by the power of God, just as one would speak to his fellow, saying, "O Jared my son, offer gifts to God for having delivered thee from the hand of Satan; and when thou bringest those offerings, so be it, that thou offerest them on the altar on which I did offer. Then also, beware of Satan; for he deluded me many a time with his apparitions, wishing to destroy me, but God delivered me out of his hand.

"Command thy people that they be on their guard against him; and never cease to offer up gifts to God."

Then the voice of Adam also became silent; and Jared and his children wondered at this. Then they laid the bodies [as they were at first]; and Jared and his children stood praying the whole of that night, until break of day.

Then Jared made an offering and offered it up on the altar, as Adam had commanded him. And as he went up to the altar, he prayed to God for mercy and for forgiveness of his sin, concerning the lamp going out.

Then God appeared unto Jared on the altar and blessed him and his children, and accepted their offerings; and commanded Jared to take of the sacred fire from the altar, and with it to light the lamp that shed light on the body of Adam.

CHAPTER XIX.

Then God revealed to him again the promise He had made to Adam; He explained to him the 5500 years, and revealed unto him the mystery of His coming upon the earth.

And God said to Jared, "As to that fire which thou hast taken from the altar to light the lamp withal, let it abide with you to give light to the bodies; and let it not come out of the cave, until the body of Adam comes out of it.

But, O Jared, take care of the fire, that it burn bright in the lamp; neither go thou again out of the cave, until thou receivest [an order] through a vision, and not in an apparition, when seen by thee.

"Then command again thy people not to hold intercourse with the children of Cain, and not to learn their ways; for I am God who loves not hatred and works of iniquity."

God gave also many other commandments to Jared, and blessed him. And then withdrew His word from him.

Then Jared drew near with his children, took some fire, and came down to the cave, and lighted the lamp before the body of Adam; and he gave his people commandments as God had told him to do.

This sign happened to Jared at the end of his four hundred and fiftieth year; as did also many other wonders, we do not record. But we record only this one for shortness sake, and in order not to lengthen our narrative.

And Jared continued to teach his children eighty years; but after that they began to transgress the commandments he had given them, and to do many things without his counsel. They began to go down from the Holy Mountain one after another, and to mix with the children of Cain, in foul fellowships.

Now the reason for which the children of Jared went down the Holy Mountain, is this, that we will now reveal unto you.

CHAPTER XX.

After Cain had gone down to the land of dark soil,* and his children had multiplied therein,† there was one of them, whose name was Genun,[21] son of Lamech the blind who slew Cain.

But as to this Genun, Satan came into him in his childhood; and he made sundry trumpets and horns, and string instru-

---

* Lit. black mud.

† Κάϊν—χθαμαλὸς ὤν—ὤσει δὲ τὴν γῆν, ἥτις ἐστὶ τρέμουσα [nod] χθαμαλὴν οὖσαν—he inhabited a land that is trembling, being low. Cedren., *Hist. Comp.*, p. 16.

ments, cymbals and psalteries, and lyres and harps, and flutes; and he played on them at all times and at every hour.*²²

And when he played on them, Satan came into them, so that from among them were heard beautiful and sweet sounds, that ravished the heart.†

Then he gathered companies upon companies to play on them; and when they played, it pleased well the children of Cain,‡ who inflamed themselves with sin among themselves, and burnt as with fire; while Satan inflamed their hearts one with another, and increased lust among them.

Satan also taught Genun to bring strong drink out of corn;§ and this Genun used to bring together companies upon companies in drink-houses; and brought into their hands all manner of fruits and flowers; and they drank together.

Thus did this Genun multiply sin exceedingly; he also acted with pride, and taught the children of Cain to commit all manner of the grossest wickedness, which they knew not; and put them up to manifold doings which they knew not before.

Then Satan, when he saw that they yielded to Genun and hearkened to him in every thing he told them, rejoiced greatly, increased Genun's understanding, until he took iron and with it made weapons of war.

Then when they were drunk, hatred and murder increased among them; one man used violence against another to teach him [evil], taking his children and defiling them before him.

And when men saw they were overcome, and [saw] others that were not overpowered, those who were beaten came to Genun, took refuge with him, and he made them his confederates.

Then sin increased among them greatly; until a man married his own sister, or daughter, or mother, and others; or the daughter of his father's sister, so that there was no more

---

* Eutych., *Nazam al-j.*, p. 20. † Lit. hearts.
‡ Lit. it seemed well in the eyes of. § Arab. " that is now called beer."

distinction [of relationship],* and they no longer knew what is iniquity; but did wickedly, and the earth was defiled with sin; and they angered God the Judge, who had created them.

But Genun gathered together companies upon companies, that played on horns and on all the other instruments we have already mentioned, at the foot of the Holy Mountain; and they did so in order that the children of Seth who were on the Holy Mountain should hear it.

But when the children of Seth heard the noise, they wondered, and came by companies, and stood on the top of the mountain to look at those below; and they did thus a whole year.

When, at the end of that year, Genun saw that they were being won over to him little by little, Satan entered into him, and taught him to make dyeing-stuffs for garments of divers patterns, and made him understand how to dye crimson and purple, and what not.

And the sons of Cain who wrought all this, and shone in beauty and gorgeous apparel, gathered together at the foot of the mountain in splendour, with horns and gorgeous dresses, and horse races; committing all manner of abominations.

Meanwhile the children of Seth, who were on the Holy Mountain, prayed and praised God, in the place of the hosts [of angels] who had fallen; wherefore God had called them "angels," because He rejoiced over them greatly.

But after this, they no longer kept His commandment, nor held by the promise He had made to their fathers; but they relaxed from their fasting and praying, and from the counsel of Jared their father. And they kept on gathering together on the top of the mountain, to look upon the children of Cain, from morning until evening, and upon what they did, upon their beautiful dresses and ornaments.

Then the children of Cain looked up from below, and saw

---

* Until they knew not either parents or children. Eutych., *Nazam al-j.*, p. 25.

the children of Seth, standing in troops on the top of the mountain; and they called to them to come down to them.

But the children of Seth said to them from above, "We don't know the way." Then Genun, the son of Lamech, heard them say they did not know the way, and he bethought himself how he might bring them down.

Then Satan appeared to him by night, saying, "There is no way for them to come down from the mountain on which they dwell; but when they come to-morrow, say to them, ' Come ye to the western side of the mountain; there you will find the way of a stream of water, that comes down to the foot of the mountain, between two hills; come down that way to us."

Then when it was day, Genun blew the horns and beat the drums below the mountain, as he was wont. The children of Seth heard it, and came as they used to do.

Then Genun said to them from down below, "Go to the western side of the mountain, there you will find the way to come down."

But when the children of Seth heard these words from him, they went back into the cave to Jared, to tell him all they had heard.

Then when Jared heard it, he was grieved; for he knew that they would transgress [his counsel].

After this a hundred men of the children of Seth gathered together,[23] and said among themselves, "Come, let us go down to the children of Cain, and see what they do, and enjoy ourselves with them."

But when Jared heard this of the hundred men, his very soul was moved, and his heart was grieved. He then arose with great fervour, and stood in the midst of them, and adjured them by the blood of Abel the just, "Let not one of you go down from this holy and pure mountain, in which our fathers have ordered us to dwell."

But when Jared saw that they did not receive his words, he said unto them, "O my good and innocent and holy children, know that when once you go down from this holy mountain, God will not allow you to return again to it."

He again adjured them, saying, "I adjure by the death of our father Adam, and by the blood of Abel, of Seth, of Enos, of Cainan, and of Mahalaleel, to hearken to me, and not to go down from this holy mountain; for the moment you leave it, you will be reft of life and of mercy;* and you shall no longer be called 'children of God,' but 'children of the devil.' "†

But they would not hearken to his words.

Enoch at that time was already grown up, and in his zeal for God, he arose and said, "Hear me, O ye sons of Seth, small and great—when ye transgress the commandment of our fathers, and go down from this holy mountain—ye shall not come up hither again for ever."[34]

But they rose up against Enoch, and would not hearken to his words, but went down from the Holy Mountain.

And when they looked at the daughters of Cain, at their beautiful figure, and at their hands and feet dyed with colour, and tattooed in ornaments on their faces,‡ the fire of sin was kindled in them.§

Then Satan made them look most beautiful before the sons of Seth, as he also made the sons of Seth appear of the fairest in the eyes of the daughters of Cain, so that the daughters of Cain lusted after the sons of Seth like ravenous beasts, and the sons of Seth after the daughters of Cain, until they committed abomination with them.‖

But after they had thus fallen into this defilement, they returned by the way they had come, and tried to ascend the

---

* Those rebellious souls are for death, the sword, perdition, and extinction like a lamp. *Cod. Nasor,* ii, 148.

† S. Ephrem, Serm. 1, on Par., vol. iii, p. 564.

‡ A description of Egyptian women, of that, as well as of the present, day.

§ But the Author of evil unable to curse the holy life and happiness of the children of Seth εἰς τὴν ὡραιότητα τῶν θυγατέρων τῶν ἀνθρώπων, ἤτοι τοῦ Κάϊν αὐτοὺς ἔρωσιν. Cedren., *Hist. Comp.*, p. 17.

‖ Eutychus tells the same in words that had better remain in the original.

Holy Mountain. But they could not, because the stones of that holy mountain were of fire flashing before them, by reason of which they could not go up again.[25]

And God was angry with them, and repented of them, because they had come down from glory, and had thereby [lost or] forsaken their own purity [or innocence], and were fallen[26] into the defilement of sin.[27]

Then God sent His Word to Jared, saying, "These thy children, whom thou didst call 'My children,'—behold they have transgressed My commandment, and have gone down to the abode of perdition, and of sin. Send a messenger to those that are left, that they may not go down, and be lost."

Then Jared wept before the Lord, and asked of Him mercy and forgiveness. But he wished that his soul might depart from his body, rather than hear these words from God about the going down of his children from the Holy Mountain.

But he followed God's order, and preached unto them not to go down from that holy mountain, and not to hold intercourse with the children of Cain.

But they heeded not his message, and would not obey his counsel.

CHAPTER XXI.

After this another company gathered together, and they went to look after their brethren; but they perished as well as they. And so it was, company after company, until only a few of them were left.

Then Jared sickened from grief,* and his sickness was such that the day of his death drew near.

Then he called Enoch his eldest son, and Methuselah Enoch's son, and Lamech the son of Methuselah, and Noah the son of Lamech.

---

* Νῦν δὲ ἐν χρόνοις τοῦ Ἰάρεδ καὶ ἐπέκεινα φαρμακεία καὶ μαγεία, ἀσέλγεια, μοιχεία καὶ ἀδικία. S. Epiph., Hæres., Lib. I, i, 5.

And when they were come to him he prayed over them and blessed them, and said to them, "Ye are righteous, innocent sons; go ye not down from this holy mountain; for behold, your children and your children's children have gone down from this holy mountain, and have estranged themselves from this holy mountain, through their abominable lust and transgression of God's commandment.

"But I know, through the power of God, that He will not leave you on this holy mountain,[28] because your children have transgressed His commandment and that of our fathers, which we had received from them.

"But, O my sons, God will take you to a strange land, and ye never shall again return to behold with your eyes this garden and this holy mountain.

"Therefore, O my sons, set your hearts on your own selves,* and keep the commandment of God which is with you. And when you go from this holy mountain, into a strange land which ye know not, take with you the body of our father Adam, and with it these three precious gifts and offerings, namely, the gold, the incense, and the myrrh; and let them be in the place where the body of our father Adam shall lay.

"And unto him of you who shall be left, O my sons, shall the Word of God come,[29] and when he goes out of this land he shall take with him the body of our father Adam, and shall lay it in the middle of the earth, the place in which salvation shall be wrought."†

Then Noah said unto him, "Who is he of us that shall be left?"

And Jared answered, "Thou art he that shall be left.[30] And thou shalt take the body of our father Adam from the cave, and place it with thee in the ark when the flood comes.

"And thy son Shem, who shall come out of thy loins, he it

---

* Or, on your souls.
† See Ps. lxxiv. 12, and S. Athan. *Quæst. ad A.*, Vol. II, p. 393.

is who shall lay the body of our father Adam in the middle of the earth, in the place whence salvation shall come."

Then Jared turned to his son Enoch, and said unto him, "Thou, my son, abide in this cave, and minister diligently* before the body of our father Adam all the days of thy life; and feed thy people in righteousness and innocence."

And Jared said no more. His hands were loosened, his eyes closed, and he entered into rest like his fathers. His death took place in the three hundred and sixtieth year of Noah, and in the nine hundred and eighty-ninth year of his own life; on the twelfth of Takhsas† on a Friday.

But as Jared died, tears streamed down his face by reason of his great sorrow, for the children of Seth, who had fallen in his days.

Then Enoch, Methuselah, Lamech and Noah, these four, wept over him; embalmed him carefully, and then laid him in the Cave of Treasures. Then they rose and mourned for him forty days.

And when these days of mourning were ended, Enoch, Methuselah, Lamech and Noah remained in sorrow of heart, because their father had departed from them, and they saw him no more.

CHAPTER XXII.

But Enoch kept the commandment of Jared his father, and continued to minister in the cave.

It is this Enoch to whom many wonders happened, and who also wrote a celebrated book; ‡[31] but those wonders may not be told in this place.

Then after this, the children of Seth went astray and fell, they, their children and their wives. And when Enoch,

* Or, continually.

† That is—the Ethiopic December; whereas the Arabic original has Tishrin (October), the month in which he was born and also died.

‡ Lit. by whom also there is a celebrated book.

Methuselah, Lamech and Noah saw them, their hearts suffered by reason of their fall into doubt full of unbelief; and they wept and sought of God mercy, to preserve them, and to bring them out of that wicked generation.

Enoch continued in his ministry before the Lord three hundred and eighty-five years, and at the end of that time he became aware through the grace of God, that God intended to remove him from the earth.

He then said to his son, "O my son, I know that God intends to bring the waters of the Flood upon the earth, and to destroy our creation.[32]

"And ye are the last rulers over this people on this mountain; for I know that not one will be left you to beget children on this holy mountain; neither shall any one of you rule over the children of his people; neither shall any great company be left of you, on this mountain."

Enoch said also to them, "Watch over your souls, and hold fast by your fear of God and by your service of Him, and worship Him in upright faith, and serve Him in righteousness, innocence and judgment, in repentance and also in purity."[33]

When Enoch had ended his commandments to them, God transported him from that mountain to the land of life, to the mansions of the righteous and of the chosen,[34] the abode of Paradise of joy, in light that reaches up to heaven; light that is outside the light of this world; for it is the light of God, that fills the whole world, but which no place can contain.

Thus, because Enoch* was in the light of God, he found himself out of the reach of death; until God would have him die.

Altogether, not one of our fathers or of their children, remained on that holy mountain, except those three, Methuselah, Lamech, and Noah. For all the rest went down from the mountain and fell into sin with the children of Cain. Therefore were they forbidden that mountain, and none remained on it but those three men.

* See S. Ephrem, vol. ii, p. 325, for a sermon on Enoch.

BOOK III.

CHAPTER I.

Noah noticed from his youth up, how sin had multiplied, how wickedness prevailed; how generations of men perished, how sorrow increased, how righteous men diminished.[1]

Therefore did he afflict his soul; he restrained his members, and retained his virginity; and grieved over the ruin wrought by the generations of men.

And this Noah habitually mourned and wept and was of a sad countenance; and thus he held his soul in fasting, so that the enemy had no advantage over him, and did not come near him.

This Noah also, ever since he was a child with his parents,[*] never made them angry, never transgressed against them; nor ever did a thing without their advice. And when he was away from them, if he wished to pray or to do aught else; he would ask of God, to guide him aright therein; wherefore God watched over him.

And while he was on the mountain, he did not transgress against God in any one evil thing, nor did he wilfully depart from what pleased God; neither did he ever anger God.

Many were the wonderful things which happened to him, more than to any of his fathers before him, about the time of the Flood.

* Lit. father.

And Noah continued in his virginity and in his obedience to God five hundred years; but after that it pleased God to raise him a seed; He therefore spake unto him, saying, "Arise, O Noah, and take unto thyself a wife, that of her thou mayest have children that may be a comfort to thee; for thou art left alone, and thou shalt go out of this country unto a strange land; for the earth shall be peopled with thy posterity."

Then when Noah heard this from God, he did not transgress His commandment, but took unto himself a wife, whose name was Haikal, the daughter of Abaraz, who was of the children of Enos's children, that went into perdition.

And she bare unto him three sons, Shem, Ham, and Japhet.

CHAPTER II.

After these things, God spake unto Noah about the Flood; that it should come upon the earth, and destroy all creatures, so as not to let one of them be seen.

And God said unto Noah, "Guard thy children; command them and make them understand not to have intercourse with the children of Cain, lest they perish with them.".

And Noah hearkened to God's words, and kept his children on the mountain, and would not let them go down to the children of Cain.

Then God spake again unto Noah, saying, "Make unto thyself an ark of wood that will not rot; to be a deliverance to thee and to the men of thy house.[2]

"But begin to build it in the low land of Eden, in presence of the children of Cain, that they may see thee working at it; and if they will not repent they shall perish; and the blame shall rest on them.

"But cut on this holy mountain, the trees whereof thou shalt make the ark; let the length of the ark be three hundred cubits, the breadth thereof fifty cubits, and the height thereof thirty cubits.³

"And when thou hast made and finished it, let there be in it one door above, and three compartments ;* and every compartment ten cubits high.

"The first story shall be for lions, and beasts, animals and ostriches all together. The second story shall be for birds, and creeping things.

"And the third story shall be for thee and thy wife, and for thy sons and their wives.

"And make in the ark wells for water, and openings to them, to draw water thereat, for drink to thee and to those that are with thee. And thou shalt line those wells with lead, both in and out.

"And make in the ark store-houses for corn; for food to thee and to those that are with thee.

"Then make also unto thyself a trumpet⁴ of ebony wood, three cubits long, one and a half cubit wide, with a mouthpiece of the same wood.

"And thou shalt blow it three times; the first time in the morning, that the workmen [working] at the ark may hear it, and gather to their work. Then thou shalt blow it the second time, and when the workmen hear it, they will gather to their meal. And thou shall blow it a third time in the evening, for the workmen to go and rest from their labour."

And God said unto Noah, "Go about among the people and tell them that a flood shall come and shall overwhelm them; and make the ark before their eyes.

"And when they question thee about the making of the ark, tell them: God has commanded me to make it, that we may get into it, I and my children, and be saved from the waters of the Flood."

But when Noah went about among them and told them, they

---

* Or, stories.

laughed at him, and only committed adultery and revelled together all the more, and said, "That twaddling old man! Whence will ever the waters come, above the tops of high mountains? We never saw water rise above mountains; and this old man says, a flood is coming!"

But Noah did all his works, as God had told him concerning them.

CHAPTER III.

And Noah begat his three sons, during the first hundred years he worked at the ark.

During these hundred years he ate no food, whence blood flows; the shoes on his feet were neither changed, nor worn, nor grown old.

During these hundred years also, he did not change his garments from off him, neither did they wear out, in the least; he did not change the staff in his hand, nor did the cloth about his head grow old; and the hair of his head neither increased nor grew less.

As to those three sons of Noah, the first of them is Shem; the next is Ham; and the third is Japhet. They married wives from among the daughters of Methuselah; as the wise LXXII interpreters have told us; as it is written in the first [sacred] book of the Greeks.

The life also of Lamech, Noah's father, was five hundred and fifty-three years; and when he drew nigh unto death, he called unto him his father Methuselah and his son Noah, and he wept before his father Methuselah and said unto him, "Dismiss me, O my father, and bless me."

Then Methuselah blessed his son Lamech, and said, "Not one of all our fathers died before his father, but the father [died] before his son, in order that there should be his son to bury him in the earth. Now, however, O my son, thou diest before me, and I shall drink [the cup of] sorrow on thy account, ere I go out of the flesh.

"Henceforth, O my son, behold the world is changed, and the [order] of deaths of men is changed: for from to-day the son shall die before his father; and the father shall not rejoice in his son, nor be satisfied with him. So also shall the son not be satisfied with his father, nor rejoice in him."

Then Lamech died, and they embalmed him, and laid him in the Cave of Treasures. His death took place seven years before the Flood came; and his father Methuselah and his son Noah remained alone on the Holy Mountain.

But Noah went down every day to work at the ark, and came up at eventide. And he instructed his sons and their wives not to come down after him, and not to hold intercourse with the children of Cain.

For Noah was anxious about his sons, and said in his mind, "They are young and might be overcome by passion." So he went down by night; and gave old Methuselah directions about them.

CHAPTER IV.

But Noah preached repeatedly to the children of Cain, saying, "The flood will come and destroy you, if we do not repent." But they would not hearken to him; they only laughed at him.[5]

When the children of Seth went down from the Holy Mountain, and dwelt with the children of Cain, and defiled themselves with their abominations, there were born unto them children called Garsina,* who were giants, mighty men of valour, such as no other giants were of equal might.[6]

Certain wise men of old wrote concerning them, and say in their [sacred] books, that angels came down from heaven, and

* A corruption of the Arabic term.

mingled with the daughters of Cain, who bare unto them these giants.

But those [wise men] err in what they say. God forbid such a thing, that angels who are spirits,* should be found committing sin with human beings. Never; that cannot be.⁷

And if such a thing were of the nature of angels, or Satans, that fell, they would not leave one woman on earth, undefiled. For Satans are very wicked and infamous. Moreover, they are not male and female by nature; but they are small, subtle spirits, that have been black ever since they transgressed.

But many men say, that angels came down from heaven, and joined themselves to women, and had children by them. This cannot be true.† But they were children of Seth, who were of the children of Adam, that dwelt on the mountain, high up [or suspended], while they preserved their virginity, their innocence and their glory like angels; and were then called " angels of God."

But when they transgressed and mingled with the children of Cain, and begat children, ill-informed men said, that angels had come down from heaven, and mingled with daughters of men, who bare them giants.

CHAPTER V.

Then the ancient old man Methuselah who remained on the mountain with Noah's sons, lived nine hundred and eighty-seven years and then sickened; and his sickness was such that, on account of it, he must depart [from this world].

When Noah and his sons, Shem, Ham and Japhet, became aware of it, they came to him with their wives, and wept before

---

* The Ethiopic construction is not quite correct here. The Arabic reads " Angelic spirits."

† See S. Matt. xxii, 30, and the same in S. Mark and in S. Luke. See also note 5 from the Coran. Sur. vi, xxxvii, and liii, etc.

him, and said, "O our father, and [our] elder, bless us, and pray God to have mercy on us when thou art gone from us."

Then Methuselah said to them with a sorrowful heart, "Hear me, O my dear children; for none of our fathers are left, but you, eight souls.

"The Lord God created our father Adam and our mother Eve, and from them filled the earth [with] people in the neighbourhood of the garden, and multiplied their seed.

"But they have not kept His commandment, and He will destroy them. But had they kept His commandment, He would then have filled heaven and earth with them.

"Yet will I ask the Lord my God to bless you, to multiply you, and to spread your race in a strange land, to which ye shall go.

"And now, O my children, behold, God will bring you inside an ark unto a land to which ye have never been. And the Lord God of all our pure fathers, be with you!

"And the glorious gifts God bestowed on our father Adam from the garden in this blessed Cave of Treasures, may He bestow them on you also!

"These are the three glorious gifts which God made to Adam. The first is—kingdom wherein God made Adam king over His works. The second glorious gift is—priesthood, in that God breathed into his face a spirit of life. And the third glorious gift is—prophecy, for Adam prophesied concerning what God thought [of doing].

"But I will ask the Lord my God, to bestow those three glorious gifts on your posterity."

Then Methuselah said also to Noah, "O Noah, thou art blessed of God. I warn thee and tell thee that I am going from thee to [be with] all our fathers that have gone before me.

"But thou, who shalt be left alone with thy children on this holy mountain, keep the commandment I give thee, and forsake not anything of what I have told thee.

"Behold my God shall quickly bring a flood upon the earth; embalm my body, and lay it in the Cave of Treasures.

"Then take thy wife with thy sons and their wives, and go down from this holy mountain, and take with thee the body of our father Adam;[8] go into the ark and lay it there, until the waters of the Flood are assuaged from off the face of the earth.

"O my son, when about to die, command thy first-born son Shem, to take Melchizedec,* son of Cainan, and grandson of Arphaxad;[9] for that Melchizedec is priest of the Most High God;[10] and to take with them the body of our father Adam from within the ark, and remove it and lay it in the earth.

"And Melchizedec shall stand ministering on that mountain that is in the middle of the earth, before the body of our father Adam for ever. For from that place, O Noah my son, God shall work salvation for Adam and for all of his seed that believe in God."

Methuselah said also to Noah and to his sons, "The angel of God will go with you, until you come to that place in the middle of the earth."

Again Methuselah said to Noah, "O my son, let him who ministers unto God and before the body of our father Adam, have a clothing of skin, and be girt about his loins with leather. Let him wear no ornament, but let his raiment be poor; let him be alone,† and stand praying our Lord God to watch over the body of our father Adam; for it is a body of great value before God.

"And let him continue in his ministry, he the priest of the Most High God; for he is well pleasing unto God, and so is the ministry he fulfils before God."

After this Methuselah commanded Noah [saying], "Mind, then, all these commandments, and keep them."

Then Methuselah's hands were loosened; he ceased speak-

---

* The Arabic reads: "Melchizedec thy son's son," *i.e.*, "Son of Shem," as generally believed in the East.

† *i.e.*, single.

ing; he gradually closed his eyes, and entered into rest like all his fathers; his tears the time streaming down his cheeks, and his heart grieving at being separated from them [all]; but mostly because of that mountain of the garden, on which not one of them was left; for God was purposed to destroy all creatures, and to blot them out from the face of the earth.

The rest of Methuselah took place when he was nine hundred and sixty-seven years old, on the twelfth of Magābit on a Sunday.

Then Noah and his sons embalmed him, weeping and sorrowing over him, and laid him in the Cave of Treasures. And they wailed over him with a great wailing, they and their wives, forty days. And when mourning and grief over Methuselah were ended, Noah and his sons began to do as Methuselah had commanded them.

CHAPTER VI.

After his death, Noah, his sons, and their wives came to the bodies of our fathers, worshipped them, and blessed themselves in them, weeping and being in the deepest grief.

But Noah had finished the ark, and not one workman was left in it. And he, with his sons, continued in prayer to God, asking Him to show them the way of safety.

When Noah and his sons had ended their prayers, God said unto him, "Go thou into the Cave of Treasures, thou and thy sons, and take the body of our father Adam and lay it in the ark; likewise take the gold, the incense, and the myrrh, and lay them in the ark together with his body."

And Noah hearkened to God's voice, and went into the Cave of Treasures, he and his sons; they worshipped the bodies of our fathers, and then Noah took the body of our father Adam, and carried it in the strength of God, not requiring the help of any one *[11]

* Lit. and would (or wished) not that one should help him.

Then Shem his son, took the gold with him, and Ham carried the myrrh, and Japhet carried the incense; and they brought them out of the Cave of Treasures, their tears the while streaming down their cheeks.

But as they were bringing them out, the bodies among which Adam had been laid, cried out, "Are we then to be separated from thee, O our father Adam?"

Then Adam's body answered, "Oh, that I must part from you my sons, from this holy mountain! Yet do I know, O my sons, that God will gather all our bodies together another time.

"But wait patiently until our Saviour have pity on us."

And the other bodies went on talking together, by the power of God's Word.

Then Adam asked God that the divine fire might remain in the lamp, before his sons, until the time when bodies shall rise again.

And God left the divine fire by them, to shed light on them. He then closed the cave upon them, and left not a trace to show [where it is] until the day of the Resurrection, when He will raise them up, like all other bodies.

But the discourse Adam held, and that too, he being dead, was by the command of God, who would show His wonders among the dead and the living.

After this let none of you say, that Adam's soul had already been under Satan's judgment. It was not so; but God commanded the souls of the dead, to come from under His hand; and to speak of the wonders of God from within their bodies." Then they returned to their places until the day of the sure deliverance that shall be unto them all.

CHAPTER VII.

But when Noah and his sons heard these voices from those dead bodies, they wondered greatly, and their faith in God was strengthened.

Then they went out of the cave and began to go down from the Holy Mountain, weeping and wailing with a fervent heart, for their being thus parted from the holy mountain, the abode of their fathers.

And Noah and his sons went back and sought the cave, but could not find it. Then they broke out into bitter lamentation and deep sorrow; for they saw that from that day forth, they should have neither existence nor abode in it.

Then once more they raised their eyes and looked at the garden and at the trees [that were] in it, and they lifted up their voices in weeping and in loud crying, and said, "We salute thee in worship, O garden of joy![13] O abode of brilliant beings, a place for the righteous! We salute thee, O place of joy that was the abode of our father Adam, the chief of creation; who, when he had transgressed, fell from thee; and then saw his body in life, naked and disgraced.

"And we, behold, we depart from the Holy Mountain to the lower side of thee; neither shall we dwell in it, nor yet behold thee so long as we live. We wish God would remove thee with us to the country to which we shall go; but God would not remove thee into a cursed land.

"But God will take us, and will bring us into that land with our children, until He has ended the punishment for our transgression of His commandment."

Noah and his sons said also, "We salute thee, O cave, abode of the bodies of our holy fathers; we salute thee, O pure spot, hidden from our eyes, yet fit to have those bodies laid within thee! The Lord God preserve thee, for the sake of the bodies of our fathers!

Again they said, "We greet you, O our fathers, righteous judges, and we ask you to pray for us before God, that He will have pity on us, and deliver us out of this passing world.

"We ask you to pray for us—for us, the only ones left of your seed; We give you a greeting of peace!

"O Seth, great master, among the fathers, we greet thee

with peace! O Holy Mountain abode of our fathers, we give thee a greeting of peace!"

Then Noah and his sons wept again, and said, "Alas, for us eight souls that are left! Behold we are taken away from the sight of the garden."

And as they were coming down the mountain they greeted the stones, took them in their hands and put them upon their shoulders; they stroked down the trees, and did so weeping. And they continued coming down from the mountain, until they came to the door of the ark.

Then Noah and his sons turned their faces to the east, and requested the Lord to have mercy on them, to save them, and to command them where to lay the body of our father Adam.

Then the Word of God came to Noah, saying, "Lift up the body of Adam to the third story [of the ark], and lay it there on the eastern side; and the gold, the incense and the myrrh together with him.[13]

"And thou and thy sons shall stand before him praying. But thy wife, and the wives of thy sons, shall be on the western side of the ark; and they and their wives shall not come together."

Then when Noah heard these words from God, he and his sons went into the ark, and laid the body of our father Adam on the eastern side, and the three offerings together with him.

And Noah brought into the ark the body of Adam, on a Friday, at the second hour, on the twenty-seventh of the month of Gembot.

CHAPTER VIII.

Then God said unto Noah, "Go upon the top of the ark and blow the trump three times, that all beasts gather together unto the ark."

But Noah said, "Shall the sound of the trump reach unto the ends of the earth to gather together the beasts and the birds?"

Then God said unto him, "It is not the sound of this trump alone that shall go forth, but My power shall go with it, to make it come into the ears of the beasts and of the birds.*

"And when thou blowest thy trump, I will command My angel to blow the horn from heaven; and all these animals shall be gathered unto thee."

Then Noah made haste and blew the trump, as God had told him. Then the angel blew the horn from heaven, until the earth quaked, and all creatures on it trembled.

Then all the beasts, birds and creeping things were gathered together at the third hour, on a Friday; when all the beasts, lions and ostriches went into the lower story at the third hour. Then at midday, came the birds and creeping things into the middle story; and Noah and his sons went into the third story, at the ninth hour of the day.

And when Noah, with his wife, his sons and their wives came into the upper story, he commanded the women to dwell on the western side; but Noah and his sons, with the body of our father Adam, dwelt on the eastern side.

CHAPTER IX.

And Noah stood asking God to save him from the waters of the Flood.

Then God talked to Noah, and said to him, "Of every kind of birds, take one pair, male and female of the clean; and of the unclean also one pair, male and female. But also of the clean take six [more] pairs, male and female."

---

* "All these beasts, birds, and creeping things, shall come to thee by the hand of the angel who shall take and bring them to thee to keep them alive. *Targ. Jonathan*, in Gen. vii.

And Noah did all this. Then when they all had got into the ark, God shut to the door of the ark upon them by His power.

He then commanded the windows of heaven to open wide, and to pour down from them cataracts of water. And so it was; by God's order.

And He commanded all fountains to burst open, and the depths to pour forth water, upon the face of the earth. So that the sea all round rose above the whole world, and surged, and the deep waters arose.

But when the windows of heaven opened wide, all stores [of water] and depths were opened, and all the stores* of the winds, and the whirlwind, thick mist, gloom and darkness spread abroad. The sun and moon and stars, withheld their light. It was a day of terror, such as had never been.

Then the sea all round, began to raise its waves on high like mountains; and it covered the whole face of the earth.

But when the sons of Seth, who were fallen into wickedness and adultery with the children of Cain, saw this, they then knew that God was angry with them; and that Noah had told them the truth.

Then they all ran round the ark, to Noah, begging and entreating him to open for them the door of the ark; inasmuch as they could not climb the Holy Mountain, by reason of the stones thereof, that were like fire.

But as to the ark, it was closed and sealed by the power of God.[14] An angel of God sat upon the ark, and was like a captain to Noah, to his sons, and to all inside the ark.

And the waters of the flood increased on the children of Cain and overwhelmed them; and they began to sink, and the words of Noah were fulfilled, which he preached to them [saying], the waters of the Flood should come and drown them.

And the waters continued above and below over Noah and

* Lit. locks.

his sons, until they were suspended in the ark; and by the strength of the water, the ark rose from the earth; and the flesh of every moving thing perished.

And the water rose until it covered the earth, and until it covered all high mountains;[15] and the waters rose above them, and above the tops of high mountains fifteen cubits, by the cubit of the Holy Ghost, which is equal to* three cubits [of man]. So that the number of these were forty-five cubits [above the highest mountains].

And the water increased and bare the ark, and brought it to the lower side of the garden, which the waters, the rain, the whirlwind and all that went about on the earth—did worship. As did also Noah and his sons and all that was in the ark—they bowed in worship to the holy garden.

And the water returned to its former state, and destroyed every thing that was upon the earth and under heaven.

But the ark was floating on the waters and rose up before the winds; while the angel of God steered and led it from east to west. And the ark thus moved about on the face of the waters a hundred and fifty days.

After that, the ark stood upon the mountains of Ararat,[16] on the twenty-seventh day of the month of Tkarnt.

CHAPTER X.

Then God sent again His order to Noah, saying, "Be quiet and wait until the waters are assuaged."

Then the waters parted asunder and returned every water to its own place, where it was at first; the fountains ceased to pour forth† over the earth; the depths that are on the face of the earth, ceased to rise; and the windows of heaven were closed. For floods of rain fell from heaven at the beginning of the Flood forty days and forty nights.

* Lit. rendered by. † Or, spread.

But on the first day of the eleventh month the tops of high mountains were seen; and Noah waited yet forty days, and then opened the window he had made on the western side of the ark, and let go a raven, to see if the waters were assuaged from the face of the earth or not.[17]

Then the raven went forth, but returned no more to Noah; for the harmless dove is the sign of the mystery of the Christian Church.

But Noah waited yet a little while after the waters were assuaged, and then sent out a dove, to see if the water had retired or not.

But when the dove went out, she found not a place whereon to rest her foot, and no abode; and she returned to Noah.

Then Noah waited seven days more, and sent out the dove to see if the water had retired or not. And the dove came back to Noah, about eventide; and in her mouth was an olive-leaf.*

The meaning of the dove is, that she is taken as a figure of the old and of the new [covenants].[18] The first time when she went out, and found nowhere to rest her feet, that is, a place of rest [is a figure of] the stiff-necked Jews, in whom no grace remained, nor any mercy whatever. Wherefore Christ, the meek one, who is figured in the dove, did not find among them rest for the sole of His feet.

But the second time when the dove found a place of rest [is a figure of] the nations that have received the glad tidings of the holy Gospel, and among whom Christ has found a resting-place.

CHAPTER XI.

In the six hundred and seventh year of Noah's life, on the second day of the month Barmudeh, the water dried from off

---

* Plucked on the Mount of Olives. *Targ. Jonath.*, in Gen. viii.

the earth.[19] And in the next month, which is Gembot, on the twenty-seventh day thereof, which is the day on which Noah went into the ark, on that self-same day did Noah also come out of the ark, on a Sunday.

But when Noah, his wife, his sons and their wives went out of the ark, they again came together, and did not part asunder one from another; at first, when they went into the ark, the men and the women remained apart, Noah fearing lest they should come together. But when the Flood was over, they again came together, the husband with his wife.[20]

God also had sent great quietness over the beasts, the lions that were in the ark, and over the birds and creeping things, not to disagree among themselves.

Then Noah came out of the ark, and built an altar upon the mountain. And he stood, and requested the Lord to show him of what sacrifices he ought to take, and bring them unto Him in offerings.

Then God sent His Word to Noah, saying, "O Noah, take of the clean kind, and offer of them upon the altar before me; and let the animals go out of the ark."

Then Noah went into the ark, and took of clean birds as many as God had commanded him; and offered them up in offerings upon the altar before the Lord.*

CHAPTER XII.

Pattern of the covenant God made with Noah, when He showed him the bow on the cloud in heaven.

And God smelled the smell of Noah's offerings, and He made a covenant with him, that the waters of the flood should not again come upon the earth, henceforth and for ever.

---

* This was the altar built by Adam, on which he, Cain and Abel had offered sacrifices. *Targ. Jonathan*, in Gen. viii. It was injured by the Flood; but Noah repaired it. *Ibid.*

And this is the covenant God made with Noah :—

God said unto Noah, "I will make the bow of My covenant come out in the cloud; and when it appears, then men shall know that it is done in truth.

"And if I was wroth, when the bow was seen in the cloud, then [it would show] that My anger and the punishment I meant to bring upon men were over.

"Then, again, O Noah, I have made this bow of My covenant to be seen in heaven, in order that all creatures should see it, and think of the trials and afflictions that came upon them at first, and repent, and turn from their evil ways."

And God accepted Noah's offering, and blessed him and his sons, and said unto them, "Be fruitful and multiply, and replenish the face of the earth."

Then God commanded the earth to bring forth herb as it did of old, for beasts, for birds, and for all that moves on the earth.

Then Noah worshipped before God, with his sons and their wives; and they praised Him for the salvation He had wrought for them.

CHAPTER XIII.

After this Noah took his sons, and built them a city and called it Semanān;[21] as they were eight souls that came out of the ark.

And Noah and his sons dwelt on that mountain about a hundred years, until he had children and children's children.

And Noah took a root of vine and planted it, and dressed it until it yielded fruit.[22] It was sweet, and Noah took some of it, and pressed wine out of it, and took it one night and drank of it, and was drunk.[23] And he came in to his wife unawares.

Then Ham, his son, came into the house in the morning and saw his father uncovered, and drunk with wine, and without sense to know anything.

Then Ham his son kept on laughing at him, and said, "What is this thou hast done, O thou old man?"

But the old man understood not what he said; only Noah's wife understood it well.

Then Ham went out laughing at his father, and told his brothers Shem and Japhet what his father had done; and laughed at his parents.

But his brothers were angry with him, and rebuked him well for so doing; because they were afraid of him, as regards the old man; for Ham was rough and hard in his talk.

Then Shem and Japhet rose quickly, and took with them a coverlet, and put behind their backs that coverlet that reached unto their feet; and they walked backwards, and turned their face towards the way they had gone, until they came to their parents. Then they threw the coverlet over them, and went from them in haste, so as not to see them.

But on the morrow after this, Noah's wife told him what Ham had said and what he had done.

Then was Noah very angry with his son Ham[*] for what he had done; and he cursed him, and made him servant of his brothers.

But Noah blessed Shem and Japhet, his sons, because they had behaved well to him.

Then Noah married another wife, who bare him seven children. And he continued to dwell on that mountain until the days drew near when he must depart [this life]. And Noah lived three hundred and fifty years after he came out of the ark.

Then he called his first-born son Shem, and conversed with him, saying, "O my son, hearken unto what I command thee.[34]

"Behold [what] I command thee now [is], to hold good until I die and ye bury me. Then, when ye have ended mourning for me, go into the ark in which we were saved from the flood; then bring out of it the body of our father Adam; but

---

[*] See the Coran, sur. v, and Hotting., *Hist. Or.*, p. 35, sq.

let no one know of it but one that is of thy seed. Then make a beautiful case for it, and lay it therein.

"Then take with thee some bread to be for provision unto thee by the way, and wine whereof to drink on thy way; for the land to which thou shalt go is rough and hungry.

"Then take Melchizedec the youngest son of Cainan,* thy son; for God has chosen him from all generations of men, to stand before Him to worship and to minister unto Him, by the body of our father Adam.[25]

"Then lay the body of Adam in the midst of the earth; and set Melchizedec to stand by it; and show him how to fulfil his ministry before God."

Moreover Noah said unto Shem his son, "If ye will keep my commandment and go [as I tell you], an angel of the Lord will go with you, and show you the way, until ye come to the place where ye shall lay the body [of Adam] in the midst of the earth; for in that self-same place shall God work salvation for the whole world.

"But, O my son, I know that our children forsook this good commandment, and went down the Holy Mountain, and mingled with the children of Cain, and that they perished with them in the waters of the Flood.

"Know, O my son, that from Adam until this day, every one of the ancients, gave commandments to one of the rest, at the time of his resting from the flesh, and that they taught [these commandments] among themselves.

"The first, O my son, who taught this commandment and made it plain, was our father Adam; he gave it to his son Seth, who received it.

"Then Seth handed it to his son Enos who kept it. And Enos gave it to his son Cainan who kept it. Then Cainan gave it to his son Mahalaleel, who kept it, and handed it to his son Jared.

"And Jared kept it and gave it to his son Enoch, who also

* Here the Arabic has Arphaxad, instead of Cainan see above, p. 149.

kept this commandment and gave it to his son Methuselah, who kept it, and gave it to his son Lamech who kept it, and who gave it to me, his son; and I have kept it.

"But my grandfather Methuselah also gave me a great commandment which I have kept; and which I give thee likewise. So, then, receive my commandment, and hold fast my words; and hide this mystery within thy heart; but reveal it not to one of all thy kindred. But go, and lay the body of our father Adam in the earth; and let it remain there unto the day of salvation."

CHAPTER XIV.

But the ark was closed during the days of Noah; neither was any one allowed to touch it. Yet they went to it, blessed themselves in it, and talked about it.

Noah, however, went into it every evening, to light the lamp which he had made before our father Adam, and blessed himself in that body.

And he did not neglect his office regarding the lamp, as it was at first in the Cave of Treasures.

But as Noah knew that after him, the ark would not remain whole, and that his children would part asunder and not return to look after the body of our father Adam, and that wickedness would increase in the earth and abominations among men, therefore did he command his son Shem to hasten to take the body of our father Adam,* and to remove it unto the middle of the earth; according to God's order.

CHAPTER XV.

Then when Noah had ended giving orders to his son Shem, concerning the body of our father Adam, Noah said to his son

* See below, ch. xviii.

Shem, "Bring hither to me thy brothers, and make them come near me."

Then when they came to Noah, he looked at them and said unto them, "O my sons, after my death ye shall part asunder, and sore troubles shall happen to your race.

"But I will from now, divide among you the earth into three portions; as every one of you shall be settled in his own portion.

"Unto Shem my first-born son, shall his lot be from Jerusalem which is a great city, as far as Qardayun and Andika.* It takes in the border mountain that reaches unto Gefur, between the land of Egypt and that of the Philistines.

"Unto my next son Ham, his portion shall be from Aris towards the south, unto Fardundan and unto Gaduriun, and unto the borders of the west.

"And unto my third son Japhet, his portion shall be from the corner of the west towards the south unto Damatha, a large tract of country; and all the north also as far as Aris."[26]

He then said to them, "Let every one of you take a portion different from that of his brothers; and let every one of you dwell in his own portion." And they settled in it, as he commanded them.

And they all had sons and daughters during their father Noah's lifetime. And Noah divided the earth among them by God's order, in order that there should be no enmity between the three brothers.

Then when Noah had ended his commandments to Shem and to his brothers, his hands dropped, his tongue became dumb, his eyes closed and he died, like his fathers. He died aged nine hundred and fifty years,[27] on a Wednesday, the second day of the month Gembot, on the mountain on the which was the ark; and there he will remain until the day God reveals [his resting-place].

And they mourned for him forty days.†

* That is, Bactriana and India.   † Eutych., p. 45.

CHAPTER XVI.

After they had ended mourning for Noah, an angel of God appeared unto Cainan father of Melchizedec, and said unto him in a vision, "Knowest thou me?" And Cainan answered, "No, my Lord."

Then the angel said to him, "I am the angel whom God has sent unto thee, to give thee this commandment. And transgress not the command of God."

When Cainan heard this from the angel of God, he wondered and said unto him, "Speak, O my Lord!"

And the angel of God said unto him, "I am the angel who brought gold to thy father Adam, when he was below the garden; I am the angel who entreated God together with him, when he offered his own blood upon the altar.

"I am Michael the angel who received the soul of Abel the just; I am the angel who was with Seth when he was born in the cave.

"I am the angel who was with Enos and Cainan, and Mahalaleel and Jared and Enoch, and Methuselah and Lamech, and with Noah. But since he entered into rest, I stand by his first-born son Shem.

"And, behold, God has sent me to thee, to take thy son Melchizedec, and to remove him to the land, in which God shall lay the body of our father Adam, and that he may be high exalted before God. Let not thy heart be grieved at his going away."

When Cainan heard these words from the angel, he worshipped before him; and said unto him, "The will of God be done! Behold, I and my son are in His hands. Let Him do what He pleases."

This angel appeared unto Cainan, not on account of Cainan's righteousness and purity, but on account of Melchizedec, and of his righteousness and purity.

Then the angel said unto Cainan, "Commit not this mystery to any one but to Shem alone."

And the angel departed from him.

CHAPTER XVII.

Then the angel of God came unto Melchizedec that night while he was lying on his bed.

And he appeared unto him in the figure of a youth like him, who smote him on the side, and awoke him out of his sleep.

When Melchizedec heard it, he rose up, and saw the house full of light, and a figure standing before him. And he was afraid, for he was not accustomed to see angels, but this once only.

But the angel prevented fear from overcoming him, and anointed him on the head and on the breast, and said unto him, "Fear not, I am an angel of God; and He has sent me to thee with this message, that thou fulfil it unto thy God."

Melchizedec then said unto him, "What is that message?" For he was a youth of a perfect heart.

And the angel said unto him, "It is that thou go with the body of our father Adam, unto the middle of the earth; and that thou stand ministering before it there; and that thou serve God; for He has chosen thee from thy childhood. For thou art of the seed of the blessed."

Then Melchizedec said unto him, "Who will bring the body of my father Adam, and me with it, unto the middle of the earth?"

And the angel said unto him, "Shem, the son of Noah thy father's grandfather."

Then the angel strengthened his heart, and comforted him tenderly one whole hour, and then said unto him, "Commit not these hidden words to any but to Shem only;[38] lest the report of it spread abroad; and they hang on to the body of Adam, and not let it go to the land, to which God has commanded [it to be taken]."

And the angel departed from him.

CHAPTER XVIII.

Then the angel went to Shem the son of Noah and said unto him, "Arise, and take the body of Adam, as thy father Noah gave thee commandment; and take with thee Melchizedec and go with them to the place ordered by God; and tarry not."

When it was day, Shem made a beautiful case and hid it close to the ark. He then prepared bread and wine and provisions, and came to Cainan; and inquired for his son Melchizedec. Then Cainan began to tell him all that the angel had said unto him; and he gave him up his son Melchizedec, with a good heart.

Then Shem said to Cainan, "Keep this mystery secret, and reveal it to no one."

Then Shem took Melchizedec and they saddled an ass between them, and they went to the ark. But they had no key wherewith to open the ark; for Noah had fastened it with a padlock, after he had come out of it.

When, therefore, they came to the ark, they bethought themselves how to open it. Then came Shem to the door, and said to Melchizedec, "Come, open it, O thou great God."

Then came Melchizedec to the door when he heard [Shem's voice], and seized the padlock; and at once the door was opened.

But a voice cried from within the ark, and said, "Rejoice, O thou priest of the Most High God, for that thou hast been found meet to enter upon the office of priest of God; the first created by Him in the world."

This voice was from the Holy Ghost.

And Melchizedec knew that voice when it breathed into his face; he knew it also through great grace that was in him.

He then marvelled, and said to Shem, "O my Lord, I know by the breathing in my face, though I saw no form, and heard no voice speaking to me; for I saw no one. This voice is from the body of our father Adam."

And Shem remained trembling, not knowing what to say to him.

But while they were wondering at the door of the ark, the Word of God came, that said, "I am He that made thee priest and that breathed of My Spirit into thee. Thou art My righteous priest; and thou art worthy to bear the body of Adam whom I created, and into whom I breathed of My Spirit. And I made him priest and a king, and a prophet. Go in first, and bring out his body."

Then Melchizedec went into the ark, and bowed in worship to the body of our father Adam; he blessed himself in it, and brought it out; the angel Michael, helping him the while to carry it.

And Shem went in also, and brought out the gold, the incense and the myrrh, and laid them together with the body of our father Adam; he then placed the body within the case, and shut it upon the body. And then he shut the door of the ark, as it was at first.[29]

CHAPTER XIX.

Then Shem and Melchizedec took the body of Adam, and went on their way; and the angel of God went with them and showed them whither to go. And so they went on that day until the evening; and alighted at a certain place to rest.

Then Shem and Melchizedec stood up to pray; and while they prayed there came a voice from inside the coffin of Adam, that said, "Glory to God who created me, who gave me life, who made me die; and who again returns me to the earth out of which He took me!"

And the voice blessed the youth Melchizedec and said unto him, "Of all our race, God chose no one but thee; neither did He anoint any one of them priest with His own hand, but thee; neither did He breathe into the face of any one His pure Spirit as He breathed it into thee; and I rejoice, O my son, that thou hast been found worthy of such honour from God."

Then the voice withdrew from Melchizedec, who wondered at this voice that came forth from a dead man. But it was done by the power of God.

But when Shem saw this first wonder wrought on Melchizedec, he kissed his face, and rejoiced greatly on his account. But as for Melchizedec, he tasted nothing that night, for the joy that filled his heart; but he continued standing before the coffin of Adam, praising God and praying until morning. This vision happened to Melchizedec in the fifteenth year of his age.

Then Shem and Melchizedec put the coffin upon the ass, and went on their way; and the angel of God went with them. And it was so that when they came to rough places, the angel bare them up by the power of God, and made them pass over them, whether they were lands or mountains.

And so they went on their way until the evening of the second day, when they alighted to rest, after their custom.

Then Shem and Melchizedec stood up to pray; and as they were praying, behold a great light shone over them, wherefore Melchizedec did not feel* aught of fatigue, by reason of the strength of God, that was in him; but he rejoiced like one that is going to his wedding.

But they stood praying as they were wont before the coffin of our father Adam. Then came a voice from the top of the coffin, that said to Melchizedec and to Shem, "Behold, we are drawing near to the place our Lord has decreed for us."

* Lit. know.

And the voice said unto Melchizedec, "Upon the land to which we are going, shall the Word of God come down; and suffer and be crucified on the place in which my body is laid.

"The crown of my head shall be baptized with His blood; and then shall my salvation be wrought; and He shall restore me to my kingdom, and shall give me my priesthood and my gift of prophecy."

Then the voice was silent by the power of God.

But Melchizedec and Shem marvelled at the voice that talked with them. And Melchizedec remained the whole of that night praying joyfully until the day dawned. Then they put the body of Adam on the ass, and went on their way.

And the angel of God went with them, until they neared the place.

Then he went before them, and stood before the ass, and took down from her the coffin, himself alone; and not as on the two former occasions, when Melchizedec took it down [from the ass].

But when the coffin reached the rock, the rock split asunder into two parts,—that was the place for the coffin; and Melchizedec and Shem knew thereby that it was the place God had appointed.

Then the angel went up from them into heaven, while saying unto God, "Behold, the body of our father Adam has arrived, and is come to the place Thou didst choose. I have done that which Thou didst command me."

Then came the Word of God to the angel, saying, "Go down to Melchizedec and strengthen his heart; and command him to abide by the body of Adam. And when Shem enters into rest, tell Melchizedec to go, and to take from Shem the bread and wine he has with him, and to preserve them."

CHAPTER XX.

Then the angel came down from God, in the figure of a man, who appeared to Melchizedec and to Shem, and strengthened their hearts.

He then laid the body of our father Adam in its place; and said to Melchizedec, "Take from Shem the bread and the wine." And he took them, as the angel told him [to do].

But Melchizedec and Shem stood praying by the body of our father Adam until the evening, when a great light came down upon the body, and angels ascended and descended in that place upon the body of our father Adam.

They were rejoicing, and praising, and saying, "Glory be to Thee, O God, who didst create the worlds; and madest men of the dust of the earth, to exalt them above heavenly beings."

And the angels thus praised God over the body of our father Adam, the whole of that night, until the dawn of day.

But as the sun rose, the Word of God came to Melchizedec, and said to him, "Arise, and take twelve of these stones; make of them an altar, and offer upon it of the bread and wine that was with Shem; and offer them, thou and he."

Then when Melchizedec heard the Word of God, he worshipped between his hands; and he hastened, and did as God commanded him.

And at the time he was offering the gift upon the altar, and asked God to sanctify it, the Holy Ghost came down upon the offering; and the mountain was filled with light.

And angels said unto him, "This offering is acceptable unto God. Glory be to him who created earthly men, and has revealed great mysteries unto them!"

Then the Word of God appeared to Melchizedec, and said

unto him, "Behold, I have made thee priest; and thou and Shem shall offer this offering thou didst make first; and in like manner as thou didst set up[30] these twelve solid foundation stones, will I raise twelve apostles to be the pillars of the world. And they are firm.

"In like manner also, as thou didst make this altar, will I make thee an altar in the world; and like as thou didst make an offering of bread and wine, will I also present the offering of My Body and Blood, and make it [to be] unto forgiveness of sins.

"And this place on which thou art standing and in which the body of Adam is laid, will I make a holy place; all creatures on earth shall be blessed in it; and in it I will grant forgiveness unto all who come hither."

Then the Word of God, blessed Melchizedec—named him priest—and then went up from him into heaven in glory and rejoicing with His angels.

CHAPTER XXI.

Then Melchizedec praised God; and he and Shem made an offering. And Shem stayed with him that day, to rest from the toil of the journey.

But when the day dawned, it seemed good to Shem to depart. Then Melchizedec wished him God speed, and blessed him, and said unto him, "The Lord God who led us to this place, be with thee; and guide thee until thou come to thine own place."[31]

Melchizedec said also to him, "When they inquire of thee about me, direct them not in the way; that they come not to me. And when my father and my mother ask thee about me, say to them, 'He has departed [on a pilgrimage]; and I do not know the place of his pilgrimage.'

"So that, when thou sayest so to them, their hope of me will be cut short; and they will feel it is of no use thinking of me; so that they will not press thee, and make thee come to me."

Shem, then departed, and returned to his kindred;[32] while Melchizedec remained standing before the body of our father Adam, ministering unto God, and worshipping Him evermore.

And an angel abode with him, who protected him and brought him food, until the time of Abraham the patriarch.

And the raiment of this Melchizedec was of skins, with a leathern girdle around his loins. And he ministered unto God, with much praying and fasting.

CHAPTER XXII.

But Shem and his brothers, multiplied abundantly upon the earth; and begat sons and daughters; and went on this way, until Shem was five hundred and fifty years old, when he died.[33]

Then they embalmed him, and continued mourning for him forty days.

After this, Arphaxad, son of Shem, lived four hundred and eighty-five years, and then died; and they embalmed him and mourned for him forty days.

Then after him was Cainan, son of Arphaxad and father of Melchizedec, who lived five hundred and eighty-nine years, and then died.[34]

After him Saleh, son of Cainan, and brother of Melchizedec lived four hundred and eight years, and then died.

After him Eber* his son, lived four hundred and thirty-four years, and then died.

Then Phalek was born when his father was two hundred and seven years old. In the days of Phalek, the earth was divided a second time among the three sons of Noah; Shem, Ham, and Japhet.

* Eber took to wife Azurad Nebrud's [Nimrud's] daughter. Kufale, c. viii, p. 34.

THE DIVISION OF TONGUES.

Wherefore were they much aggrieved through this division among themselves; because during their father's life-time, they were gathered together. But now they were divided asunder, and much affliction befell them on that account.

But Phalek died, and they buried him in his own city Phalek. For they had built a city, and had called it after his name.

But after his death, which happened when he was four hundred and thirty years old, there were great disturbances, and men gathered together within fenced cities.

And after this, tongues (there are seventy-two) were divided; for God divided them when men built the tower in Sennaar;[35]* but it was destroyed over them.[36] And God divided their languages; and what remained of them He dispersed over the earth; because they built without a fixed plan. Therefore God dispersed them and scattered them, and brought upon them the division of their languages; until if one of them spake, no other understood what he said.[37] And the number of languages is seventy-two.

And when they were thus divided, they had over them seventy-two rulers, one to every tongue, and to every country, by way of a king. And of the seed of Japhet were six peoples.

CHAPTER XXIII.

Then Ragu, Phalek's son, lived two hundred and thirty-two years, and died. But when Ragu, Phalek's first-born son, was one hundred and thirty years old, there reigned one of the first kings that ever reigned on the earth, whose name was Nimrud, a giant.

That Nimrud saw a cloud of light under heaven; a mere apparition of Satan. And he inclined his heart to it, and coveted its beauty; and then called to one whose name was

* Nimrud provided them with food from his hunt. Abul-pharaj. Dyn. *Arab.*, p. 18; and *Syr.*, p. 9.

Santal, a carver, and said to him, "Carve me a crown of gold, after the pattern of that cloud."[38]

Then Santal made him a crown [of gold] which Nimrud took and placed upon his own head. Wherefore was it said that a cloud had come [down] from heaven, and overshadowed him. And he became so wicked, as to think within himself that he was God.

And in those days Ragu was one hundred and eighty years old, and in his one hundred and fortieth year, Yanuf* reigned over the land of Egypt.

He is the first king that reigned over it; and he built the city of Memphis, and named it after his own name. That is Misr; whose name is rendered Masrin.

This Yanuf died; and in his stead, in the days of Ragu, one from the land of India reigned, whose name was Sasen; and who built the city of Saba. And all the kings who reigned over that country were called Sabæans, after the name of the city.

And it was so, until the days of Solomon, son of David.

Then again Phar'an reigned over the children of Saphir, and built the city of Saphir† with stones of gold; and that is the land‡ of Sar'ania, and because of these stones of gold, they say that the mountains of that country and the stones thereof are all of gold.

Then the children of Lebensa of the country of India, made king over them, one named Bahlul, who built the city of Bahlu.

Then Ragu died in his two hundred and eighty-ninth year.

CHAPTER XXIV.§

After [him] came Serok[39] his son, in whose days idol-gods of stone, were openly worshipped in the world. The children

---

* Called Panophis [Apop, Apophis] by Bar. Hebr., *Syr.*, p. 8.

† Sophir (Ophir) is the Coptic word for "India." ‡ Or, city.

§ The whole of this chapter is given, almost word for word, by Eutychus, in his *Nasam al-jawahir*, pp. 58, 60.

of men began to make idols of stone, the first of which were Kalithon and Helodon.

And the children of men multiplied upon the earth, and their wickedness increased also; for they had neither law nor order; and no teachers to guide them in the way of righteousness; nor any one to be judge among them.

Wherefore they grew worse and worse, and wandered farther from the way of God; every one of them did what he himself listed; and they made for themselves idol-gods, which they worshipped.

They had no hope in the resurrection of the dead. But whenever one of them died, they buried him, and set up an idol over his grave; and said, that was his god, that would show him mercy in his grave. They said also, as regards the dead, that when his god was set up over his grave, the remembrance of him, would not be cut off from the face of the earth.

This was a common saying brought out by Satan; and the earth was thus filled with idols; and those idols were of divers kinds, men and women.

After this Serok died two hundred and thirty years old; and they embalmed him in Sar'ania his city, that was built in his name.

After that Nahor, when twenty-nine years old begat Terah. And when Nahor was eighty-six years of age, God looked down upon the children of men, [and saw] that they were ruined and worshipped idols.

Then God sent forth winds, and the whirlwind, and earthquakes on the earth, until the idols were broken one against another. Yet the children of men did not repent of their sins, neither did they turn to God from their iniquities that He might save them; but rather increased in wickedness.

And in the twentieth year of Terah's life, the worship of idols spread over the earth in the city of Aarat, which Barwin, the son of Eber, had built.

And at that time there was a rich man living in it, who died; and his son made an idol of gold in the likeness of his father, and set it up on his [father's] grave.

He then ordered one of his servants, to stand by the idol, and to minister unto it; to sweep the ground around it, to pour water to it and to burn incense.

But when Satan saw this he entered into the idol of gold, and talked to the servant, like his master's father that was dead; and said to him, "Thou doest well thus."

After this a thief took by surprise the house of the youth, son of the man who was dead; who then came to his father's grave, weeping.

And he said, "O my father, they have carried away all my goods."

Then Satan answered him from within the idol, and said, "Do not stay here, but go and bring thy son, and offer him up in oblation to me, and then I will return to thee all thy goods."

Then that youth went, and did with his son, as Satan had commanded him. And at that time Satan entered into him, and taught him to practise enchantments, and magic, the mixture of drugs, and divination.

That was the first evil example [of the kind] set to men, to take their children and to offer them up in oblation to idols and to devils.

CHAPTER XXV.

Then in the hundredth year of Nahor, God looked down upon the children of men [and saw] that they sacrificed their children to idols.

Then God commanded the stores of winds to open, and to send forth the whirlwind, and gales, and darkness upon the whole face of the earth, until all the idols and images, and figures were brought together [by the winds] in mountains upon mountains high. And the idols remained buried under them until this day.[40]

Many wise men have written about this wind, that it was the wind of the Flood; and many of them say it was the water of the Flood that thus brought together these mountains [of idols].

But they erred, and said what is false concerning it; because ere the water of the Flood came upon the earth, there were no idols in it. But the Flood came upon the men at that time because of their adulteries, and of the sins which they committed among themselves; both the children of Cain, and those who followed them.

Moreover at that time the whole earth was not filled with people; but only the land of the garden, in which dwelt the children of Seth; and the place inhabited by the children of Cain; besides that, the whole earth was bare [of inhabitants].

But when the Flood came, it bare the ark, and brought it to this land of trouble. And this earth was filled with people; and that land was laid waste.

Then in those days, king Nimrud saw a flaming fire in the east, which arose from the earth.*

Then said Nimrud, "What is that fire?"† He then went towards it; and when he saw it, he bowed to it in worship, and appointed a priest to minister before it, to burn incense to it, and to sacrifice victims to it. From that day the men of Fars began to fill the earth.

Then Satan the worker of idols saw a fountain of water near the fire-pit, and he came to it, and looked at it, and made a horse of gold, and set it up on the edge of the fountain of water; and it so happened that all those who came to wash in that fountain of water, bowed in worship to that golden horse;

---

* Joseph., *Ant. Jud.*, lib. i, c. iv, 2, 3.
† The whole of this paragraph is told word for word by Eutychus, *Nazam al-j.*, p. 62, sq.

and from that time, the people of Fars began to worship horses.

But the priest* whom Nimrud appointed to minister to the fire and to burn incense to it, wished to be a teacher, and wise of the same wisdom as Nimrud, whom Barwin, Noah's fourth son had taught.

That priest, therefore, kept on asking Satan, while standing before the fire, to teach him this evil ministry and abominable wisdom. So, when Satan saw him doing his best in the service [of the fire], he talked to him, and said, "No man can become a teacher, or wise, or great before me, unless he hearkens to me, and goes and weds his mother, his sister and his daughter."

Then that priest hearkened to Satan in all that he commanded him, and taught him all manner of wisdom and of wickednesses. And from that time, the people of Fars have committed like sins unto this day.

And Nimrud built great cities in the east; and wrought all manner of iniquities in them.[41]

* That priest was called Ardeshan. *Nasam al-j.*, p. 65.

BOOK IV.

CHAPTER I.

THEN when Terah was two hundred and thirty years old, he fell sick, and called Abraham[1] his son,[2] and said unto him, " O my son, I wish to die."

But Abraham stood up and comforted him, paid him all due honour, and did not aggrieve him about his being a maker of idols.

For Abraham his son, was a righteous man, and could not bear idols;[3] but he paid him all due respect, as being his father.

Then Terah died; and Abraham and Nahor buried him in a mountain.

But when Abraham was grown up, God said unto him, " O Abraham, come out of thy land, of thy kindred and of thy father's house, and go to the land that I will show thee."

Then Abraham arose, and took Sarah his wife, and Lot his brother's son,* and they came to the land of the Amorites.[4] And Abraham was seventy years old when he saw this vision; and this was his first wandering from the land of the east, to the western side of the river Euphrates.

So Abraham came, and dwelt among kings; and those kings rose up against his brother's son, and carried him away

---

* Lot was the son of Haran, Abraham's brother, who perished in trying to put out the fire set by Abraham to the idol temple at Ur. Abul-pharaj., *Dyn.* Arab. p. 20. Cedrenus, *Hist. Comp.*, p. 48.

captive.* Then Abraham took his servants, and all those who were about him, and came to his brother's son, and delivered him out of their hands.

At that time Abraham was eighty years old, and no son was born to him, because that Sarah his wife, was barren.

Then as he was returning from the war with those kings, the grace of God drew him, until he had passed over the hill of Nablus; and from the hill of Nablus, he came near to Jerusalem, ere it was built.†

Then Melchizedec, priest of the Most High God, came out, and welcomed him with joy. And Abraham, when he saw Melchizedec, made haste and bowed to him in worship, and kissed him on the face; and Melchizedec gave him a good blessing.⁵

Then Abraham gave Melchizedec a tenth of all he had with him.‡ After that Abraham communed with Melchizedec of the holy mysteries which Melchizedec had consecrated with his own hand. For that was an exalted place, not by man's hand, but God Himself had anointed it.

But after Abraham had communed with Melchizedec, God said unto Abraham, "Fear not, great is thy reward with Me; and in like manner as Melchizedec My high priest blessed thee, and made thee partaker with himself of Holy Mysteries, so will I make thee partaker with him of heavenly grace."

Again did God say to Abraham, "In blessing will I bless thee, and in multiplying will I multiply thy seed upon the face of the earth."

---

* Og, King of Bashan, who had been saved by sitting on the top of Noah's ark, and who was among those kings, came and told Abraham that they had taken Lot captive. *Targ. Jonathan,* in Gen. xiv.

† The *Kufale* dwells at great length on the history of Abraham, borrowed chiefly from the Scripture account. But whether by accident or otherwise, it makes no mention of Melchizedec, but only of priests and of tithe, as an institution of God for ever.

‡ Entych., *Nasam al-j.,* p. 66.

CHAPTER II.

After this there was a famine in the land of Palestine; and Abraham went down into the land of Egypt.

And Sarah his wife was with him, and she was good-looking.

So Abraham said to her, "Say not, I am Abraham's wife, lest they kill me, and take thee from me. But say, I am his sister."

Then when they came into the land of Egypt,[6] men spake to Pharaoh king of Egypt, and said to him, "Behold a man has come hither; and with him is his beautiful sister."

Then Pharaoh sent and took her from Abraham, who remained weeping.

But God in His mercy sent an angel who smote Pharaoh, and said to him, "Send back to Abraham his wife, lest God kill thee."

Then in the morning, Pharaoh called Abraham, and said unto him, "Forgive me." He then gave him his wife Sarah; and gave to Sarah, Hagar the Egyptian, and gave her many presents.

After this Abraham took Sarah his wife, with Hagar her maid-servant, and returned to Palestine.

And after that, Abraham took to himself Hagar to wife,* who bare him Ishmael, when Abraham was eighty-seven years old.

But in that Abraham said, "Sarah is my sister," he did not lie; inasmuch as Terah, his father, married two wives; one of which was called Tona,† the mother of Abraham, who died shortly after he was born.

Then Terah married again another wife whose name was Tahdif,‡ who bare him Sarah, whom Abraham married, and

---

* She was the daughter of Pharaoh, son of Nimrud who had cast Abram into the fiery furnace. *Targ. Jonathan*, in Gen. xvi.

† Called Yuna, Eutych., *Nazam al-j.*, p. 65.   ‡ Called Tohwait, Eutych., *ibid.*

who, for that reason, said, "She is my sister"—on my father's side, but not on my mother's.

After this, when Abraham was dwelling in tents, the Lord came to him with angels of His, and gave him a sign of the birth of his son Isaac,[7] who was born to him when he was a hundred years old. The Lord showed him also many mysteries.

Then days after this, God said to Abraham, when Isaac was fourteen years old, "Offer unto me thy son Isaac, in oblation."[8]

Then Abraham fortified himself and took courage for this trial; and brought his son to offer him in oblation to God.[9] But God redeemed Isaac with a lamb that was tied to a bush.

And the bush to which the lamb was tied, is the very place into which the tree of the Cross was planted. And the lamb that saved Isaac from death, was a figure of the Lamb of God who saved us all from death.

That mountain also, on which king David saw an angel standing with a sharp sword of fire in his hand, as if going to smite Jerusalem with it—is the place where Abraham saw with the eye of the Holy Ghost, the Son of God, hanging on it.

For this reason did the Lord say to the Jews, "Abraham, your father, rejoiced and longed to see my day, and he did see it, and was glad."

Again, this is the place, as the blessed Paul said, "For the sake of Jesus Christ my Lord am I minister of the circumcision"—where Christ was circumcised on the eighth day.*

That is also the place where the patriarch Abraham offered up an oblation to God.

And again, as it was in the days of Moses, when they offered up a lamb for the sins of the people, to cleanse them from their sins—so also did the Lamb of God offer up Himself in oblation for us, to set us free from our sins.

---

* The translator or writer of the book evidently thought Christ was circumcised in the Temple. This clause seems ill-joined with the rest.

CHAPTER III.

After this Melchizedec showed himself to men, who saw him, and who were comforted by his words, everywhere.

The kings of the earth and peoples, when they heard his voice, did gather together; a multitude of creatures and of kings ;* that numbered twelve hosts.

They came to him and bowed to him in worship, and were blessed by him, and asked him, saying, " Come, let us make thee king over us."

But Melchizedec king of Salem, and priest of the Most High God, would not.

And the kings wondered at his beauty; their hearts were drawn to him by his discourse, and they fell down at his feet in worship; and they asked God, that Melchizedec might dwell among them in their palaces.

But Melchizedec would not, and said unto them, "I cannot leave this place, and go to another one."

So those kings said among themselves, " Let every one of us who can, come, and let us build a city on this mountain for Melchizedec."

They all took pleasure in the work, brought together materials in abundance, and built the City of Jerusalem, that means " the middle of the earth."

Then Melchizedec continued to dwell in it, at that place; and the kings came, and were blessed by him, until the day of his departure, when his life ended in this world.

CHAPTER IV.

After this, Abraham ordered one of his servants,† to take a

---

* They were twelve in number. Eutych., Nas. al-j., p. 66, sq., where the same story is told.

† Eliezer, of Damascus, son of Mesek, one of Abraham's servants, Kufala, c. xiv., p. 55, ὁ δὲ υἱὸς Μασὲκ τῆς οἰκογενοῦς μου, οὗτος Δαμασκός Ἐλιέζερ, lxx, Gen. xv, 3.

wife for his son Isaac; and adjured him not to marry Isaac, but to one of his own kindred.

And Abraham entered into rest when one hundred and seventy-five years old; and Isaac and Ishmael his sons buried him.[10]

Then Isaac married when he was forty years old; and Esau and Jacob his sons, were born unto him when he was about sixty years of age.* And God blessed Isaac greatly.

Then after this Jacob went to the land of Haran, to Laban, his mother's brother, and married his two daughters Leah and Rachel.

He had by Leah, Reuben, Simeon, Levi, Judah, Issachar, and Zebulun; and by Rachel he had Joseph and Benjamin.

Then he had also by Zilpah, Leah's maid-servant, Gad and Aser; and by Bilhah, Rachel's maid-servant, he had Dan and Naphtali.

And about twenty years after Jacob's return from the land of Haran, before his father Isaac died, Joseph was sold by his brothers, because they were jealous of him.

But when Isaac died, his two sons Esau and Jacob came to him, embalmed him, and laid him in the sepulchre of his father.

Then six years after the death of Isaac, Rebecca died; and they buried her by Sarah, Abraham's wife. And when, after that Leah, Jacob's wife died, they buried her by the side of them.

Then after this Judah took to himself a wife whose name was Habwadiya, that means, "house-wife;"† but in the law her name is Sewa.

She was of a Canaanitish family, and Jacob's heart suffered

---

* Rebecca, when with child and before the birth of Esau and Jacob, went to consult Melchizedec, who told her she had two nations in her womb, and that the elder should serve the younger. Eutych., *Nazam al-j.*, p. 77.

† And in the Arabic original it is rendered, "Sahaniyeh," that means a black linen girdle.

much on that account; and he said to Judah his son who had married that wife, "The God of Abraham and of Isaac will not allow the seed of this Canaanitish woman to mingle with my seed."

But some days after this, Sewa bare three sons unto Judah, whose names were Er, Onan, and Selah. And when Er was grown up, Judah married him, his first-born son, unto a woman named Tamar, daughter of Kadesh Levi.

And Er continued with her a long time, and behaved after the manner of the men of Sodom and Gomorrah. But God looked down upon his evil deeds and killed him.

Then Judah married his son Onan to Tamar, saying, "He shall raise seed unto his brother."

But him also did God kill because of his evil deeds; on account of Jacob's curse, "That no Canaanitish seed should mingle with his own." So God would not let any of it mingle with that of Jacob the righteous.

Therefore did Tamar go to Judah her father-in-law, who had intercourse with her, not knowing she was his son's wife; and she bare unto him twins, Pharez and Zarah.

CHAPTER V.

After this Jacob went to Joseph, and continued fourteen years in the land of Egypt, where he died at the age of one hundred and fifty-seven; when the good Joseph was fifty-three years old.

Then when he was dead, Joseph called cunning Egyptian embalmers, who embalmed him beautifully; and then Joseph carried his body to the land of Canaan, and buried him in the sepulchre of his fathers Abraham and Isaac.

After this Pharez begat Judah, and Judah begat Ezrom, and Ezrom begat Aram; and Aram begat Aminadab; and Aminadab begat Naasson.

And this Naasson was great among the sons of Judah; and the daughter of Aminadab married Eleazar the son of Aaron, who prayed to God, until His wrath abated.

Thus, O my son, have I told thee in detail the genealogies from the first until now.

CHAPTER VI.

After this, there began to issue a race from Naasson, who was great among the sons of Judah; and from him began a kingdom and a priesthood, and the Jews became celebrated through him.

Then Naasson begat Salmon, and Salmon begat Boaz of Rahab. And thou must know that from Boaz and Ruth the Moabitess, began the kingdom whereby Lot, the son of Abraham's brother, obtained a share [in the generations] of the kingdom [of Judah].

For God denied not seed to Lot, neither would He cut it short. For this Lot was righteous, and shared all Abraham's troubles with him; and received the angels of God in Sodom and Gomorrah.

Therefore did God give to Lot's children fellowship in the kingdom, and that was [reckoned] for righteousness unto Lot the righteous. For this reason also were [Lot's children] mentioned among the genealogies of the kingdom of Abraham and of Lot; for Christ was born of their seed.

Then, again, Obed, Ruth's son, was of Lot's seed, on his mother's [side]; and Obed begat Jesse; and Jesse begat David the king. And king David begat Solomon; all these are of Ruth the Moabitess.

Again, Amnan,* the daughter of [Dan], king of the Ammonites, was of Lot's seed; and Solomon the king took this

---

* Naamah. 1 Kg., xiv, 21, 31.

daughter of Dan to wife; and had by her, Rehoboam, who reigned after Solomon.

But king Solomon took to himself many wives, seven hundred daughters of kings, three hundred concubines, one thousand in number.

But although Solomon took to himself these many wives, they did not bare him a single male child, but Rehoboam, of Amnan, the daughter of Dan, king of Ammon; who was of a blessed race.

Thus, again, God would not allow the seed of Canaanites to mingle with that of strange peoples, which God had made strangers. And this shows that Christ came of the seed of Abraham the blessed father, and of Lot his brother's son.

And all the families of the children of Israel in the land of Egypt, were Levi, Amram, Moses, Joshua, and Caleb, son of Jephunneh; all these were great chiefs over their peoples.

CHAPTER VII.

As to Moses, when they had thrown him into the river, Sephurah, the daughter of Pharaoh, took him up thence, and brought him up. She it is, whom the Hebrews call Mariam, the mother of Moses.

And Moses abode forty years in Pharaoh's house; and other forty years in the land of Midian, ere God spake to him.

Then, again, when God spake to Moses from within the bush his tongue faltered; and [his] tongue was—as God said, "From the time that I spake to My servant Moses, he was of a faltering tongue."

And Moses dwelt forty years in the land of Egypt, and forty years in the land of Midian, with the priest Jethro, his father-in-law; then forty years more in the wilderness; when Moses died, aged one hundred and twenty years.

Then after him arose Joshua, the son of Nun. He was

twenty-seven years judge over the children of Israel, and exercised judgment over them; he was prophet among them, and kept them, and led them in the right way; and he entered into rest and died, when sixty years old.

Then after him arose Kusarat the judge, eight years, and he died; and after him Phutamiral, the son of Kaba, judged the children of Israel forty years, and died.

After him Naod, son of Phuru, judged the children of Israel eighty years. But in the twenty-fifth year of Naod, ended four thousand years since Adam. Naod died, and Sikar judged the children of Israel. But in his days a king of Canaan rose against Sikar, wishing to make war against him. But God gave Sikar victory over him, whom he defeated; and Sikar judged forty years.

After him Yarod was judge over the people of Israel, forty years; and after him Abimelec judged ten years, and died.

And after him Banu, son of Yuorani, judged twenty-three years, and died. After him Yar of Phila, judged twenty-two years, and died.

After him the son of Aminadab, judged fifty-eight years, and died. And after him the daughter of Nasyamu judged seven years, and died.

After her, Ansyus judged seven years, and died; and after him the Philistine judged forty years. But God gave him into the hands of the champion Samson, who slew him. Then the champion Samson arose and was judge over the children of Israel twenty years, and then died.

Then the children of Israel were left without a judge twelve years, when Eli the priest began to judge; and judged them forty years, and then died.

After him Samuel was judge over the children of Israel forty years, and died. Then after him, Saul reigned over them forty years, and died.

Then after him, David reigned over the children of Israel forty years, and then died. And after him, his son Solomon arose, who also reigned forty years over the children of Israel, and then died.

He wrought more wonders in the earth than all other kings, who were before him. For he was the first whom God filled with wisdom. So that he made [and did] many things peculiar to him; so far as to make a ship, and go in it to the city of Saphir; [where] he wrought gold in ornaments, and brought it to Jerusalem.

During his reign, there was great peace; there was no trouble; but there was peace between him and Hiram king of Tyre; who reigned five hundred years over the city of Tyre, and whose kingdom lasted from the reign of Solomon, to that of Zedekiah; until, from the length of his days and of his years, and from the greatness of his kingdom, he exalted himself and said, " I am God, and no man."[11]

God was wroth against him because of his evil deed; and God looked down upon it, and delivered him into the hands of king Nebuchadnezzar who put him to death; removed his army, and took his spoil.

CHAPTER VIII.

But we will inform thee of the things king Solomon[12] gave every day in his house. On account of his many wives, they made bread in his house of thirty cores of fine flour; one hundred cores of wheat flour, which hardly sufficed. And they slaughtered in his house daily, ten bullocks well-fatted, and twenty fat oxen, and one hundred sheep; besides what they slew of buffaloes, gazelles and wild deer, which they hunted every day. And in Solomon's house they drank daily four hundred basins of wine. And many other things did they.

And Solomon reigned over his large kingdom with the greatest wisdom ever found. But he did not keep his soul; but inclined his heart to the love of women, and forsook God who had created him, and who had given him this kingdom. And he died in his denial of Him, and in his sins.

After him reigned Rehoboam, his son, seventeen years, and did evil. He defiled Jerusalem with abominable sacrifices, and sacrificed to Satan; and adultery increased greatly in his days. Wherefore God cut off his kingdom swiftly; and took it from the house of David.

But in the fifth year of Rehoboam, a king whose name was Susakim came up against Jerusalem. He took all the spoil of the temple, and spoiled all Roboam had, and spoiled all the house of David, and removed them and took them to his own country.

And he boasted, and said to the Jews, "The things I have taken from you as spoil, are goods that belonged to my fathers, of which your fathers spoiled them, when they came out of the land of Egypt, and which they brought unto this place; and behold, I have taken them from you."

And Rehoboam died in his denial [of God]; and after him, his son Abius, reigned twenty years over the children of Israel. But he, too, walked in his father's ways, by reason of Makia his mother, the daughter of Absalom; wherefore, did he many wicked things, and then died.

After him arose Asaph his son, who reigned forty-one years over the children of Israel. He did what was right, just and good before God; he brake down the idols that were in his day, and removed their images from the face of the land; and he took his wicked mother Anna, and threw her down from the roof [of her house] and she died, because of her adulteries.

After that, came Eleazar a black king, who was king of Endena, to fight Asaph. But God delivered him into the hands of Asaph, who defeated him.

Then Asaph died; and his son Jehoshaphat reigned in his stead. He also did that which is just and good before God, and pleased God all his days, and then died.

Then his son Aram reigned in his stead; but he transgressed the commandments of God, and forsook His law, and sacrificed unto idols.

Then Zambri rose up against him, made war against him, and he died in his denial [of God].

Then Yusia, his son, reigned [after him]; but on account of his transgressions, God delivered him into the hands of his enemies, who put him to death. But when he was dead, his mother rose up against all the royal children and put them to death, and said, " I will take the kingdom from the house of David."

Then Yusabet daughter of the king of Aram, arose, took Agragarina, and slew him before the eyes of the royal children that were left. But when she had put him to death, she feared, and hid herself and those with her, under a bed. And Gotholia was queen over the children of Israel, and died.

Then the whole people of Israel said, " Whom shall we make king over us ?"

Then when Yuda the high priest heard they spake thus, he gathered together the whole of the Jews within the Temple, and waited until the messengers of thousands and the messengers of hundreds came; and then Yuda the high priest, said to them, " What do you require of me, and who is he whom ye will make king over the house of David ?"

Then they said to him, " Thou hast authority."

Then Yuda rose and took Barsia, and brought him before them, and said to them, " Does this one suit you for a king ?"

The people were pleased with him; so Yuda brought him into the house of God, and set him over the kingdom; then all the people rejoiced, and the whole country was quiet in his days; and he was king in Jerusalem forty years.

But Barsia did not bear in mind all the good things Yuda the priest had told him; but he took him and put him to death. After this, enemies rose up against Barsia and put him also to death.

CHAPTER IX.

After him his son Amazias reigned twenty-nine years, and put to death those who had killed his father; but he did not put to death their children, so as to fulfil the law of Moses, that says, "Ye shall not put to death children for the sins of their fathers."

Then Amazias died, and after him Ozia reigned fifty-two years, and in his reign exercised justice and judgment, and right before God. Yet did he do one wicked act, and that was that—without due orders,* he offered sacrifices unto God, and oblations that did not become him. So he died.

After him Yonathan his son, reigned sixteen years. But during his reign, he did evil before God, and angered his Creator, and forsook His commandment and His law; and burnt incense to idols, and sacrificed unto them. For this reason did God deliver him to death, into the hands of Caran, king of Elmosal.†

And when the king of Elmosal led him away [captive], he [Yonathan] took all the vessels he found in the house of God, and sent them all to the great king of Elmosal; and left nothing in the house of God.

In the days of this king, did the children of Israel, go the first time into captivity. He removed them to his own country, and the land of Israel remained bare.

Then the king of Elmosal, sent people to dwell in the land and to till it, instead of the children of Israel who had left it.

But when those people came to dwell in that land, [wild] beasts rent them asunder and devoured them, and prevailed against them in all the borders of the land.

Then they sent word to the king in their own tongue, and asked him to send them Urias the priest, to give them the

* Or, being ordained. † *i.e.*, Mosul or Assyria.

law, so that wild beasts should no longer come near them, and hurt them.

When the king heard this he sent them Urias the priest, and commanded him to give them a law, for them to keep, so that the wild beasts hurt them not.

Urias the priest came, and did as the king had commanded him, and he gave the people the law of the Jews; it was in their hands, they recited it and ruled themselves after it. And those were the Samar; whom the king, of whom we have just spoken, had sent to till the land of Israel.

Then Yunathan died, and after him reigned Akaz his son, who did well before God, and then died.

After him reigned his son Hezkias, when he was twenty-five years old; and he reigned twenty-two years; and did good, and judgment, equity and justice; and he pleased the Lord; he kept His law and His commandments; he brake down the idols, and destroyed their houses.

But in the fourth year of his reign, came Sanakreb king of Assarium, and took away captive all that were left and sent them to Babylon.

But Hezkias served the Lord God, and fulfilled His law, until he fell sick and became very weak, and was in great distress by reason of his sickness; his heart suffered, and he said to himself, "Woe is me! I shall die without a son to reign after me."

And in his sickness he wept before God and said, "Woe is me, O Lord! behold, I die without a son; and behold the promise Thou madest unto David, shall fail in me; and the kingdom shall pass from the house of David."

Then God looked upon his sorrow of heart, and upon his sickness, for his sickness was sore. And God had pity on him and gave him fifteen years over and above the rest of his days; and he recovered from his sickness.

Then three years after he had recovered, and God had raised him from his sickness, he begat Manasseh. And he died, rejoicing greatly at having a son born unto him, to sit upon his throne.

CHAPTER X.

After him Manasseh his son reigned twelve years in Jerusalem. He did much evil, and made the people of Jerusalem worship idols.[13]

Then when he had thus transgressed the law of God, Isaias the prophet came to him and rebuked him for the wickednesses he had wrought.

Then Manasseh was angry with him, and commanded valiant and wicked men to take Isaias the prophet, and to saw him asunder with a saw of wood,* from his head down to his feet, among the trees of the wilderness; and then to cast him to the beasts [of the field] to devour him. And they did so to him.[14]

Isaias was then one hundred and twenty years old. His raiment was of shaggy goat's hair upon his body; and he fasted regularly every second day [of the week] all the days of his life.

Then Manasseh died; and after him reigned his son Amots, who did evil before God; for he offered sons and daughters in sacrifice unto idols.

Then Amots died; and after him reigned Yusias his son. He was twenty years old when he [began] to reign, and continued twenty-two years in his kingdom in the city of Jerusalem. He did justice and right before God; and kept the Passover of the Lord, such as the children of Israel never were able to keep, except the one Moses kept for them in the wilderness. This king purified Jerusalem of all wickedness.

But Pharhon the lame, king of Egypt, killed Yusias in Carmelos.

* i.e., a saw used in sawing or felling trees.

CAPTIVITY OF BABYLON.

Then after him Akaz reigned three months. But Pharhon bound Akaz in chains and sent him into the land of Egypt; and he died in that place.

After his death Yuakem his brother reigned fourteen years; but in the third year of his reign, Nabukadanatsor came to the city of Jerusalem, and God delivered Yuakem into his hands; and Yuakem was under his orders, bowed unto him, and paid him tribute; he then sickened and died.

After him reigned his brother Yekonias three months; then came Nabukadanatsor who took captive Yekonias and all his army, and sent them to Babylon.

On the way thither, Daniel's mother gave him birth. Anania, Azaria, and Misael, sons of Yekonias, were also born on the first transportation of Yuakem.

Then Yekonias died, and after him Zedekias reigned twelve years. This was the end of kings that reigned over the children of Israel, and all Judah; after them no king was left to them.

And at the end of the fourteenth year of Zedekias, Nabukadanatsor came and transported all the people of Jerusalem, as far as the west, and as far as the river Euphrates, and as far as the great river. He laid waste Tyre, and burnt Hiram king of Tyre with fire, who had reigned five hundred years.

Then after this Nabukadanatsor went into Egypt, and put to death Pharhon; destroyed his army, and laid waste the land of Egypt; and then took the city of Jerusalem. And God delivered Zedekias into his hands, whom he took, and brought out before idols, and set him before the people, and slew his children before him, without pity. He then put out his eyes, bound his hands with chains and his feet with fetters; and sent him to Babylon, because of his folly, and of the evil he had done to Irmias* the prophet, by casting him into springs of water in a marsh.[15]

---

* Jeremiah.

After this Nabuzaradan captain of the king's army, destroyed the walls of Jerusalem, burnt the House of God with fire; and did all manner of evil to Jerusalem.

But Simeon the priest, found favour and grace with the captain of the king's army, and requested him to give him the house* of records; and he gave him a command accordingly.

Then Simeon the priest came in and gathered together the ashes of the books, and laid them in a pot in a vault, and he took a censer of brass, and put fire therein, and threw pure incense upon it, and hung it in the vault over the place in which the ashes of the books lay.

But [Nebuzaradan] laid waste Jerusalem, like a wilderness.

And Jeremiah the prophet sat weeping and mourning over Jerusalem twenty years, after which this prophet Jeremiah went into the land of Egypt, and died there.

But the writers and the interpreters destroyed the writings, and the Hebrews changed the writings; and the Syrians and the Greeks rejected many sections of those writings. So that the children of the people could not ascertain [their kindred], neither could men or women hear who were their fathers or their mothers, except very few of them;

And this was because of the laying waste of Jerusalem; so that until this day, nothing certain is found among the writings, except the chief writings alone, which writings had been translated before the ruin of Jerusalem.

Then again since some of the writings were altered, people could not ascertain how they were married, and could not know who were their wives or daughters; they did not know their names or their kindred; nor the order of generations; neither did they know that of the priesthood.

And Jechonias remained twenty-seven years bound in prison at Babylon. After that he was released by Marzuk king of Babylon, who gave him to wife, a woman called Dalilah daughter

---

* Or, repository, ark, chest.

of Eliakim, by whom he had Salathiel in Babylon. But Jechonias, Salathiel's father, died at Babylon.

Then Salathiel took to wife Hadast, daughter of Elkanah; and had by her Zerubbabel. And Zerubbabel married a woman whose name was Malka, daughter of Ezra the scribe; but he had no child by her in Babylon.

Then in the days of Zerubbabel, who was elder among the children of Israel, a Persian king, called Cyrus, who reigned over Babylon, took to wife a woman called Meshar, sister of Zerubbabel, elder among the children of Israel; and he made her queen after the manner of the queens of Persia. And when she became queen, she found favour with the king, and asked him to show mercy to the children of Israel, and to send them back to the city of Jerusalem.

CHAPTER XI.

But Cyrus loved much Meshar, sister of Zerubbabel, [even] as his own soul.

So he gave an urgent order that they should go about the whole land of the Chaldæans, and gather together the children of Israel into Babylon, the house of the kingdom; and they gathered them according to the king's order.

Then Cyrus said to Zerubbabel, his wife's brother, "Take thy people and go to thy city Jerusalem; and rebuild it as it was at first.

Then when dutiful Cyrus had given this order concerning the return of the children of Israel to Jerusalem, in the land of the sanctuary;

God appeared unto him in a vision during sleep, and said unto him, "Because thou hast done this, they shall call thee Cyrus the Messiahnic; and this name, Messiahnic, shall be given thee, because thou hast sent back strangers to their own city; and because thou hast given commandment concerning the rebuilding of Jerusalem."

Then the children of Israel returned from the captivity of Babylon, Zerubbabel was elder over them; and Josiah, son of Zadok, of the sons of Aaron, was high priest over them; as the angel of God spake to the prophet Zachariah saying, "Those two sons that stand before the Lord of the whole earth shall minister unto them, as becomes their service."

Cyrus had assumed the kingdom two years, when the captivity returned from Babylon; and at the end of that year, the five thousand years [spoken of] to Adam were fulfilled.

But when the children of Israel returned from Babylon they had not the law, neither was there a book in their hands; inasmuch as the voices of the prophets had departed from among them.

So, when they came to Jerusalem and were settled in it, Ezra the scribe came to the vault in which were the ashes of the books, which Simeon the priest, had gathered together.

And Ezra found the censer that was full of fire, hanging with [smoke of] incense rising from it on high.

Then Ezra prayed to God, wept abundantly, and spread his hand towards the ashes of the books of the law and of the prophets, and all of them three times.*

Then came the Spirit of God upon him, and the [same] Spirit spake through him that had spoken through the prophets. And he wrote the law and the prophets, and made them new a second time.

And the fire which he found in the censer, is the divine fire that was all the time in the House of God.

Then Zerubbabel settled in Jerusalem as king over the children of Israel, and Josiah son of Zadok as high priest, with Ezra the scribe of the law and the prophets also, as chief over the children of Israel.

* Eutych., *Nazam al-j.*, p 226.

And the children of Israel kept a solemn Passover unto the Lord, when they returned from their captivity at Babylon.

These were the three great, full and solemn feasts of the Passover, which the children of Israel kept during their existence. The first Passover was in Egypt, in the days of Moses; the second Passover was in the days of king Josiah; and the third Passover was when they returned from their captivity in Babylon.

CHAPTER XII.

From the first transportation to Babylon, when they carried away Daniel's mother, and she brought him forth, unto the second year of Cyrus the Persian, are seventy years, during which the children of Israel were captive, according to the prophecy of holy* Jeremiah the prophet.

And the children of Israel began to build the House of God, in the days of Zerubbabel, of Josiah the son of Zadok, and of Ezra the scribe. And they were forty-six years building it, until it was finished, as it is written in the holy Gospel—that they were forty-six years building it.

Moreover, scribes arranged tables of genealogy, and recorded the names of the men; but they could not record the names of the women because they knew them not, except very few.

But, O my brethren, I have watched much, and I have searched long in the books of the Greeks and of the ancient Hebrews, and I have found the name of the women written in them.

For I found that when the children of Israel came from Babylon, that Zerubbabel begat Abiud of Maukab† the daughter of Ezra the scribe; and that Abiud took to wife Tsamita the daughter of Zadok the high priest, and she bare Eliakim.

* Or, innocent.   † Called Malka at p. 197.

And Eliakim married Hasbia, the daughter of Aram, and brought forth Azar. And Azar begat Zadok of Lebaida. And Zadok took to wife Kalem, the daughter of Waikam, who gave birth to Akim.

And Akim married Asbaidi, who gave birth to Eliud. And Eliud married Awad, the daughter of Gasulius, who gave birth to Azar.

And Azar married Hayat, daughter of Walha, who brought forth Mattan; and Mattan married Sabartyal the daughter of Phulius, who brought forth twins, namely, Jacob and Joachim.

And Jacob married Gadat, the daughter of Eleazar, who gave birth to Joseph the betrothed of Mary. And Joachim, the brother of Jacob, married Hannah the daughter of Makah; and she brought forth the pure Virgin Mary; and of her was born Christ.

The former scribes, however, could not find a good lineage for the Virgin and her father, or kindred; wherefore did the Jews crucify Christ, and taunt Him, and mock Him, and say to Him, " Show us the fathers of Mary the Virgin and her people, and what is her genealogy." Therefore did they blaspheme her and Christ.

But henceforth shall the mouth of those unbelieving Jews be closed; and they shall know that Mary is of the seed of David the king, and of that of the patriarch Abraham.

Moreover, the unbelieving Jews had no registers to guide them aright, neither did they know, how the lines of kindred ran at first, inasmuch as the law and the prophets were three times burnt [out] from them.

The first time in the days of Antiochus, who burnt down the whole House [of God]; The second time they burnt those books in the days of Qablar the great king of Mosul; And the third time* they burnt the books was at the transportation by king Nabukadanatsor when Abumirdan came and burnt the

* Eutychus attributes the last destruction of all Jewish chronicles, to Herod the Great. *Nazam al-j.*, p. 309.

House of God, and destroyed the walls of Jerusalem; when Simeon the priest asked of him the store of books, and he gave them to him.

CHAPTER XIII.

But we will make known to you all the genealogies in detail. Judah begat Pharez, and Pharez married Barayah, the daughter of Levi, and begat Esrom.

And Esrom married Kanita, the daughter of Zebulun, and he begat Aram. And Aram married Phozib the daughter of Judah; and he begat Aminadab.

And Aminadab married Thebara, the daughter of Esrom, and he begat Naasson. And Naasson married Simar, the daughter of Yuhanas, and he begat Salmon; and Salmon married Saphila, the daughter of Aminadab, by whom he had Booz.

And Booz married Ruth the Moabitess, of the seed of Mot, and begat Obed; and Obed married Abalit, the daughter of Sonas, and begat Jesse. Jesse married Habliar, the daughter of Abrias, and begat David the king.

And king David took to wife Bathsheba, the wife of Uriah, and begat Solomon. And Solomon married Nan, the same as Makiya, the daughter of Dan king of Ammon, of the seed of Lot, and begat Rehoboam.

And Rehoboam married Makin, the daughter of Bilos, and begat Abia. And Abia married Malkit, the daughter of Absalom, and begat Asaph.

And Asaph married Nirona, the daughter of Sala, and begat Joshaphat.

And Joshaphat married Malkiya, the daughter of Abiud, and begat Joram. And Joram married Phitalia, the daughter of Naphrim, and begat Osias; and Osias married Sophia, the daughter of Habralias, and begat Jotham.

And Jotham married Hadast, the daughter of Elkanah, and

begat Ahaz. And Ahaz married Bikaz, the daughter of Zachariah, and begat Hezekiah; and Hezekiah married Basyar, the daughter of Bartenas, and begat Manasseh;

And Manasseh married Amasisan, and begat Amos; and Amos married Nadyas, and begat Josias. And Josias married Dalilah, the daughter of Kermias, and begat Joachim.

And Joachim married Phurdia, the daughter of Phulek, and begat Jechonias and his brother during the captivity of Babylon.

And Marsas who reigned over Babylon, released Jechonias from prison, and gave him to wife, a woman whose name was Dalilah, the daughter of Eliakim, by whom he had Salathiel.

But Jechonias died at Babylon; where Salathiel continued forty-nine years after him, and married Hadast, the daughter of Elkanah, and begat Zerubbabel. And Zerubbabel married Maukab, the daughter of Esdras the scribe, and had by her Abiud.

And Abiud married Hadast, the daughter of Zadok the high priest, and begat Eliakim. And Eliakim married Kwebedai, the daughter of Aram, and begat Azar.

And Azar married Salambeta, the daughter of Zadok. And Zadok married Kalim, the daughter of Waikan, and begat Akim. And Akim married Zasbaidi, and begat Eliud.

And Eliud married Awad, the daughter of Gasalias, and begat Eleazar. And Eleazar married Hayat, the daughter of Thalka, and begat Matthan. And Matthan married Sabartia, the daughter of Phunius, and had by her twins, namely, Jacob and Joachim.

And Jacob married Gadat, the daughter of Eleazar, and begat Joseph the betrothed [husband] of Mary.

But Joachim married Hannah, the daughter of Makah, and begat the pure Mary; Here ends the genealogy of pure Mary.

CHAPTER XIV.

And here, O my brother, behold, I have settled for thee that which is true, and I have revealed unto thee the genealogy, and laid for thee the firm foundation, which not one of the writers and of the wise men, could make known.

But, O my brother, give me thy heart and make it clean, that I may tell thee what things remain, and how the reckoning of generations come all round to reach unto and to stand firm by the birth of Christ.

But after the birth of Christ there remained no more trustworthy reckoning [of kindred] to the Jews. For Christ was the end of the generations; He took it and gave it to us.

But let me tell thee, O my brother, that the five thousand years from [the creation of] Adam, did not end before the days of Cyrus, king of Persia. Then from Cyrus to the sufferings of our Saviour Jesus Christ, even as the faithful Daniel prophesied, saying, "After seven weeks Christ shall come, and shall be put to death."

Now seven weeks are four hundred and ninety years; for a great week is of seventy years. But in that the prophet said, "After seven years," he pointed to the ten years [that remained]; for he did not say, "Christ shall come at the end of the seven weeks," but he said, "After seven weeks [He shall come] and be put to death."

But the meaning here of "after," is—those ten years, that make up the five hundred years. And that is the fulfilment of the promise that God made to Adam, that He would save him at the end [of that time].[16]

Henceforth are the mouths of the Jews struck dumb, and to them belongs shame, because they blaspheme and say that Christ is not yet come.

But while they say so, they, of necessity, believe the first statement [of the prophets] to be true and the last to be a lie. If they say "Christ came," believing, as they do, the prophecy of the prophet Daniel, they now see that the prophecy of Daniel is fulfilled, and that the House of God is laid waste [and taken] from them; that the priesthood is abolished, and that the seven weeks were fulfilled, and that Christ came, and was put to death; and that the Holy City was laid waste by king Vespasian and his son Titus.

"But let me also tell thee, O my brother, that in the thirty-second year of the reign of Augustus Cæsar, Christ was born in Bethlehem of Judah, as it is written in the Gospel. And, behold, it is made plain to us, that Christ came when the prophecy was fulfilled.

As Micah the prophet said, "But thou, O Bethlehem, [in the] land of Judah, thou art not lower than the kings of Judah; for from thee shall come a king, that shall feed my people Israel."

Let the Jews now feel ashamed of themselves; for if they make Daniel a liar, they cannot again make the prophet Micah a liar; yet if they will make them liars still, behold, Christ was born in Bethlehem [in] the land of Judah.

And when He was born at Bethlehem [in] the land of Judah, a star in the East made it known, and was seen by Magi. That star shone in heaven, amid all the other stars; it flashed and was like the face of a woman, a young virgin, sitting among the stars, flashing, as it were carrying a little child of a beautiful countenance.

From the beauty of His looks, both heaven and earth shone, and were filled with His beauty and light above and below; and that child was on the virgin woman's arms; and there was a cloud of light around the child's head, like a crown.

But it was a custom of the Chaldæans to observe the stars of heaven; to take counsel from them; and they were numbered by them.

So when they saw the star of the figure we have just

mentioned, they were greatly troubled, and said among themselves, "Surely the king of the Helonæans is putting himself in battle array against us!"

And they inquired among soothsayers and philosophers, until they ascertained the fact and discovered that the king of the children of Israel was born.

As to this matter of the stars, the Chaldæans used to work it out, and to take counsel from the power* of the stars; so that they knew every event that should be, ere it happened. Likewise the captains of large ships, when they went on a voyage upon the seas, [knew beforehand] the signs of winds, of whirlwind, of gloom, and of thick darkness.

Thus the Magi when they read in their books, knew from them, that Christ should be born in the land of Judah.

So they went upon a high mountain in the east, while coming westward; and they took with them the presents they had prepared ere they set off on their journey; that is, gold, frankincense and myrrh—that had been with Adam in the Cave of Treasures. Gold, namely as unto a king; frankincense, as unto God; and myrrh, as for His death.

CHAPTER XV.

But when Hor, king of Persia, heard who it was they called King of kings, he prepared his chariot and mounted it. Basantar also, king of Saba, came out; and Karsundas, king of the East, got himself ready and came out also.

They were all in great tribulation, and also all other kings in the borders of the West trembled with them, and every country in the East was in great alarm at the sight of that glory.

* *i.e.*, influence.

Then the Magi while on their journey said, "This star has not risen but for some great event." And they went on their way until they came to Jerusalem.[17]

But when Herod heard of it, he was troubled, and called the Magi to him, and communed with them; and they rehearsed unto him the [whole] thing.

Then he and all his hosts trembled; and he said to the Magi, "Go ye, and inquire diligently concerning this Child; and when ye have found Him, come and tell me, that I also may go and worship Him.

Then the Magi went forthwith to Bethlehem, and found Christ, and offered Him their gifts. But they did not return to Herod; they went back to their own country.

But after they were gone, Herod was wroth, and commanded all children of two years and under, to be put to death.

Then an angel of the Lord appeared unto Joseph, and said to him, "Arise, and take the Child and His mother, and go to the land of Egypt; and abide there until I tell thee." And Joseph went into the land of Egypt.

Then Herod began to slay all children, until he had not left one. And he died of an evil death.

After his death an angel of the Lord appeared unto Joseph in the land of Egypt. And Joseph came up out of Egypt, and dwelt at Nazareth, he, the child, and Mary His mother.

And they abode at Jerusalem until Christ was thirty years of age, and was baptized by John.

This John lived all his days in the wilderness, and his food was locusts and wild honey.

And in the nineteenth year of Tiberius, our Lord Christ was crucified. He died in the body, and was buried, and rose again from among the dead on the third day; as it is written.

And He went down into hell, and saved Adam and Eve, and all their righteous seed, according to His first and firm promise.

And thus He fulfilled all that the prophets had prophesied concerning Him.

He then went up into heaven; whence He will come again with His holy angels, to judge the quick and dead.

Unto Him be glory, and thanksgiving, and honour, and power and worship for ever. Amen.

NOTES TO BOOK I.

1 " He rooted up from elsewhere, trees no larger than the horns (antennæ) of locusts, and planted the garden full of them." (*Bereshith Rabbah*, sect. fol. 18, ed. Frkf.; and *Yalkut Rubeni*, fol. 13, ed. Armst.) R. Abarbanel, however, denies that; and says that God did not take trees from elsewhere to plant them there; but the meaning is, that the garden and the trees thereof, were a plant of His own planting, to take pleasure therein—the perfection of His creation. (*Comm. in Pent.*, fol. 22.) *Yalkut Rubeni* (fol. 13, ed. Amst.), quotes from the Bk. *Zoar*, that as God made two Paradises, one on earth for Adam, and one above for the righteous who are to be there girt with light, so also has He made two Gehennas; one under the earth, and one above it. The one below, is for all who do not believe in God, and have not entered into covenant with Him. But the Gehenna above is for all Israelites who have broken the commandments, and care not to repent.

2 The Angel of the Face revealed unto Moses the creation of the world, and how on the third day God created the waters, dry lands, woods, fruit trees, and the Garden of Eden, for delight. (*Kufale*, p. 7; and R. Maim., *Sanhed. X.*)

3 R. Abarbanel renders מלקדמין (Targum *Onk.*, Gen. iii, 8), by מזרח בארץ the utmost limit of the earth created at the beginning (*Comm. in Pent.*, fol. 22). It was planted on a mountain [the Holy Mountain] in the north; eastward; whence flowed the rivers down into the world. (*Sode Raza*, in *Yalk. Rubeni*, fol. 13.)

4 S. Ephrem had a different idea of Paradise. In his first sermon on this subject (vol. iii, p. 564), he compares Paradise to the orbit of the moon, that embraces within itself both the earth and the seas. (S. Chrys., *Hom.* xiii, in Gen.)

5 Then the Lord God [the Word of the Lord, *Targ. Hier*] said to the ministering angels: " Behold, Adam is alone in the earth as I am alone in the high heavens, and men shall come from him who shall know good from evil. Had he kept My commandment he would have lived and continued [stood] like the Tree of Life, for ever. But now since he has transgressed, let us decree to drive him out of Eden ere he take of the Tree of Life. And God drove Adam from the Garden of Eden, and he went and dwelt on Mount Moriah, to till the ground from which he had been taken. (Targ. *Jonathan*, in Gen. iii.)

The Jews, says S. Basil (*Hom. in Hexaemeron*, ix, c. 6), being reduced to great straits, πολλά, φασίν, ἔστι τὰ πρόσωπα πρὸς οὓς ὁ λόγος γέγονε τοῦ Θεοῦ, say there were many persons to whom God addressed the words, " Let us make man;" namely to the angels παρεστῶσιν αὐτῷ, who waited on Him. Ἰουδαϊκὸν τὸ πλάσμα, but it is a Jewish fiction and fabulous—for is the image of God and of angels one and the same ?

In the *Coran*, sur. vi, 14, Mahomet inveighs against *al-mushrikin*, those who gave companions to God, and worshipped them, in the shape of angels, together with Him. And in sur. xxxvii, 153, and elsewhere, he further blames them—and the former inhabitants of Mecca in particular—for believing that angels were of the female sex, and daughters of God. " Have we created angels females," says he, "and do we prefer daughters to sons ?" etc.

6 Adam and his wife were seven years in the Garden of Eden, tilling and keeping it, " and we," says the Angel of the Face, " gave him work and taught him everything needful [lit. visible] for husbandry; and he laboured at it, and gathered the fruit thereof, and laid it in store for himself and his wife." (*Kufale*, p. 13.)

7 The air of Paradise is full of sweet and fragrant smells; Adam drew breath from it, and grew thereby. (S. Ephrem, *Serm. X, on Par.*, vol. iii, p. 595.)

8 Adam the first man, king of all that is on the earth, was created on the Friday of the first week in Nisan, the first month of the first year of the world (Bar. Hebræus, Syr., *Dyn.* i, p. 3). After having created everything, God said to His angels: " Let us create man after our own image and similitude, knowing good and evil, and with the power of doing either." Then there appeared an open right hand, with particles of the four elements in it; into which God breathed a living soul, whence Adam came into existence. (Abulpharaj. Arab. *Hist. Dyn.*, p. 5.)

God created Adam in the last hour of the first Friday. He created him of the surface of the earth, taking a handful of earth of all colours, He mixed it up with divers waters (ἀπὸ τῆς πυρρᾶς γῆς φυραθείσης ἐγεγόνει Joseph. *Ant. Jud.*, lib. i, c. i, p. 2); red earth being virgin soil; and having formed him, He breathed a breath into him, and he became a living and sensible creature, after having been a senseless vessel of clay. (Jelal, and Jahias on *Coran*, sur. ii, 39.) At sur. lxxvi, 1, on the words *hal ata 'ala 'l insâni*, Jelal says (according to Maracci, p. 769), that Adam had been forty years a form of clay no one ever mentioned, for there was nothing remarkable or to be noticed (remembered) —in it, until God breathed into him the breath of life.—Truly such writers, and their readers, are easily pleased ; for if, Jelal says, Adam was created on the Friday of the creation, where had he been, as a figure of clay, during those forty years ?

Pyrrhon in his history, says indeed, that Adam came into the Garden of Paradise on the fortieth day [of his creation] ἀλλ'οὐκ οἶδα ποῦ διέτριβε πρότερον ὁ 'Αδάμ, ἔξω τοῦ παραδείσου τεσσαράκοντα διάγων ἡμέρας, but I don't know, says M. Glycas, where Adam could have been spending forty days outside Paradise. (*Annal.* i, p. 156.) This legend was probably derived from the λεπτὴ Γένεσις, or Ethiopic *Kufale*, where we read in ch. iii, p. 12, " When Adam had passed forty days in the land in which he was created, we, the Angel of the Face, brought him into the Garden of Eden; and Eve his wife, after eighty days. Wherefore it is written in the tables of heaven, that a woman continues forty days until cleansed, for the birth for a man-child, and eighty days for that of a female.

Philo (*Quæst.* xxv, Armen. in Gen.) alludes to this, when he says that " man's " formation being more perfect than woman's, *gisu bidètsav jamanagi*, only required half the time, that is forty days ; but woman's nature being less perfect, took *grgnagi avurts* twice as

210   THE BOOK OF ADAM AND EVE.   [BOOK

many days—eighty." [This may have been clear to Philo, but to no one else.] Targ. Jonathan in Gen. ii. says that God took dust from בית מקדשא the sanctuary and from the four winds [quarters] of the world, mixed it up with waters from the whole world, and made man סומק שחים וחיור brown, black and white—and He " breathed into him a living soul, to light up his eyes, and to quicken his ears to hearken." Ebn-Ali adds that while Adam was thus a figure of clay—either forty nights or forty years [τεσσαρακοστῇ ἡμέρα Geo. Syncell. from λεπτὴ Γένεσις, or Kufale] Satan came and kicked it; and as it gave a sound, he said, " This is not created, but to rule and govern." And God said to His angels, " When I have animated it, ye shall fall down and worship him." They did so, but Satan would not, etc. (Maracci, p. 22). Man was as high as a palm-tree, and the hair of his head was long and thick, etc. (Jahias, p. 270.)

But Masudi (Maruj es-sahabi, p. 50, sq.) improves upon this account, and says, that God having finished the earth, peopled it with [jins] genii or demons, one of which was Eblis—before He created Adam. They began to fight among themselves, and were driven to distant islands; while Eblis was made regent of the sky [the heaven of the world], but harboured pride in his breast, and refused to worship Adam when created. Then God sent Gabriel and Michael, and after them the Angel of Death, who took a handful of clay of red, black and white colours; whence men are of different complexions. The first man was called Adam [from adim, surface], and left forty years, some say one hundred and twenty years, a figure of clay. The angels passed by and stared at it, and Eblis himself was astonished, and gave it a kick that made it resound. Afterwards, when commanded to worship Adam, he refused, saying to God, " I am Thy vicar on earth, created of fire, with wings and a glory round my head—but this one is of clay." Then God cursed Eblis, hurled him down from heaven, but gave him respite, until a fixed time—the day of the resurrection, etc.

R. Meir says God made the first man of dust gathered from the whole world; and R. Oshaya says his body was made of dust from Babel (or Babylon), his head from the land of Israel, and his other members from different lands. But R. Jochanan Bar Hanina says that there being twelve hours in the day : At hour one, God gathered the dust ; at two, He formed the mass ; at three, He spread out his members; at four, He put breath into him; at five, He set him up on his feet; at six, he called the names [of the beasts] ; at seven, He joined him to Eve ; at eight, they begat twins ; at nine, they were ordered not to take food from the tree ; at ten, they transgressed ; at eleven, they were judged ; and at twelve, they were driven from Paradise. (Talmud Bab. Sanhedrin, p. 75, 76, ed. W.) The same story is also told in P. Avoth. of R. Nathan. fol. 2. Philastrius (Cotel., Pat. ap., vol. i, p. 642) speaks of heretics, who taught that Adam was created blind. Τυφλὸς κτίζεται, and ἄνθρωποι τυφλοί. (S. Clem., Homil. iii, 39 and 24.) See also Simon Magus and S. Peter arguing on this at Rome—αὐτίκα γοῦν ὁ καθ'ὁμοίωσιν αὐτοῦ (τοῦ Θεοῦ) γεγονὼς 'Ἀδὰμ καὶ τυφλὸς κτίζεται κ. τ. λ.—to which S. Peter replies : εἰ τυφλὸς ἐπλάσθη ὁ 'Ἀδάμ, ὡς λέγεις, if Adam was formed blind as thou sayest, how could God have commanded him, showing him the tree of good and evil, if it had not been plain to him ? etc. (Credrenus, Hist. Comp., vol. i, p. 364.)

9 When God drove Adam from Paradise, He in His mercy made Adam

dwell in a lower land (valley or plain) away from it. (S. Ephr., vol. iii, *Serm. I, on Par.*, p. 554.)

10 Quando expulsi sunt de paradiso fecerunt sibi tabernaculum, et fuerunt vii dies lugentes et lamentantes in magna tristitia, etc. (*Vita Adæ et Evæ*, p. 37, ed. Meyer.)

11 God drove Adam and Eve from the Garden of Eden abroad in the earth, at the ninth hour of the same Friday on which they had been created at the first hour. (Abulphar. *Dyn.* i, p. 6; Geo. Syncellus, *Chron.* p. 5.)

S. Chrysostom (*in S. Matt.*) says, τῇ ἕκτῃ ἡμέρᾳ τῆς πρώτης ἑβδομάδος, τοῦτ'ἔστι τῇ αὐτῇ ἡμέρᾳ τῆς πλάσεως αὐτοῦ, λέγει τόν ' Ἀδάμ ἐκβληθῆναι τοῦ παραδείσου καί τήν Εὔαν. If driven from Paradise at the sixth hour on the Friday, how could they have been created at the eleventh hour on that day, according to the Coran?

12 According to the *Kufale* Adam and Eve left the Garden of Eden exactly seven years, two months, and seventeen days, after having been brought into it from the land of Elda, where they had been created, and to which they now returned. On this day [the 10th of May, Syncel.] Adam offered a sweet smelling sacrifice of incense and other spices, at sun-rise; and on this day were all creatures driven from the garden, and their speech taken from them. For until the day Adam was driven from the garden, all animals, birds, and reptiles, had one speech of their own. (*Kufale,* p. 14, 15.) Geo. Syncellus adds to this from the λεπτὴ Γίνεσις (p. 15, ed. Dind.) "that all animals ὁμόφωνα εἶναι —τοῖς πρωτοπλάστοις spake the same language as Adam and Eve before their fall (so also Joseph. *Ant. Jud.*, lib. i, c. i, 4); for the serpent spake to Eve with a human voice"—a statement Syncellus did not believe; albeit he says, "we do not doubt the serpent was four footed before the fall, and afterwards, became creeping."

Speaking of the λεπτή Γίνεσις, the probable Greek original of the Ethiopic *Kufale,* of Jewish authorship, and possibly alluding to this present work of Christian origin, Geo. Syncellus says, "he was driven to quote from them against his will, on account of the naming of the beasts by Adam, of the fall, etc., εἰ καὶ μὴ κύρια εἶναι δοκεῖ although such particulars do not seem to be authentic" (p. 7).

13 And the King of Light commanded me Æbel Zivo [who with Anush and Shetel, attended Adam] saying, "Go to the world of darkness which is full of evil, and bring out every thing to light —let the earth be formed, and bring forth food and every living thing, male and female. Let man and woman be, and call them Adam and Eve; and let all things, even the Angels of Fire, serve him. With the aid of Fetahil [Demiurgus] the world will come to light." Adam and Eve were then created, and a soul given them, in the garden. "Go then, Æbel Zivo [Brilliant Ruler] and cause Adam's heart to shine, and establish him so that his mind shine; converse with him, thou and the two angels that are to go about with him in the world. And teach him and Eve and their children, to eschew evil and Satan, and to practise righteousness in the earth," etc. (*Codex Nasaræus* i, p. 62, 64, 66.)

Adam was clothed in the brightness of life, and three pure Genii—Æbel, Anush and Shetel were given him for companions, etc., i, p. 193; ii, p. 120, etc. [See a long quotation from *'Emeq hammelech* on this subject, in Eisenmenger's *Entdecktes Judenthum*, vol. i, p. 459.]

14 "The world was created by God the Father through His only Begotten Son," says Syncellus (p. 1, 2, ed. D.), "on the first of Nisan, or 25th of March,

14*

or 29th of Phamenoth. On the same day the angel Gabriel appeared to the B. Virgin Mary, and on that day also did Christ rise from the dead, τοῦ ιφ'λ'δ 'ἴτους ἀπὸ κτίσεως κόσμου, being 5534 years from the creation of the world; a matter I will diligently try to prove" (the discrepancy between 5500 and 5534 is explained further on). The general opinion among Jews has always been that this world will last 7000 years. Thus in *Avoda Zara*, p. 17, we read, "6000 years will be to the world—2000 years תֹהוּ of emptiness; 2000 years תּוֹרָה of the law; 2000 years, the days of the Messiah in our manifold afflictions." These, adds the commentary, are determined according to the days of the week, and the last 1000 years are the Sabbath. This account of the first 2000 years does not agree with what is said elsewhere, that "the law was given before the creation, and that Adam and the Patriarchs had it."

Τίνος δὲ χάριν τὴν ζ' ἡμέραν εὐλόγησε ὁ Θεός; "Why then did God hallow the seventh day?" asks Cedrenus. "Because whereas every other day had within itself the blessing resting on the works done therein [that were very good] the seventh day had no such distinction. God, therefore, hallowed it as a day of rest, καὶ ὡς τύπος τῆς ἑβδόμης χιλιετηρίδος, and as a figure of the seventh thousandth of years [or millennium] as told by Josephus, and in the λεπτὴ Γίνεσις (Eth. Kufale) ἥν καὶ Μωσέως εἶναί φασί τινες ἀποκάλυψιν, which some say is the Revelation of Moses." (Cedrenus, *Hist. Compend.*, p. 9, ed. D.)

15 And the Lord called me [Æbel Zivo], and said, "Go, tell Adam, with a clear voice, of the most high King of Light; of the kings of praise, who stand praising Him; of the creatures of light, that live for ever. Teach them to pray and to give thanks, to stand praying to the King of Light, Lord of all creatures, three times a day and twice in the night, etc. (*Codex Nasar.* i, p. 68.)

Targum *Onkelos* (Gen. ii. 7), says of "the living soul," that it became (or was) in man לרוח ממללא a speaking spirit — προφορικὸς λόγος [which no " missing link " possesses].

16 After God had given His commandment to Adam and Eve, not to touch the tree, Satan said within himself, I shall not be able to make Adam fall, but I can make Eve do so. He then drew near to her, and while whispering in her ears, he shook the tree with his hands and feet, until the fruit thereof fell to the ground; so that Eve should take of it without touching even the root of the tree. (*Pirke Avoth* of R. Nathan, fol. 2.)

Quoniam in hora gloriæ ejus intravit serpens, et invenit Evam solam, et decepit Evam. (*Protoev. Jacobi*, c. xiii, ed. Thilo.)

And S. Ephrem (in *Gen.*, vol. i, p. 31), says that, Eve trusting to what the serpent said, ate the fruit first, hoping thereby to obtain divinity, and thus to become superior to her husband, whom she wished to rule, rather than obey. When, however, she found herself deceived, she gave him of the fruit, in order that he should fare as she did. And she did not die at once, lest Adam should be terrified at the sight of her death, and so, not eat of the fruit.

S. Ephrem's opinion agrees in part with the words of Eve: Δεῦρο, κύριέ μου, Ἀδάμ, ἐπάκουσόν μου καὶ φάγε ἀπὸ τοῦ καρποῦ τοῦ δένδρου, οὗ εἶπεν ὁ Θεός, τοῦ μὴ φαγεῖν ἀπ' αὐτοῦ καὶ ἔσῃ ὡς Θεός. "Come hither, my lord, Adam, and hearken to me and eat of the fruit of the tree, of which God told us not to eat; and thou shalt be as God," which she said, when disappointed and mortified at her own disobedience and transgression ('Αποκάλυψις, in *Vita Adæ et E.*, p. 54, 55).

17 R. J. Abendana (*Leqet Shecha*, ad loc.) remarks on "one of his ribs," Gen. ii, 21, that צלע "a rib," is feminine, and means עד "side," that confirms the opinion of Rabbis of blessed memory, that Adam was created די פרצופין δι-πρόσωπον, with two sides, or-faces ; the one male, the other female. See notes 18 and 24.

Targ. *Jonathan*, in Gen. ii, does not agree with that; but says that the rib taken out by God was עלעא תליסרית דמן סטר ימינא the thirteenth rib on the right side.

18 But R. Jeremiah B. Eliezer says, that in the hour God created Adam, He made him אנדרוגינוס, ἀνδρόγυνος man and woman ; as it is written : "male and female created He them," Gen. i, 27. But R. Shemuel Bar Nathan, holds that God created Adam דיו פרצופין, δι-πρόσωπον, with two faces ; the one looking one way, and the other looking the other way. He then sawed them asunder, into two backs, a back to the one and a back to the other, etc. (*Bereshith Rab.*, fol. 9 ; and *Yalk. Shimoni*, fol. 6, 20), to which *Matnoth Kah.* adds, that one side was male and the other female. The same story is told in Talmud Bab. (*Berachoth*, p. 121, ed. W.) where the commentary (R. Shelomoh) adds, that God did not "saw" Adam asunder, but split (צלח) him in two, and made Eve out of one half. And elsewhere (*Erubin*, p. 35), R. Jeremiah Ben Eliezer, repeating the same thing, founds his belief on Psalm cxxxix. 5, "Thou hast beset me, behind and before."

Adam and Eve were twenty years old when created. עפר "dust" is masculine and אדמה "earth" is feminine; and He who formed them made them thus of the dust of the earth, male and female. And God made Adam גולם מן הארץ עד חרקיע in bulk (reaching) from earth to the firmament and then put breath into him. For "soul" is understood in five different ways :—(1) Spirit ; (2) breath ; (3) intelligent single use of double members ; (4) life ; (5) and soul which is blood, as it is written : "For blood is the soul." (*Beresh. Rab.*, fol. 17.) [This is treated at length in R. Sh. Palkeire's *Sepher Nephesh*, on Hebrew psychology, 1864; and by Maimonides, in his preface to *Pirke Avoth*.] R. S. Ben Melech (*Miclol Yophi*, Gen. i) understands "in the image of God" אלהים, in the image of angels, like an angel, with breath given him from on high.

And S. Macarius, *Hom.* xv, p. 88, οὐ γὰρ περὶ Μιχαὴλ καὶ Γαβριὴλ, τῶν ἀρχαγγέλων εἶπεν, ὅτι ποιήσωμεν κατ' εἰκόνα καὶ ὁμοίωσιν ἡμετέραν: ἀλλὰ περὶ τῆς νοερᾶς οὐσίας τοῦ ἀνθρώπου τῆς ἀθανάτου λέγω ψυχῆς.

R. Abarbanel (*Com. in Pent.*, fol. 17) explains this, saying, Adam alone was created after the image and similitude of God [circumcised, according to R. Nathan, in *Yalk. Shimoni*, fol. 5, 16], being as it were the perfection of His creatures. And that, as some say, Adam was אנדרוגינוס a Greek term, means that he had both the name and the form within him; wherefore is he also said to have had שניפרצופין two faces (or sides) the one male and the other female ; but the male was actually wrought out, whereas the female was בכח *in posse*.

חזהר על התורה (in *Gen.*, fol. 22, ad Liv.) explains it thus : God said to His companions, "O ye that are with Me, is not this Adam a male emanation, with the female hidden within him ?" So was Adam. διπρόσωπος, דיפרצופין אצל לחאי לית ביה צלם ודמות yet in reality he had neither form nor similitude, but was very high exalted, with a name that reached up to an idea of God—clad in the light God created at first.

R. M. Maimonides (quoted in גדולות מקראות, fol. 9) says, that God addressed the earth when He said, "Let us make man." The earth was to give him all his earthy matter, and God, all his spiritual and intellectual faculties. The same is also told in כלי יקר, fol. 15; and again repeated by R. Bekai. See note 25.

19 The tree had not in itself good and evil, for there could be nothing evil in Paradise; ὅρος δὲ ἐτέθη ἐπὶ τῷ φυτῷ πρὸς γυμνασίαν τῆς ἐλευθεριότητος; but the tree was set up as a mark (or limit) in order to bring out Adam's freedom of action—whether to obey (good) or to disobey (evil). For his knowledge of either was before the commandment given, not to touch of the fruit of the tree. (Cedrenus, Hist. Compend., p. 13.)

20 When God said to his angels: "I, indeed, will put a [khaliph] vicar in the earth"—and commanded them to worship him, and they did so. But Eblis [Satan] would not; he (Coran, sur. ii, 30, sq.) was proud, and became one of the infidels—then God asked him: "Why wilt thou not worship Adam?" "Because," replied Eblis, "I am better than he; Thou didst create me of fire, but him of mud," etc. (Coran, sur. vii, 12 and 9). Then Satan, or the serpent, made Adam and Eve fall from Paradise to the earth: Adam in Serandib [Ceylon; Adam's Peak] and Eve at Jeddah in Yemen, where she was buried (ibid. ibid.) [I visited her tomb in 1841; her head is said to be at one end of the burial ground, her body under the wely in the centre of it, and her feet at the farther end, some hundred yards apart. The Arab who took me to see it, could not help saying: Yā Khawājah, hí thaweelé, wallāh! O sir, she was long indeed!]

Ibn-Batutah (Travels, vol. iv, p. 179, sq.) gives a description of Adam's Peak in Serandib, of the two ways, for Adam and Eve, to the summit; of the print of the foot, sunk into a black rock; of trees whose leaves when eaten, restore old age to youth, etc.

Masudi tells the same story, but adds, that some of the fig-leaves with which Adam was girt about, having been scattered by the wind in his fall from Paradise, those leaves became the sweet spices for which Ceylon is celebrated. (Masudi, ch. iii, p. 60, 61.)

21 R. Eliezer improves upon the account given in Beresh. Rabbah, quoted above (note 18), and says the first man reached from earth to the sky, and from east to west when he lay down. But after his transgression God laid His hand upon him ומעיטו and made him small; as it is said Psalm cxxxix. 5, "Thou hast beset me, etc., and laid Thy hand upon me." So also R. Jehudah avers in the name of all the Rabbis of blessed memory that it was so. (Talmud Bab. Hagigah, p. 23.) While reading the Kandjur, I often wondered there could be men found to write and to believe such things. But they are not more absurd than the lore of the Talmud, whereof we read among other warnings: "My son, give heed to the words of the writers (Rabbis) rather than to the law itself." (Erubin, p. 42.) "For he who has only מקרא the text of the Bible, without the Talmud, is like one that has no God." (Share tsedek, fol. 9 Eis.) And "to contradict such teaching, is כחולק על השכינה like one who would differ from, or contradict the Shekinah" (Presence of God, or Holy Ghost, according to Sepher Yesirah, p. 112, ed. Rittang). And for a man to go from the Talmud and to מדבר חלכח לדבר מקרא return to the Bible (or text) there is no more peace! (Talm. Bab. Hagigah, p. 17.)

22 At ch. xxvi (ii, p. 276) Masudi tells of a wonderful cup said to have belonged to Adam, that always remained full, however much was drunk out of it, whose virtue Alexander the Great tried on his visit to Ceylon. And Ibn Batutah (vol. iv, p. 167, sq.) relates his adventures on his pilgrimage to Adam's foot, the print of which is of an enormous size. [But is it not also Buddha's foot ?] Hyde in his notes to Peritsol (*Itinera Mundi*, p. 25) refutes the etymology of Taprobana from Div (isle) Rohan—the name for Adam's Peak in the *Coran*; and proposes to bring "Serandib," from Selen, or "Seilan-dib," island of Seylan—Singhala.]

El-kazwini (*Ajaib* i, p. 165), speaks of Jebel Serandib upon which Adam alighted—which shines with gold up to heaven, and is seen from a great distance by sea-faring men. There is the print of Adam's foot sunk in the stone and about seventy yards long. The reason for which there is only one foot is—that Adam rested the other on the bottom of the sea.

23 On the second week, says the Angel of the Face, we brought all the beasts to Adam, by command of God. On the first day, beasts ; on the second, cattle; on the third, birds; on the fourth, all that moves (creeps) on the face of the earth ; and on the fifth, all that moves in the waters; and Adam called them all by their names, and that which he called them, was their name. (*Kufale*, p. 11.)

24 Immediately after the transgression, Adam and Eve lost the angelic vision and intelligence they had before they transgressed God's commandment. And now their sight and power of discerning became limited only to matters corporeal and sensible. (S. Ephrem, vol. i, p. 139.)

Bereshith Rabbah (Gen. ii, 7; and *Yalkut Rubeni*, fol. 13), says "That God gave Adam a twofold nature, partly of things above or divine, and partly of things earthly, such as eating, drinking ; and as to heavenly gifts, he was to stand over 'ministering angels.'" [These were called מלאכי השרת who were appointed to wait on him, namely, Æbel, Shetel, and Anush (*Cod. Nasar.*, p. 192, etc.). They were, however, frightened at Adam's size, that reached from earth to heaven (*Yalk. Rubeni*, fol. 10) and so went up terrified, to ask God what He had created," according to *Yalkut Shimoni*, on Gen. i.

It must then have been when they came down back into Paradise, that according to R. Jehudah (*Yalkut Shimoni*, fol. 4; and *Avoth* of R. Nathan, fol. 2), "they waited on Adam, roasted his meat, and mixed his wine," [מסנכין לו יין.]

"Other heavenly gifts of Adam were speech, understanding, and faculty to look on the 'ministering angels ;' for animals cannot do it. For God said : "If I make him only of the earth (earthy) he will die ; if of heaven only, he will live." So his Creator made him up of those, and gave him a twofold nature knowing good and evil ; for animals know not the good." [See also Talm. Bab. *Berachoth*, p. 61, on this same subject.]

But R. S. Ben Melech (*Miclol Yophi* and *Yalk. Shimoni*, fol. 6, 20, on Gen. i) says, that God made use of the expression : "Let us make man," etc., merely as a mark of respect, being about to create Adam in presence of the four elements, and to make him partly of עליונים heavenly things, and partly of תחתונים things of below, earthy. Instead of the four elements, Talmud Bab. (*Sanhedrin*, p. 78), says they were רב שע" the great of the world ; and *Midrash Nehelam* (quoted in *Yalkut Rubeni*, fol. 10, ed. Amst.) says, that " the Wheel, the Angel, and the Throne (Ezech. i) joined together, saying, "Let us make man to be in fellowship with us, his breath from the Throne; his spirit from the Angel, and his soul from the Wheel, in blessing, sanctification, and unity." *Yalk. Rubeni, id.* however, quotes another Midrash to show that God gathered together all things above and all things below, in fellowship with Himself, to take their share in the creation of man.

25 R. Bekai (*Pĭrush 'al atth.*, fol. 8, ed. Crac.) sums up these and other explanations of "Let us make man," etc. (1) על דרך הפשט—according to the text or simple sense, it is God and the earth, He as Creator and the earth as the mother of man; (2) as R. Kimchi says, it is an expression of majesty; or, it is an address of God to Moses, when He told him to write, etc.

26 When God, says R. Akha, came to create man, He took counsel with the ministering angels, and said to them: "Let us make man." Then they asked Him: "What will be his property?" "His wisdom shall be greater than your own," said God; and He brought before them beasts and birds, and asked them what they were. The angels did not know. God then asked Adam, who said, "This is an ox, an ass, a horse, and a camel." And what is thy name? said God. "It befits me to be called 'Adam,' because I was made of the earth." "And what is My name?" said God to Adam. "It befits Thee," said Adam, "to be called the Lord of all Thy [creatures]." Then God said: That is My name given Me first by Adam. (*Beresh. R.*, sect. xvii, fol. 20.)

And God said to the ministering angels who were created on the second day, and who ministered before Him:— "Let us make man after our own image and similitude—with 248 members, 365 nerves;" He spread a skin over them, and filled the whole with flesh and blood, etc. (Targ. Jonathan, B. Uzziel in Gen. i.)

[For a learned treatise on צלם and דמות with reference to Gen. i, 26, see *More Nevukim*, sect. i, c. i, of R. Maimonides.]

"When God set about creating the world," said R. Jehudah, "He created one legion of ministering angels, and said to them: 'Is it your good pleasure that we should create man?' To which they replied: 'What is man that Thou art mindful of him?' Then God thrust His finger between them and consumed them. And so with a second legion. But the third said to Him: 'What the first angels said availed nothing; the world is Thine; do what seemeth the best.'" (*Yalkut Shimoni*, ed. Crac., fol. 4.)

"There is another tradition," says R. Eliezer, "that God said to the Law [which, according to the Talmud, was created before the world], Let us make man!" To which the Law answered: "What, he the ruler of the world? his days will be shortened through sin; a child of wrath; and unless Thou be long suffering, it will be as if he had not been." "Am I then long suffering in vain?" said God. "He then took some earth, red, white and greenish, from the four corners of the world; red, *adom*, for Adam; white, for his intestines; and greenish for his body," &c. (*Ib. ibid.*, fol. 4.)

27 After Adam's transgression God brought him, Eve, and the Serpent to judgment: He said to the Serpent: "Because thou didst that, thou shalt be cursed among all the beasts of the field; upon thy belly shalt thou go, ורגליך יתקצצין thy legs shall be cut short; and thou shalt shed thy skin once in seven years; a deadly venom shall be in thy mouth, and thou shalt eat dust all the days of thy life. I will put enmity between thee and the seed of the woman; those who keep the Law, shalt smite thee on the head; and

thou shalt bite them in the heel. But there will be a remedy for them, ועתידין למעבד שפירותא בעיקבא ביומי דמלכא משיחא and they will apply that healing power to their heel, in the days of King Messiah. But when the Lord God said to Adam, "Thou shalt eat the herb of the surface of the field," Adam answered and said: "By the mercies that are of Thee, O Lord, let me pray that we be not reckoned as beasts of the field, to eat grass that grows thereon; Let us arise and toil with the labour of our hands, to eat our food from the yield of the earth; so that from now a difference be made between the children of men and the beasts of the field," &c. (Targum, *Jonathan*, in Gen. iii.)

In *Bereshith Rab.*, sect. xix, we are told that R. Meir taught "that the serpent was wonderfully high;" R. Jonathan, "that he was erect, and his feet like canes;" R. Jeremiah, "that he was אפיקורוס (Epicurus) a heretic or infidel;" R. Simeon, "that he was like a camel;" &c. Maimonides (in *More Nevukim*, sect. ii, c. 30) calls attention to a passage in the *Midrash*, where it is said "that חנחש נרכב the serpent was being ridden, and was like a hairy camel; and that he who rode him was he who beguiled Eve, namely, Samaël, or Satan." And, again: "When the serpent seduced Eve, Samaël was riding him; but God shall laugh at the serpent and at his rider." Also, "When the serpent came to Eve, he sprinkled his filth over her;" it will be wiped off the Israelites who stood on Mount Sinai: but the Gentiles retain it. (*ibid.*) The same story is told somewhat differently by R. Eliezer, in *Yalkut Shimoni*, fol. 8, 25. According to *Bereshith R.*, sect. 20, and to *Yalk. Shimoni*, fol. 9, 31, the ministering angels came down and קצצו ידיו ורגליו cut off his hands and his feet, and his cries were heard from one end of the world to the other.

28 What did that old serpent, that was jealous of Adam's glory, surrounded by ministering angels, think at the hour that he tempted Eve? "I will go and kill Adam and the woman his wife, and I shall be king of the whole world; and I shall walk erect, and enjoy all the pleasures of the world." Then God said to him: "Therefore will I put enmity between thee and man; therefore shalt thou alone be cursed of all beasts; therefore, also, because of thy pride, and wish to walk erect and to enjoy all the pleasures of earth, shalt thou creep on thy belly all the days of thy life." (*P. Avoth* of R. Nathan, fol. 2; and Bk. Zoar in *Yalkut Rubeni*, fol. 16.)

The Rabbis hold that the serpent had intercourse with Eve, whence Cain was born and with him, sundry female infirmities; and that Samaël, not being able (not having strength or power) to seduce Adam, turned to Eve as to the weaker of the two. (*Zoar*, in *Yalk. Rubeni*, fol. 16.)

29 S. Ephrem (in *Gen.* vol. i, p. 35) says the serpent was made to crawl on its belly, "for having increased the pangs of childbearing, through the seduction of Eve." And at p. 135, "that the serpent was deprived of feet because it had hastened on them to come to Eve, and had sought to be chief among beasts."

30 It is said, however, by R. Eliezer (quoted in Eisenmenger's *Entd. Jud.* i, 377), that Adam had a staff which he gave to Enoch, Enoch to Noah, Noah to Shem, Abraham, Isaac, Jacob, and Joseph; after Joseph's death his house was plundered, and the staff came into the hands of Pharaoh, who planted it in Jethro's garden. But when Moses was grown up he found it there covered with written characters; he then took it

and told Jethro this rod should deliver the children of Israel out of Egypt, &c. In דברי הימים של משא רבינו Paris. 1628, fol. 8, we read that "Moses having fled to Midian, and having become known to Jethro as an exile from Egypt, was by him put in prison. Moses, however, having pleased Zipporah, she fed him in prison, where she always found him standing on his feet, praying (fol. 9). She then told her father that divine vengeance would overtake him, if he maltreated his prisoner. Jethro at once brought him out; and gave public notice that whosoever would come and root out the rod that was planted and growing in his garden, to him would he give his daughter Zipporah to wife. Many came, small and great, kings, princes, great men, and men of valour, but could not root it up. But Moses, while walking in Jethro's garden, saw that rod of sapphire (or diamond) שם המפורש חקוק עליו, with the glorious name of Jehovah, engraved on it. He then rooted it up thence, at once, and it became a rod in his hand; and he returned home with it in his hand. Jethro seeing this, marvelled much, and gave his daughter Zipporah to wife unto Moses, etc. [Another story says that the inscription on that rod was the initials of the ten plagues of Egypt.]

But in the *Deburitho* of Mar Salomon of Botsra, c. xvii, we are told that Adam's stick was a branch of the tree of the knowledge of good and evil, which he broke (or cut) off the tree as he was leaving the Garden of Eden. (Assem, *Bibl. Or.*, vol. iii, p. 212.)

31 The Talmud and Josephus, as we have seen, teach that at first all animals had speech; and Philo (*Quæst.* xxxii, Armen, in Gen.) is of opinion that "in the beginning of the existence of the world, all animals (or living creatures) *wotch anmasn kol i panavoruthènd*, were not altogether deprived of reasoning power; although man excelled in this respect and in a clearer voice." Thus attributing a voice to the serpent, given it at the time, in order to seduce Eve; which the gloss, however, says, *ipr shtchmamp*, was only a hissing, understood by Eve for what it meant.

32 Our father Adam wept before the gates of Paradise, and the angels said unto him, "What wilt thou that we do to thee, Adam?" He then answered, "Behold, ye cast me out; I therefore intreat you to give me some sweet spices from Paradise, that when I am driven out of it, I may offer a sacrifice to God, that He may hear me." Then at the request of the angels, God gave Adam leave to gather from the garden, κρόκον καὶ νάρδον καὶ κάλαμον καὶ κινάμωμον καὶ λοιπὰ σπέρματα εἰς διατροφήν αὐτοῦ, saffron and spikenard, and sweet-cane and cinnamon, and other seeds for his support. Having gathered them, he left the garden and dwelt in the land. ('Αποκάλυψις in *Vita Adæ et E.*, p. 57.)

33 "Nam et Magos reges fere habuit Oriens" (Tertull. *Adv. Jud.*, c. ix), and (*Adv. Marc.*, c. xlii) "reges, dixit toparchas urbis alicujus aut regionis—quales in sacris paginis occurrunt sæpenumero. Hujus modi reges variis per orientem urbibus magos fere fuisse ait Septimius; hoc est, siderum astrorumque scientiæ peritos."

We read in the History of Georgia (*Kart'hlis tskhovreba*, ch. x, p. 39), that in the first year of king Aderki, *ishwa up'hali chweni Yeso Kriste*, our Lord Jesus Christ was born in Bethlehem of Judah; and that Magi came to bring him presents. Then news came to Mtzkhet'ha—the capital of Georgia at that time—about this coming of the Magi, "that an army was come to destroy Jerusalem." This caused great wailing among the Jews of the place, until the year after, other news was brought that "the army was not come to destroy the Holy City, but had with them presents they brought and offered to a certain male child, respecting his birth. This caused great joy among the Jews; until some fourteen years later, a certain disciple called Anna came from Jerusalem, with other Jews of Mtzkhet'ha, and told the people that the child, to whom Magi had offered gifts, was now grown up, and called Himself the Son of God, and proclaimed a new law and service," etc. See on this subject the last chapter of this work, and the notes thereon.

34 Χρυσὸν γοῦν αὐτῷ γεννηθέντι, βασιλείας σύμβολον προσεκόμισαν οἱ Μάγοι (Clem. Al. Pædag., lib. ii. p. 176.) Τὸν μὲν χρυσὸν ὡς βασιλεῖ, τὸν δὲ λίβανον—ὡς Θεῷ, τὴν δὲ σμύρναν—ὡς μέλλοντι γεύσασθαι θανάτου. (Theophyl. in Matt. ii, etc.) S. Ephrem (in Nativ. Dom., Serm. iii,) omits "the incense," and Tertullian (Adv. Marc., c. xiii,) omits "the myrrh," but in De Idol., c. ix, he mentions, the gold, the incense, and the myrrh.

35 Et dixit Adam ad Evam : surge et vade ad Tigris fluvium—et sta in aqua fluminis xxxvii dies; ego autem faciam in aqua Jordanis xl dies ; forsitan miseretur nostri Dominus Deus. Et transierunt dies xviii. Tunc iratus est Satanas et transfiguravit se in claritatem angelorum et abiit ad Tigrem flumen ad Evam, et invenit eam flentem ; et ipse diabolus quasi condolens ei cœpit flere et dixit ad eam: Egredere de flumine et de cetero non plores ; jam cessa de tristitia et gemitu, Quid sollicita es tu et Adam vir tuus ? Audivit Dominus gemitum vestrum, et suscepit penitentiam vestram—et misit me ut educerem vos de aqua et darem vobis alimentum, quod habuistis in paradiso et pro quo planxistis. Nunc ergo egredere de aqua et perducam vos in locum, ubi paratus est victus vester.

Hæc audiens autem Eva credidit et exivit de aqua fluminis et caro ejus erat sicut herba de frigore aquæ. Et cum egressa esset, cecidit in terram et erexit eam diabolus et perduxit eam at Adam. Cum autem vidisset eam Adam et diabolum cum ea, exclamavit cum fletu dicens: O Eva, Eva, ubi est fructus penitentiæ tuæ ? Quomodo iterum seducta es ab adversario nostro, per quem alienati sumus as habitatione paradisi et lætitia spiritali. Hæc cum audisset Eva cognovit quod diabolus suavit exire de flumine et cecidit super faciem suam in terram et duplicatus est dolor et gemitus et planctus ab ea. (Vita Adæ et Evæ p. 39, 40.)

36 Surgamus, ait Adam, et quæramus nobis, unde vivamus, ut non deficiamus. Et ambulantes quæsierunt novem dies et non invenerunt sicut habebant in paradiso, sed hoc tantum inveniebant, quod animalia edebant ; et dixit Adam ad Evam : hæc tribuit Dominus animalibus et bestiis, ut edant: nobis autem esca angelica erat. Sed juste et digne plangimus ante conspectum Dei, ut. (Vita Adæ et Evæ, p. 38.)

37 מן לבוש טופרא דאתבריאו ביה of the raiment, "onyx" (sweet perfume), "in which they were created," says Targ. Jonathan, in Gen. iii.

38 It seems as if the legend of the golden rods, and of these figs and fig-trees of an enormous size, reached farther east than Egypt, where the original of this Ethiopic translation was probably written. For R. M. Maimonides, speaking of the Sabæans (or Zabians), says : They all believed in the antiquity of the world, for heaven (the heavens) are to them instead of God. They also believed that the first man Adam was born of a man and a woman, like all other men. But they extolled him greatly,

saying he was a prophet-apostle for the moon, and called men to the worship of the moon; and that יש לו חבורים בעבודת האדמה there are books of his extant on the tillage of the land. They say of Adam, moreover, that when he came from the [climate] land of תשאם [Tasom, or Tasham], near India, and dwelt in the land of Babylon, he brought with him wonderful things; among others, a tree of gold that yielded branches, leaves, and flowers [of gold]; also a like tree of stone, with leaves that fire could not burn, and that could shelter 10,000 men as tall as Adam. And he brought with him two leaves, each of which could cover two men. But they also say that Seth departed from Adam's worship of the moon, etc. (*Mors Nevukim*, sect. iii, ch. 29.)

They also say that Adam relates in his book on the tillage of land, that there is in India a tree, whose branches, when thrown upon the ground, wriggle and creep like a serpent, etc. (*Ibid.*)

39 In Targum *Jonathan*, however, we read that God made for Adam and Eve לבישין דיקר robes of honour of the skin of the serpent, which it had sloughed off; and God covered their skin withal, instead of their own beauty of which they were stripped. (In *Gen.*, iii.)

40 Si cui igitur eorum, qui certant vel lumen, vel figura quæpiam ad similitudinem ignis appareat, ne amplectatur hujusmodi visum; est enim fallacia inimici manifesta; quæ quidem res multos fefellit, qui propter ignorantiam, a via virtutis deflexerunt. Nos autem scimus quod quamdiu sumus in hac mortali vita, aliquid cœlestium miraculorum ejus videre aspectu corporis non possumus. (B. Diadochus, *de perfect. spirituali*, c. xxxvi.)

41 Before the law fell on Adam [doom, after his transgression] he ate no food; but after the law had fallen on him, he and his family [Abel was born to him before the fall, II, p. 122] arose, and ate of all the fruits, vegetables, and living things Fetahil had prepared for him. (*Cod. Nasar.* ii, p. 134.)

42 This account agrees with that of Abul-pharaj or Bar. Hebræus (*Dyn.* Arab., p. 6 ; *Chron.* Syr., p. 3), who calls Cain's sister Climia, and Abel's Lebuda. Arab writers on the *Coran*, however, say that Eve always brought forth twins; a boy and a girl (Maracci, sur. v); while *Sidra l'Adam* (*Codex Nasar.*) of the Mandæans (ed. Norberg ii, p. 120, sq.), says that after Fetahil had created the world and Adam and Eve, to whom he gave feet to walk and a mouth to speak, he made for Adam a son like unto himself—pure and sinless, called Abel; before Abel the son of Eve. But after Adam and Eve had returned to the land (Elda) in which they had been created, Eve brought forth twins, son and daughter, three years following, etc. According to the *Kufale* (p. 15), however, Cain was born in the third week (of years) of the second Jubilee (seventieth year from creation, Syncell.), Abel in the fourth ; and his sister Awan (Aswam, Asauna, Syncell.) in the fifth. But according to Methodius (Bar. Hebr., Syr.) called Mar Thudiusi in Arabic, (*Dyn.*, p. 6), Cain and Climia were born thirty years after Adam and Eve came out of the garden ; Abel and Lebuda thirty years later. It was seventy years after, that Adam wishing to marry them one to another, Cain slew his brother.

Targ. *Onkelos* in Gen. iv, 2, renders the Hebrew text correctly ; but Targ. *Jonathan*, says that after the birth of Cain, Eve brought forth his twin sister and Abel—although it is not easy to understand how that could be.

Eve, says S. Ibn-Batrik (Eutychus), conceived and brought forth a son called Cain and a daughter called Azrun. Then she conceived again and gave birth to a son called Abel, and to a daughter called Awain, but in Greek, Laphura. (*Nasam al-j.*, p. 14.)

43 Or, grudged it. "He," says Philo on this, "who slays a victim [or, sacrifice], after dividing it, pours out the blood about the altar, and takes home the meat. But he who brings an offering, gives it whole, as we see, to him who takes [or, receives] it. Thus he who is selfish [a lover of self] like Cain, parts or divides [his offering]; but he, who like Abel, is a lover of God, devotes [to Him] his gift." (*Quæst. in Gen.*, Armen. lxii.)

44 According to Saîd Ibn-Batrik (Eutychus) when the sons were grown up, Adam said to Eve: "Let Cain take Owain, that was born with Abel, and let Abel take Azrun who was born with Cain." Then, said Cain to Eve his mother, "I will take my sister, and Abel shall take his sister; because Azrun was fairer than Owain." But when Adam heard these words, he was greatly perplexed, and said to Cain : "It is against the commandment that thou shouldest marry the sister that was born with thee." (*Nasam al-j.*, pp. 14-17.)

According to S. Epiphanius, *Hæres.* xl, 5, the Archontici, heretics in Palestine, held that ὁ διάβολος ἐλθὼν πρὸς τὴν Ἐῦαν, συνήφθη αὐτῇ ὡς ἀνὴρ γυναικί, καὶ ἐγέννησεν ἐξ αὐτοῦ τόν τε Κάϊν καὶ τὸν Ἄβελ—and that the two brothers did not fall out on account of God's preference for Abel, but because they both wished to have the same sister in marriage. Therefore did Cain kill Abel. For a Gnostic account of this, see S. Irenæus, *Hæres*, lib. i, p. 110 (ed. Grabe); concerning which statements Theodoritus says (*Hæres*, lib. i, 11), "were I to repeat them κοινωνεῖν τῆς φλυαρίας ὑπίλαβον, I might be thought to share in their folly."

45 Why then did Cain and Abel quarrel together? Because, answers R. Arona, the fairest twin sister was born with Abel. Cain, then said, "I shall take her to wife because I am the eldest." But Abel said : "But I will have her because she was born with me." (*Bereshh. Rabbah*, sect. xxii, fol. 26.)

Said Ibn-Batrik relates that Adam then said to Cain and to Abel, "Take ye of the fruits of the earth, and of the young of your flock, and go to the top of that holy mountain, and make an offering there; and then take your wives to yourselves." Cain offered of the best fruits of the earth; and Abel of the best of his flock. Meanwhile, as they were going up the mountain, Satan entered (the heart) of Cain to kill his brother because of Azrun his sister. Therefore God did not accept Cain's offering. (*Nasam al-j.*, p. 17.)

This is contrary to Scripture. Targum *Onkelos*, renders the Hebrew ; but Targum *Jonathan* says, that "Cain and Abel made their offering on the fourteenth of Nisan, and that Cain's offering was מדרע כירתא of flaxseed." Gen. iv, 2, sq. Or, according to Bk. *Zoar*, quoted in *Yalk. Rubeni*, fol. 21, Cain's offering was of פשתן flax, his thoughts dwelling on covering his nakedness from before the Lord.

Josephus (*Antiq.* i, c. 2) says, Abel offered γάλα, καὶ τὰ πρωτότοκα τῶν βοσκημάτων milk, and the firstlings of his flock.

46 God said to Cain, "Why is thy countenance sad ? If thou doest well, shall not thy guilt be forgiven thee ? But if thou doest evil in this life, thy sin shall be reserved unto the great day of Judgment, and thy sin shall lie at the door of thy heart. Behold, I have made over to thee רשותיה דיצרא בישא power (or, authority) over [thy] evil nature ; the desire of it will be unto thee [it will solicit thee to evil]; but thou shalt rule over it, whether for good [purity] or for sin " [lit. between

purity (or, holiness) and between sin].
(Targ. *Jonathan* in Gen. iv.)

47 Then Cain said to Abel, " Let us go down into the vale." Hence we see either that they were living on the slope of the mountain of Paradise, whence Cain led his brother into the plain below, or that Abel was tending his sheep on the hill, whence Cain brought him down into the vale, suited to him by reason of the standing corn and mud ; among which Cain could easily hide and bury his brother. (S. Ephrem, in Gen., vol. i, p. 41.)

48 Cain said to Abel his brother, Let us go into the field. When there Cain said, " There is no judgment ; there is no Judge ; there is no world to come, and there is neither reward for the righteous nor retribution to the wicked." But Abel replied, " There is a Judgment and there is a Judge ; there is a world to come, and there is both a reward to the righteous, and a punishment to the wicked." And as they were disputing about this in the field, Cain rose against his brother, stuck a stone into his forehead and killed him. (Targ. *Jonath. and Jer.*, in Gen. iv.)

49 Josephus (*Antiq.* i, ℔. 2) says, that Cain τὸν νεκρὸν αὐτοῦ ποιήσας ἀφανῆ λήσειν ὑπέλαβεν ; and S. Ephrem as stated above, says that as Abel tended his sheep on a hill, Cain allured him into the plain, where he might easily hide his body among the tall ears of corn, and *b'medrā thamre hwo*, and cover it with mud. But in the *Coran* (sur. v, 37) we read : *faba'ath allāhu ghurāban yabhathu fi-llardh*, that God sent a raven that scratched the earth to show Cain how to hide his brother's corpse. Jelal, however (Maracci, p. 229) says that this raven had a dead one in its beak, which it hid in the earth after having dug it with its beak and claws. But Masudi (ch. iii, p. 64) says that God sent forth two ravens, one of which killed and buried the other. Seeing this, Cain repeated the words of the *Coran*, sur. v, 34 : " Wretched man that I am, why cannot I be like this raven and hide my [shame or] guilt against my brother ? " He then buried him. *Midrash Tankhuma* (p. 6, ed. Amst.) however, says that they were עופות טהורים two clean birds, one of which killed its fellow, then dug the earth with its feet and buried it, in the presence of Cain, and in order to show him how to bury his brother, and to hide his blood.

R. Eliezer (*Pirke*, etc.), however, as quoted in *Yalkut Shimoni*, fol. ii, says that, the חכלב שהיה משמר צאנו של הבל dog who kept Abel's sheep, watched by his corpse to ward off beasts and birds of prey from it. And that as Adam and his help-meet sat by the corpse, wailing aloud over their son who lay dead, not knowing what to do, a raven that had killed its fellow said to them, " I will show you what to do." It then began to dig in the earth, and buried the bird. Then Adam said to Eve, " Let us do the same ; " and they dug the earth, and buried Abel.

I, Enoch, came to a place where I saw the spirits of the departed ; and I asked Raphael who was with me, " What spirit is it whose voice reaches me and accuses ? " And Raphael answered: " It is the spirit of Abel, whom Cain his brother killed; and who will accuse him until his seed is destroyed from off the face of the earth, and from the race of men his seed defiles." I then asked Raphael about him and about the day of judgment, and why he was separated from the rest [or one from another]. Then he answered: " These three separations, by chasm, water and light above, have been made between the spirits of righteous men, from sinners—when they are buried in the earth ; and great is the suffering of sinful spirits, until the great Day of Judgment, etc. (Book of Enoch, c. xxii, p. 14, 15.)

Before Cain had killed his brother, the land yielded fruit like the Garden of Eden; but after that murder, the land turned to yield only thorns and thistles. (Targ. *Hieros.* in Gen. iv.)

50 Targum *Jonathan*, however, says this sign was שמא רבא ויקירא of the great and precious Name. (In Gen. iv.)

NOTES TO BOOK II.

1 Masudi (i, ch. iii, p. 65), gives a popular ditty said to have been composed by Adam, while mourning for Abel. "How changed is the land and those who dwell in it! The face of the earth is now but hideous dust; Everything has lost both flavour and colour; Mirth and gladsome faces are gone; And our family has taken the tamarisk and other weeds, for the sweet and lovely plants of Paradise. Around us [watches] a relentless foe, accursed, at whose death we should breathe freely. Cain has slain Abel cruelly [or with violence]; Oh, sorrow—over that beautiful countenance! How should I not shed floods of tears, while the grave embraces Abel? There is now for me but a life-long sorrow; for what relief could I find from it?"

To which Eblis, who was at hand, though unseen replied:—

"Go from this land, and from its inhabitants, for the earth is now too narrow for thee. Thou, Adam wast in it with thy wife Eve, happy at being safe from the woes of this world; But my wiles and my craft rested not, until thou wast deprived of those goods. And unless the mercy of the Most High protected thee, the wind alone would carry thee far from the everlasting Paradise."

See Fabricius *Cod. Apoc. V. T.*, vol. i, p. 21, sq., for "The Psalms of Adam and Eve."

2 R. Abarbanel, *Comm. in Pent.* p. 30, says that Eve conceived twins in the Garden of Eden; and that what is told in the *Midrash* is true, that she must have brought forth twins [though not so stated in Scripture], otherwise Cain could not have taken a wife, and have had children by her, whose name was Ana, etc.

3 When Eve conceived Seth, her forehead shone, light brightened up her features, and her eyes flashed rays of light; and when the time came that she should be delivered, she brought forth Sheit [Seth] an eagle among men, who excelled them in grace, beauty of form, perfection of gifts, nobleness of disposition; and resplendent of light which, passing from Eve into him, shone on his forehead, and enhanced his beauty; so that Adam called him *Hibbet Allah*, "Gift of God." When Seth was grown up, Adam taught him his high calling as depository of God's will concerning his race, etc. etc.—Masudi i, ch. iii, pp. 67, 68.

In the two hundredth year of Adam, says Syncellus, Seth was taken up by angels and taught the falling away of the Watchers, the destruction of the earth by the Flood, and the coming of the Saviour. When after forty days' absence he returned among men, he then declared to Adam and Eve what he had seen and heard, etc. Seth was then forty years old; he was beautifully formed, as all his children were after him. They dwelt in a high land not far from Eden, etc. (*Chron.* p. 16, 17; and Cedren. *Hist.*, *Comp.* i, p. 16.)

Adam when two hundred and thirty years old, begat a son whom he called Seth, of a beautiful countenance, tall, and of a perfect stature like his father Adam. (Said Ibn-Bat. *Nasam al-j.*, p. 17.)

The Archontici say (S. Epiph. *Hares.* xl, 7), τὴν Δύναμιν σὺν τοῖς ὑπουργοῖς τοῦ ἀγαθοῦ Θεοῦ 'αγγέλο ις מלאכי השרת) καταβεβηκέναι καὶ ἡρπακέναι αὐτὸν τὸν Σήθ καὶ ἀνεγηνοκέναι ἄνω που κ. τ. λ.

4 Adam knowing in his own wisdom that this son would not, like Abel, seek after glory and kingdom, and that he would not be like Cain, eager after possessions, and a tiller of the ground—but that he would give himself to spiritual and intellectual pursuits—called him שֵׁת, Seth, because שֶׁמֶּמֶנוּ יִוָּשַׁת הָעוֹלָם he saw that the world would be founded on him. (R. Abarbanel, *Comm. in Pent.*, fol. 31.)

Seth was weaned when twelve years old, says Cedrenus (*Hist. Comp.* i, p. 16); and his face shone so brightly that they called him a god!

5 This chapter looks like a Christian version of the story of Lilith (לילית), a night owl, but also "lamia," a she devil, often mentioned in Rabbinical writings. Elias Levita (*Tishbi*, ed. Isn., su. 6, v), says, "one finds written that during the one hundred and thirty years Adam was separated from Eve, demons (שדים) visited him, conceived and bare him demons, unclean spirits and wicked sprites (מזיקין)."

And R. Eliezer adds, "When God created the first man alone, He said, 'It is not good for man to be alone.' He created for him a woman out of the earth whom He called Lilith, who bare him every day a hundred children, that were dispersed abroad among the lands, seas, mountains," etc. (Ben Syra in Buxtorf, Lex. v, p. 114, s. 1.)

And elsewhere we are told in agreement with such stories, that "Adam was driven from Paradise on the Sabbath-eve, down into the lowest of the seven earths (ארץ התחתונה) where he spent the whole Sabbath in terror and in utter darkness. But when he had repented of his sin God brought him up to (אדמה) the ground above that, where a light lighted the firmament of heaven, etc. As regards the inhabitants of that earth (Adamah) they are all Anakim of immense size, which the first man begat together with demons, spirits and Liliths (לילין) which Lilith bare unto him, when she overcame him against his will, during the one hundred and thirty years he was separated from Eve," etc. ('*Emeq hammelek*, fol. 179, quoted in Eisenmeng., vol. i, p. 459.)

6 Postquam factus est Adam annos dccccxxx, sciens quoniam dies ejus finiuntur dixit: Congregantur ad me omnes filii mei ut benedicam eos, antequam moriar—congregati sunt, et interrogaverunt eum: Quid tibi est pater, ut congregares nos? et quare jaces in lecto tuo? Et respondens Adam dixit: Filii mei, male mihi est doloribus. Et dixerunt ad eum omnes filii ejus: Quid est pater, male habere doloribus? Et respondit Adam et dixit: Audite me, filii mei, Quando fecit nos deus me et matrem vestram—posuit nos in Paradiso—dedit nobis Dominus Deus angelos duos ad custodiendos nos. Venit hora ut ascenderent angeli in conspectu Dei adorare. Statim invenit

locum adversarius diabolus dum absentes essent angeli; et seduxit diabolus matrem vestram, ut manducaret de arbore illicita et contradicta. Et manducavit et dedit mihi. Et statim iratus est nobis Dominus Deus et dixit ad me Dominus : Eo quod dereliquisti mandatum meum et verbum meum quod confortavi tibi non custodisti, ecce inducam in corpus tuum lxx plagas; diversis doloribus ab initio capitis et oculorum et aurium usque ad ungulas pedum, et per singula membra torquemini.

Quum vidisset eum flentem in magnis doloribus, cœpit ipsa flere, dicens : Domine Deus meus, in me transfer dolorem ejus, quoniam ego peccavi. Et dixit Eva ad Adam. Domine mi, da mihi partem dolorum tuorum, quoniam a me culpa hæc tibi accessit. (*Vita Adæ et Evæ*, p. 48, 49.)

7 "When Adam's death," says Eutychus, "drew near, he called his son Seth, Enos, the son of Seth, Cainan, the son of Enos, and Mahalaleel, the son of Cainan, and commanded them saying, 'Let this commandment be to your children. When I am dead embalm my body with myrrh, incense and cassia [or, cinnamon] and lay me in the Cave of Treasures. And whichever of your sons is living at the time of your leaving the borders of the garden (Paradise), let him take my body with him, and place it in the middle of the earth ; for from thence will come my salvation and that of all my children.'" (*Nazam al-j.*, p. 18.)

Adam, the first man created, having heard John discoursing of Christ in the region of darkness, said to Seth his son, "O my son, I desire thee to tell the ancestors of our race and the prophets, whither I send thee, when I fell sick unto death." Then Seth said, "Patriarchs and prophets hearken. My father Adam when he fell sick unto death, sent me to make a request unto God, close to the gates of Paradise, that He would guide me through the leading of an angel, to the Tree of Mercy (that is, of the oil of mercy) that I take some of the oil, and anoint my father, and raise him from his sickness. That, I have done.

"Then, after my prayer, the angel of the Lord coming to me, said, What is thy request, O Seth ? Thou askest for the oil that raises the sick, or for the tree whence that oil flows, for thy father's sickness. Thou canst not find it now. Go thy way, and tell thy father, that when five thousand five hundred years from the creation shall be fulfilled, the Only Begotten Son of God, shall come upon earth in a human body, and that He will anoint him with that oil ; and that He will wash him and his children (πλυνεῖ) with water and with the Holy Ghost ; and that thy father will then be cured of every disease. For the present, this is impossible. The patriarchs and prophets hearing this, rejoiced greatly." (*Evangel. Nicodemi* Græcè, c. xix, ed. Thilo.) The Latin copy, as given by Fabricius, *Cod. Apocr. V. T.*, vol. i, p. 278, which is followed by the A.-Saxon version (ed. Thwaites, Oxon, 1698) differs from the Greek in some respects. Sée also Cotel. *Pat. Apost.*, vol. i, p. 497, note.

8 Adam having in the six hundredth year, repented of his transgression, received by revelation through Uriel, who is set over those who repent,—a knowledge of the Watchers, of the Flood, and of other things to come. (Sync. *Chron.*, p. 18.) He died aged nine hundred and thirty, on the same day as that on which he had transgressed. Inasmuch as one thousand years are as one day among heavenly witnesses, as it was written on the Tree of Knowledge that he should die on the day he ate of its fruit, Adam did not complete the day of one thousand years, by seventy years, but died on that same day. (*Kufale*,

p. 19.) Adam also learnt of Uriel about the prayers sent up on high, day and night, by the whole creation, through Uriel who presides over repentance. At the first hour of the day—prayer in heaven; second hour—prayer of angels; third hour—of birds; fourth hour—of cattle; fifth hour—of wild beasts; sixth hour—angels attend, and set in order the whole creation; seventh hour —angels go into the presence of God, and come out thence; eighth hour— praises and offerings of angels; ninth hour—prayers and supplications of men; tenth hour—prayers of heavenly and earthly beings; eleventh hour—confession and rejoicings of all; twelfth hour—men's intercessions accepted by God. (Cedren. *Hist. Comp.*, p. 18; and M. Glycas, *Annal.*, p. 228; also Fabric., *Cod. Apoc. V. T.*, vol. i, p. 14, sq.)

9 After Seth, Adam begat nine more children. (*Kufale*, p. 16.) And when he died he left thirty-three sons and twenty-six daughters; having been chief of his kindred all the days of his life. (Syncell. *Chron.*, p. 19.)

10 All the time Adam lived, says Said Ibn-Batrik (Eutychus), was nine hundred and thirty years. He died on a Friday, in the fourteenth night from the new moon, being the sixth of Nisan, which is Barmudeh, at the ninth hour of that Friday. That is the hour at which he was driven from Paradise. When Adam was dead, his son Seth embalmed him, as he had commanded him. And Seth took his body up the mountain, and buried it in the Cave of Treasures. And they mourned over him forty days. (*Nazam al-j.*, p. 18.)

Et sicut prædixit Michael archangelus, post sex dies venit mors Adæ. Cum cognovisset Adam, quia hora venit mortis suæ, dixit ad omnes filios suos, Ecce sum annorum dcccxxx, et si mortuus fuero, sepelite me contra ortum dei magnum habitationibus. Et factum est eum finisset omnes sermones illius, tradidit spiritum. Et videt Seth manum domini extensam tenentem Adam. Et sepelierunt Adam et Abel, Michael et Urihel angeli in partibus paradisi, videntibus Seth et matre ejus et alio nemine. (*Vita Adæ et E.*, pp. 58 and 66.)

11 The Life [He who is Life—eternal life, also called Supreme Life, as distinguished from the second or lesser life—that of mortals], the Supreme Life having taken counsel, sent deliverance to Adam, from his body, and from this world of sorrow. Then his soul was severed from the body, to which it said, "Why do we tarry, in this foul body ? The Deliverer will come and set us free." Then the Deliverer came —touched Adam, and said to him : " Arise, O Adam, shake off thy foul body, house of clay, which the seven star-angels made for thee ; the Life sends me to fetch thee back to the place whence thou camest, where thy parents live." Hearing this, Adam began to weep, and said : "My father, if I go with thee, who will take care of this world—of Eve my wife—of the crops I have sown—of this house which I occupied—of the fruits of my garden ? Who will draw water from the Euphrates and from the Tigris to water my plants ? Who will bind the ox to the plough—put the seed in the earth— and gather in the harvest ? Who will befriend the orphan and the widow, clothe the naked, and set free the captive ?"

"Come, come," said the Deliverer to Adam ; " come, and put on thy garment of light, where the sun never sets ; wear on thy brow the crown of glory ; gird thyself with water wherein is no pain, and sit on the throne, made ready for thee by the Eternal Life," etc. "But Father," said Adam, "if I go with Thee who will take care of my body—wake it up where it lies, and give it food to eat, or shelter it from the storm—or keep the beasts of the field from devouring it, or the birds of the air from nestling themselves in the hair of my head," etc., etc. (*Cod. Nasar.*, pp. 140-142.)

12 Then the Messenger of Life came, took Eve away from an evil crowd, and put an end to her sorrow. She then fell upon her face before him and said, " Welcome art thou, O Lord; take me to Thy company above, and bring my soul out of this body." " I am come," said the Messenger of Life, " to fetch thee—thou shalt rest in light, and thy countenance shall shine for ever," etc. (*Cod. Nazar.*, iii, p. 166, sq.)

Post sex dies vero quod mortuus est Adam, cognoscens Eva mortem suam, congregavit omnes filios suos et filias suas, qui fuerunt Seth cum xxx fratribus et xxx sororibus, et dixit eis Eva : Audite me filii mei—dixit nobis Michael archangelus : propter prævaricationes vestras generi vestro *superinducet* dominus noster *iram judicii sui* primum per aquam, secundum per ignem; his duobus judicabit Dominus omne *humanum* genus.

Facite ergo, tabulas lapideas et alias tabulas luteas, et scribite in his omnem vitam meam et patris vestri quæ a nobis audistis et vidistis. Si per aquam judicabit genus nostrum, tabulæ de terra solventur et tabulæ lapideæ permanebunt si autem per ignem judicabit genus nostrum, tabulæ lapideæ solventur, et de terra luteæ decoquentur. Hæc omnia cum dixisset Eva filiis suis tradidit spiritum. Postea cum magno fletu sepelierunt eam—et cum essent lugentes quattuor dies tunc apparuit eis Michael archangelus dicens ad Seth : homo Dei, ne amplius lugeas mortuos tuos quam sex dies, quia septimo die signum resurrectionis est futuri seculi requies.—Tunc Seth fecit tabulas. (*Vita Adæ et E.*, pp. 58, 59, 66.)

13 After the death of Adam, the family of Seth severed itself from the family of Cain the accursed. For Seth, taking with him his firstborn son Enos, with Cainan the son of Enos, and Mahalaleel the son of Cainan, with their wives and children, led them up the mountain to the top, where he buried Adam. But Cain and all his children abode in the vale, where he had slain Abel. (Eutychus, *Nazam al-j.*, pp. 20, 21.)

But Cain, after many wanderings εἰς τόπον τινὰ Καϊνᾶν ὀνομαζόμενον ἦλθε, came to a certain place called Cainan, where he committed all manner of crimes, laying wait for way-faring men and putting them to death, and heaping up wealth untold from his spoils of them. (S. Eustath. Antioch, in *Hexaemeron*, fol. 749, ed. M.)

14 The children of Seth lived on that mountain in the practice of purity [or, of innocence], and were in the habit of hearing the voices of angels, from whom they were not far apart, and with whom they joined in worshipping and praising God; and they, with their wives and children were called " Sons of God." They did no work, neither sowed nor reaped ; but their food was fruits of trees. There was among them neither envy, injustice, nor lying ; and their bond (pledge or faith—*imânhum*) was, " No, by the blood of Abel." They went up to the top of the Holy mountain every day, and worshipped before God, and blessed themselves in the body of Adam. (Said Ibn-Bat.,*Nazam al-j.*, p. 21.)

15 Then when the death of Seth drew near, he adjured his children by the blood of Abel, that not one of them should go down from this holy mountain, and not to let one of their children go down to the children of Cain the accursed. All the time Seth lived was nine hundred and twelve years. (Said Ibn-B., *Nazam al-j.*, p. 21.)

16 R. Maimonides is not of the same

opinion; for he says not only that in the days of Enos men went far astray and the mind of thought of wise men became stupified, but that ואנוש מן עצמו הן חמועים Enos himself was among those who erred. [This, too, is far from Philo's distinction between Adam and Enos. *Quæst.* Armen. in Gen.] And the error, says Maimonides, was this, that they worshipped and honoured the heavenly bodies and built temples to them on high places, etc. [R. Maimonides seems to take Gen. iv, 26, "או הוחל לקרא ב" as other Hebrews do, to mean—then was the calling on the name of God profaned —and Targ. *Onkelos* חלו מלצלאח "ב men fell away from praying in the name of the Lord. Targ. *Jonathan*, "That was the age in whose days, men began to go astray, who made to themselves idols, and called them by the name of the Lord." But the LXX read: 'Ενώς, ούτος ήλπισεν έπικαλείσθαι τὸ ὄνομα κυρίου τοῦ Θεοῦ.] (R. Maimonides, *Halekot 'Avod. kokav*, etc. Opp., vol. i, fol. ed. Amst.)

R. Abarbanel, however, *Comm. in Pent.*, fol. 31, understands it to mean that in the days of Enos they began to pray in the name of God in all their works, because until then, Adam, Abel, and Set חיו משרים במציאות האל lived in intercourse with God who was present among them.

17 Cain, says Geo. Syncellus (*Chron.*, p. 19), died the same year as Adam (A.M. 930), killed by the stones of his house that fell upon him, λίθοις γάρ καὶ αὐτὸς τὸν 'Αβὶλ ἀνεῖλε—for himself had killed Abel with stones. The *Kufale*, whence this account is taken, adds: "that he was thus killed by righteous judgment; for it is decreed on the tables of heaven, that with what weapon a man slays another, with such also shall he be slain." (*Kufale*, p. 19, 20.) Cedrenus quotes this legend from the same source, at p. 16 of his *Hist. Compendium*, where he also says, that Abel having been righteous, his body ἀφανὶς γεγονέναι, disappeared [from the sight of man] in order to give those who came after him a good hope [of everlasting life].

18 Here follows in the Ethiopic text : " Then Lamech stood [or, remained] grieved for what he had done; the cattle went away from him into the open country, and he knew not what to do. But the narrative would be long [or, tedious]." Yet the Arabic original gives even a longer account, says Dr. Trumpp in his note—that Lamech lay there a long time, hungry and thirsty, not knowing whither to go, blind as he was. Then all his people turned out to look for him over hill and down dale; and at last found him lying on the ground, by the side of the two corpses; himself half-dead from hunger and thirst. So they brought him home; gathered the cattle together, and having covered Cain and the young shepherd in gay apparel, they buried them in the neighbourhood, as being the first of the Cainites that had died, and they mourned over them forty days and forty nights. Here, however, the Arabic adds also, "But the story would be [too] long."

In the three hundredth year of Enos, Cain the accursed, Adam's son, who had slain his brother Abel, was himself slain. For a seventh descendant from Cain, called Lamech who was a shepherd, shooting an arrow in play, hit his ancestor Cain through the heart and killed him. For Cain was bewildered and wandering in the open country, not being able to rest in any one place. (Eutych. *Nazam al-j.*, p. 22.)

R. S. Jarchi, in his *Comm.* on Gen. iv, 23, relates this story thus : "Lamech's wives had separated themselves from him, for his having slain

Cain, and Tubal-Cain his son. For Lamech was blind, and was led about by Tubal-Cain, who seeing Cain coming and looking like a wild beast, told Lamech his father, to bend his bow, wherewith he killed Cain. When Lamech found that it was Cain his ancestor, he struck his hands together; but Tubal-Cain's head happening to be between them, he also was killed by Lamech. On this account did Lamech's wives leave him. But he quieted them, saying, 'Hear ye my voice,'" etc. (*Comm. ad l.*, fol. 7, ed. Buxtf.) [The same story is also told in *Sepher ayashar*, *Shalsheleth akkabbala*, etc. See Eisenm. *Ent. Jud.*, vol. i, p. 471.]

Cedrenus and S. Ephrem (in Gen., vol. i, pp. 45 and 143) relate two traditions, in substance like the above account. It is also given in the Armenian *Desuthyun badmuthyants Asdw.* Survey of the histories of the books of Holy Scripture, vol. i, c. 2, p. 13, Cedrenus, however, gives another version of the story, and says "that Lamech committed two murders—of a man and of a child, both of whom were brothers of Enoch, who earnestly prayed God not to let him see such slaughter, and for that, was taken up into heaven." (*H. Comp.*, p. 15.)

Midrash Tankhuma (fol. 6) tells the story pretty much as it is in the Ethiopic; but adds that the little boy said to Lamech, "I see כמין חית something like a wild beast." Lamech shot an arrow and killed it. Then the boy seeing Cain with a horn on his forehead, lying dead, said, "O father, this beast is like a man with a horn on the forehead!" Then Lamech clapped his hands together, and so doing, killed the boy. He then went home and said to his wives, " I have slain a man to my wounding, and a young man to my hurt!" Adah and Zillah then said, they would no longer live with him; so that Lamech had to go with them to Adam for judgment.

19 Joseph B. Gorion, being in a certain island in the neighbourhood of India, "found there men like women, who lived on live fish, and who told him they had in their island the sepulchre of a very ancient king, called Kainan, son of Enos, who lived before the Flood, and ruled the whole world, spirits, demons, etc. In his wisdom he knew that God would bring a flood [and overwhelm the earth] in the days of Noah. Wherefore he wrote what was to happen after him on tables of stone; and lo they are there; ויכתוב את העתיד להיות מזח על לוחות אבן וחנם שם and the writing is in Hebrew. And he also wrote therein that in his days the ocean overwhelmed a third part of the world; and so it happened in the days of Enos, the son of Seth, son of Adam the first man." (*Jos. B. Gorion*, lib. ii, c. 18.) There seems to be some confusion between this legend and the one told in a note on Cainan, son of Arphaxad, to which the reader may refer.

20 When the death of Cainan drew near, he called Mahalaleel and adjured him by the blood of Abel, not to let one of his children go down from the mountain to the children of Cain the accursed. All the days of Cainan were nine hundred and ten. (Eutych., *Nazam al-j.* p. 22.)

21 This word is of Arabic origin, and is either for the collect, pl. *jinnun* genii, pl. of *junnun*, a demon, devil; or, it may stand for *junnun*, folly, etc. Anyhow, the "j" being pronounced and transcribed "g" by the Ethiopic translator, shows that the work was done not far from Egypt, where "j" is pronounced "g" hard.

According to Targ. *Jonathan*, in Gen. v, Lamech had three sons, Jabel and Tubal, sons of Adah; and Tubal-Cain and his sister Na'amah, children of Zillah. One account says that the young shepherd slain by Lamech, was

Zillah's son; and that for that reason she and Adah would no longer live with him. Jenun or Genun, might then be for Tubal-Cain.

22 Abulpharaj, however (*Dyn.* Arab., pp. 8, 9) says that, the daughters of Cain were reported to have first made instruments of music and sung to them: wherefore a *song* is called *quinto* in Syriac, and in Arabic *quaīnah* means a singing girl.

Cain, says S. Eustath. Antioch (in *Hexaëmeron*,) invented μίτρα καὶ σταθμούς, καὶ ὅρους, measures, weights and the division of land, and the building of cities.

23 Meanwhile the children of Cain played on instruments of music, until the sound and clamour of them, reached unto the top of the Holy mountain. Then a hundred men of the children of Seth gathered together to go down to the children of Cain the accursed. Jared then adjured them by the blood of Abel, not to go down from the Holy mountain; but they would not hearken to him, and went down. And when they were come down and saw the daughters of Cain the accursed, those sons of Seth committed adultery with them, and perished in consequence. Of these adulteries giants were born. (Eutych. *Nazam al-j.*, pp. 25, 26.)

24 Then Enoch the scribe said to the Watchers, who had left heaven, and had defiled themselves with women, after the manner of men: "I have written your petition [to the Most High], but in my vision I have seen that it will not be granted you; judgment has been passed on you, and ye shall not be. And from henceforth, ye shall not go up into heaven, so long as the world endures; for it has been decreed that ye shall be bound in the earth, all the days of the world.

"But before this, ye shall behold the destruction of your beloved children; ye shall not possess them, but they shall fall before you by the sword. And ye shall pray for them, but your prayer shall not be heard," etc. (*Book of Enoch*, c. xii—xiv, pp. 7, 8, 9.)

It was in the four hundredth year of Jared, that the Watchers [ἐγρήγορες] went down the Holy mountain and begat giants of the daughters of Cain. These giants not only were of immense size and awful to look at, and given to all manner of wickedness, but they also invented weapons of war, magic, dyeing stuffs, musical instruments, etc., as taught by Azael, one of their chiefs. But αὐτοὺς δρακοντόποδάς τινες προσηγόρευσαν, some say they were dragons (or, serpents) with feet; because in waging war against the children of Seth who were above on the mountain, they had to creep on their hands and feet, lying flat on the ground, etc. (Cedren. *Hist. Comp.*, p. 18.)

25 But when the sons of Seth who had gone down to the daughters of Cain the accursed, wished to ascend the Holy mountain, the stones of the mountain were made fire, so that they could find no means of again going up the mountain. Then after these, companies after companies went down from the Holy mountain to the daughters of Cain the accursed. (Entych. *Nazam al-j.*, p. 26.)

26 R. Abarbanel (Quæst. vi, Comm. in Pent., fol. 31) says that "sons of God," is explained to mean, kings, princes or judges, skilled in knowledge and endued with power—or men possessed of divine knowledge; and that the Nephilim [said by some to be the same as the Anakim] were so called from their fall from heaven (נפל) into sin, on earth.

27 And it happened in a certain year of this Jubilee (twenty-fifth) that angels of God saw the daughters of men that they were fair, and took them

to wives who bare them giants, etc. (*Kufale*, c. v, p. 20.)

After the death of Adam, Seth ruled the race of men then living. Then two hundred of his children called Watchers, in the one thousandth year of the world, four hundredth of Jared, and seven hundred and seventieth of Seth, having gone astray went down from the mountain, and took to themselves wives, who bare them giants, as Scripture says. As some doubt this, adds Syncellus, I will bring proofs of it from the Book of Enoch, Moses and S. Peter the chief of the Apostles. (*Chron.*, p. 19 ; *Bar. Hebr.*, pp. 4, 5 ; Abulphar. *Dyn.* Arab., pp. 8.)

Concerning the Watchers (from the Ethiopic *Book of Enoch*, sect. ii, c. 7).

"And it happened when the children of men multiplied in those days, that daughters were born unto them fair and beautiful. And angels, sons of heaven saw them, and desiring them, said among themselves : 'Come let us choose for us wives from among the daughters of men, and beget children for ourselves.' Then Samyaza, chief among them, said : 'I fear lest ye will not do this thing, so that the whole retribution of this sin fall upon me.' And they all answered : 'We will swear with an oath and bind one another with curses, that we will not turn from this deed, but do it amain.' They then swore and bound themselves together with curses, for this thing. And they were two hundred. Then they came down to Ardis, which is on the top of Mount Hermon, and called it Hermon by reason of the oaths and curses wherewith they had bound themselves [חרמון, חרם] And these are the names of their chiefs :

1. Samyaza, chief of all.
2. Urakibarameel.
3. Akibeel.
4. Thamiel.
5. Ramuel.
6. Dan'el.
7. Ezekeel.
8. Sarakuyal.
9. Asael.
10. Armars.
11. Bathraal.
12. Anani.
13. Zakebe.
14. Samsaweel.
15. Sartael.
16. Thurael.
17. Yumyael.
18. Arazyal.

"These were the captains of the two hundred, and the rest were with them. Every one chose a wife for himself, who taught him sorcery, divination, etc.; and they brought forth giants, whose stature was three hundred cubits, and who injured all creatures, devoured men and committed such sins as reached unto heaven. Then Michael, Raphael, Gabriel, Suryal, and Uriel looking down upon the blood shed on the earth, addressed the Most High, on behalf of men, etc. (c. 8.)

"These angels of God, with whom He was angry, for their having thus fallen, did the Lord command us, says the Angel of the Face, to bind into the depths of the earth until the Day of Judgment." (*Kufale*, c. v, p. 21.)

And Syncellus adds from Zosimus of Panopolis, in his book Imuth—that these fallen angels taught secret arts, and that the first book on the subject was called χημεῦ, ἔνθεν καὶ ἡ τέχνη χημεία καλεῖται, whence the art is called *chemia*=chemistry. (*Chron.*, p. 24.)

28 But when the death of Jared drew near, he called unto him his son Enoch and Methuselah the son of Enoch, and Lamech the son of Methuselah, and Noah the son of Lamech, and said unto them: "See that not one of you go down from this Holy mountain; for your sons have erred and have perished. And I know that God, powerful and glorious, will not leave you on this Holy mountain. Therefore whosoever of you shall go out of this place, let him take with him the body of Adam, and these gifts, and place them wherever God shall tell him." And all the days Jared lived was 962 years. He died when Noah

was 206 years old, on a Friday about sunset, the third day of Adar, which is Barmahat. Then his son Methuselah, Lamech and Noah embalmed him and laid him in the Cave of Treasures, and mourned for him forty days. (Eutych. *Nazam. al-j.*, pp. 29-32.)

29 Then the Most High spake and sent Arsyalalyur to the son of Lamech, and said unto him: "Tell (him) in My Name: hide thyself. And reveal unto him the destruction of all flesh by the waters of the Flood, that will come over all the earth, and destroy all that is in it. And teach him how he may save himself and establish his seed in the whole earth."

Then He sent Raphael to bind Azazeel in the lowest pit, until the Day of Judgment; Gabriel and Michael to punish the wicked inhabitants of the earth.—Let all flesh perish. Then after it has been cleansed, vines shall be planted and bear fruit.—Peace and righteousness shall reign therein, and all the sons of men shall be righteous, and all nations shall bless Me and do Me service, etc. (*Book of Enoch*, c. x, p. 5, 6, 7.)

These are the names of the holy angels who watch.

Uriel, one of the holy angels—over thunder and terror.

Raphael, one of the holy angels—over the spirits of men.

Raguel, one of the holy angels—over the punishment (restraint) of the world and luminaries.

Michael, one of the holy angels—over the good done to men, gives orders to the nations.

Sarakiel, one of the holy angels—over the spirits of men, whose spirits have transgressed.

Gabriel, one of the holy angels—over Akist (?) Paradise and the Cherubim. (*Book of Enoch*, c. xx, p. 13.)

30 According to *Midrash Tankhuma*, fol. 6, ever since God's curse upon the earth, on account of Adam's transgression, the ground never yielded the seed sown; but אלא חיו זירעין חמים וקיצרין קוצים when they sowed wheat they reaped thorns and thistles. Therefore did Lamech say, Noah should "comfort them concerning their work;" for after Noah's birth they reaped what they sowed; wheat if they sowed wheat, barley if they sowed barley.

31 I Enoch, scribe of righteousness, alone of all the children of men, have seen a vision of the end of all things (*Book of Enoch*, c. xix, p. 13), and have received a portion of everlasting life. They were a hundred and three parables which I took up to tell those who dwell on the earth. (c. vi, p. 20.)

In the Coran, sur. xix, and elsewhere Enoch is praised as *Edris*, the name given him by Arabic writers. He is so called probably from *darasa* דרס, on account of his skill in writing and of his learning. (See Hotting. *Hist. Or.*, p. 31, sq.; and Maracci., *Alcor.*, p. 435.)

Enoch was the first among men who taught writing, science and wisdom of all sorts. He wrote about the signs of heaven, years, months, etc., and gave laws. He also received visions of all that is to happen until the Day of Judgment. (*Kufale*, c. iv, p. 17.)

The ancient Greeks, says Abulpharaj (*Dyn.* Arab., p. 9), thought Enoch was Hermes Trismegistus, so called for the three great sciences he taught concerning the three qualities inherent in God: (1) His existence; (2) His wisdom; and (3) His eternal life. The Arabs call him Edris. The Sabians say that he got his wisdom from Agathodemon, that is Seth, the son of Adam; and others think also that Esculapius was a disciple of his, who grieved so much at Enoch's departure from this world, that he raised a statue of him which was worshipped after the Flood! etc.

As to the Book of Enoch, that contains Jude 14, 15, known to Syncellus who gives extracts from it, and to several of the Fathers, but lost sight of for centuries—it was discovered by Bruce in Abyssinia, written in Ethiopic, several copies of which he brought to Europe. It consists in visions of Paradise, of the coming of the Beloved, of the Flood, and of the end of the world. It is full of excellent sentiments and pious lore, dating probably from a little before the coming of Christ.

Enoch received thirty leaves of writing from heaven, as Adam had received thirty-one and Seth twenty-nine. (Masudi i, c. iii, p. 73.)

Οὗτος πρῶτος γράμματα μανθάνει καὶ διδάσκει, καὶ θείων μυστηρίων ἀποκαλύψεως ἀξιοῦται. (Cedren. Hist. Comp., p. 17.) Adam is also said to have written a thousand leaves on the property of plants, climate, etc. (See Quatremère's *Agricultura Nabathæorum*, quoted in Chwolson's *Die Ssabier*, i, pp. 706, 708.

32 I then inquired of the Angel of Peace who was going about with me: "For whom are the instruments I see prepared?" And he said : "For the host of Azazeel, to be delivered to the [or, cast under] the lowest condemnation—Michael, Gabriel, Raphael, and Phanuel shall be strengthened at that time—when the Lord of Spirits sends forth chastisement—then shall the stores of waters that are above the heavens burst open, on the fountains of water that are on the earth and under the earth. Those waters shall then mix together as it were in union, and shall blot out all that is in the earth, unto the borders of heaven. Thus shall they be made to know the iniquity they have committed in the earth; and thus shall they be punished." (*Book of Enoch*, c. lix., p. 30.)

"And now Methuselah my son," said Enoch, "I have made known unto thee all [that Uriel told me concerning the seasons, days, years and stars of heaven]. Keep, O Methuselah my son, the books of [me] thy father, that thou mayest transmit them to generations in the world. I have given wisdom to thee and to thy children, and to the children thou shalt have, that they may give it to those that are to come for ever. (c. lxxxii, p. 57.)

"I have made known to thee, Methuselah my son, all that I saw before thy birth; now listen to another vision I have had. As I was in the house of Mahalaleel, my father-in-law, I saw heaven fall upon the earth. And as it fell, the earth was suspended in a great abyss, mountains upon mountains, hills upon hills, great trees were wrenched off their roots [trunks] and were thrown in a heap into the abyss. And I cried, The earth is destroyed ! Mahalaleel heard my cry. I told him the vision. My son, said he, the earth will be destroyed, in a great overthrow because of the sins of men. Now then, arise, and pray the Lord that a remnant be left," etc. (c. lxxxiii, pp. 59, 60.)

33 "And now, Methuselah my son," said Enoch, "call together all thy brothers and all thy mother's sons—for a voice calls me ; and my spirit within me is troubled, to make known unto you all that shall ever happen to you." Then Methuselah brought them to Enoch, who said to all his righteous children : "Hear, O my children, the words of your father—my beloved: Love righteousness, and walk therein. Approach not right [or, integrity] with a double heart, and make no fellowship with double-hearted men. But walk in righteousness, O my children ; for it will lead you in good paths. And let righteousness be your companion.— Hearken unto me, therefore, O my children : Walk in the ways of right-

eousness, and avoid those of violence; for those who walk therein shall perish for ever." (*Book of Enoch*, xci, pp. 74, 75.)

34 "After that—I went up to heaven," says Enoch, " and I saw the sons of holy angels treading on flame of fire, whose garments were white and their faces brilliant like [hail] crystal. And I saw two rivers of fire, like unto hyacinth; and I then fell on my face before the Lord of Spirits. But Michael took me by the hand and raised me up. —But I fell again on my face, my flesh was dissolved, and my spirit was changed; and I cried with a loud voice and great spirit, I blessed, and praised, and extolled. And what I did was acceptable to the Ancient of Days— who came with Michael, Gabriel, Raphael, and Phanuel, and thousands of angels—one of which came to me and said: Thou art the son of a man, born for righteousness; righteousness has rested on thee, and the righteousness of the Ancient of Days shall not forsake thee. And the angel said to me: He will give thee peace in His name for ever—and it shall be so unto thee for ever and ever.—Thus shall be length of days with this son of sons of men, and peace shall be to the righteous ; His right path shall be to them [to follow] in the name of the Lord of Spirits, for ever." (*Book of Enoch*, c. lxxi, pp. 45, 46.)

Sed et Enoch sine circumcisione placens Deo, cum esset homo, Dei legatione ad Angelos jungebatur, et translatus est. (S. Irenæus, *Hæres.*, lib. iv, c. 30. See also Fabric. *Cod. Apoc. V. T.*, vol. i, p. 160, sq. for other authorities.)

NOTES TO BOOK III.

1 After a time, said Enoch, my son Methuselah, took for his son Lamech, a wife who bare him a son, whose body was white like hoar-frost, and red like the blossom of a rose; the hair of his head was white as wool, and as long ; he had beautiful eyes, that shone like the sun, and lighted up the whole house, when he opened them. No sooner did he leave the hands of the midwife, than he began to speak to the Lord in righteousness.

Then Lamech his father was afraid of him, and running, came to his father Methuselah, and said unto him: " A son is born unto me, strange and unlike other children of men, but like a child of angels of heaven; his nature [creation] is different, and is not like us. His eyes are like the rays [feet] of the sun ; his countenance glorious ; and, altogether, he looks as if not born of me, but rather of angels; and I am afraid some wonder will be wrought on the earth in his days. I beseech thee, go and inquire of Enoch, who is in heaven, concerning him."

Methuselah then came and found me at the end of the earth, and told me what had happened.

Then I, Enoch, said to him, that in the days of that child a great flood would destroy the earth, and all the inhabitants thereof, except that one and his three sons, whose children should beget giants, not spiritual, but carnal, etc. And tell Lamech that his son's name shall be Noah; because he shall be the one of you that shall be left after you, etc. (*Book of Enoch*, c. cv, p. 87, 88.) [Eth. *nuah*, long. The Hebrew etymology is given further on.]

2 Noah was 600 years old, when Methuselah died aged 969 years on a Friday, about mid-day, the twenty-first of Ilul, which is Tbut. Then Noah and Shem embalmed him and laid him in the Cave of Treasures, and mourned for him forty days. There was now no one left on the Holy mountain, but only Noah with his wife, whose name was Haikal, daughter of Namusa, Enoch's son, and his three sons, Shem, Ham, and Japhet, with their wives, who were of the daughters of Methuselah. Shem's wife was called Salit; Ham's wife, Nahlat; and Japhet's wife, Arisisah.

But when iniquity increased on the earth through the intercourse of the children of Seth with those of Cain the accursed, and they committed all manner of wickedness and took to all sorts of amusements, God made known to Noah, saying, I shall send the Flood over the earth and destroy everything in it. And He commanded Noah to come down the Holy mountain, and to build a ship, of square timber (some say of the wood of the Indian plane-tree), three hundred yards long, fifty broad, and thirty high, lined with pitch and bitumen both in and out, with three stories; the lower for four-footed beasts, the middle for birds, and the upper for himself and his family, with a door [opening or window] on the eastern side, with cisterns for water, and places for food. (Eutych. *Nasam al-j.*, pp. 34, 37.)

3 Philo, *Quaest.*, c. ii, p. 5, Armen. in Gen., compares the ark to the human body, after whose pattern he thinks it was made. It seems that both S. Augustine (*Contra. Faust.*, l. xii, c. 39) and S. Ambrose (*Hexaëmer.* l. vi. c. 9) were of the same opinion, which they borrowed from Philo.

4 And God commanded Noah to make a bell (*nāgus*, a flat piece of wood, suspended and beaten with a wooden clapper, commonly used in the east, to call to prayer) three yards long, of the wood of the Indian plane (*sāj*), a yard and a half broad, with a clapper of the same wood. And that Noah should beat it three times a day; in the morning, to gather men to their work; again at noon at the hour of dinner; and again in the evening, at the time of parting. "And when they hear thee," said God to Noah, "beating the bell, and they ask thee saying: What is it thou art doing? Tell them, God is about to send a flood." (Eutych. *Nasam al-j.*, p. 73.)

It is evident that Eutychus borrowed his information from the Arabic copy of this book; for he mentions the *sāj* "Indian plane," or teak tree; the wood of which Noah is said to have built the ark, because it does not rot [or, is not attacked by worms], but is passed over by the Ethiopic translator, who probably did not understand the term, as suggested by Dr. Trumpp, for he hereby rendered it "ebony."

Dionysius Bar Salibi in his *Pushoqo d'qurovo*, or "Exposition of the Liturgy," ch. iv, asks whence comes *noqusho*, the wooden clapper or bell beaten to call people to church, or the small brass bell rung, during the service: "We answer," says he, "that it is written in many histories, that when God commanded Noah to build the ark, He also told him to make a bell; which was beaten in the morning to gather workmen to their work at the ark; then at noon, for them to enjoy their meal; and again in the evening, for them to rest from their work." (Asseman, *Bibl. Or.*, vol. ii, p. 179.)

5 God raised Noah a preacher of righteousness in those days; whose words were hard (i.e., as clear) as torches. He said to them: "Repent, or the Flood will overwhelm you." But they laughed at him—That old man of the ark! and said: "A flood! whence will it come? If it is of fire, we have a thing called עליתה, Alitha, that will save us from it. If it is a flood of waters, from the earth, we have iron plates [or, hoes] wherewith to dig; and if it comes from the heaven, we have a thing called עקוב, a sponge, to souk it up." Then he said to them: "It will come from between the soles of your feet." [With a play on עקב or עקוב a sponge, and עקב sole or heel, of the foot, etc.] Talmud Bab., Sanhedr., p. 216.

6 According to the Talmud and to Jewish Rabbis, Og, king of Baahan, was one of these giants who had escaped drowning in the Flood, by being shut up in a box with a unicorn, or by sitting on the top of the ark, and fed by Noah. (Targ. Jonathan in Gen. xiv.) Others say he was the same Eliezer, Abraham's servant, whom he used to cover with the palm of his hand, etc. But in the Targum of Jonathan B. Uzziel, on Numb. xxi, 36, we read that: Og seeing the camp of the Israelites three miles long, went and fetched a mountain of that size, to throw it upon the camp. Upon which the Word of God מן יד זמין זחלא prepared at once a snail [or, worm] that ate a hole through the mountain; so that Og's head passed through it [the mountain resting on his shoulders]. He then tried to get it out: but his teeth having grown on each side of his mouth, he could not do so. Moses then took a hatchet ten cubits long, and smote him in the heel, etc.

7 It is said in the Law that Sons of God (called Beni Elohim), when they looked upon the beautiful daughters of Cain, came down to them; whence giants were born. But he errs, and knows not what he is saying, who tells us that angels came down to daughters of men (lit. of the flesh). But they were the sons of Seth who came down from the Holy mountain to the daughters of Cain the accursed, for the sons of Seth were called Beni Elohim, or sons of God, by reason of their purity, and so long as they dwelt on the Holy mountain. They err then, who say that angels came down to the daughters of men (lit. of the flesh); for the essence of angels is simple [or, single] and their nature is in no need of marriage. Man, however, is composite in his nature, who requires marriage, like other animals. If angels had intercourse with daughters of men, not one of them would remain a virgin. (Eutych. Nazam al-j., p. 26.)

8 God commanded Noah to make a ship, and when it was finished, Gabriel brought the coffin containing the bones of Adam, which was laid in the ark. (Masudi i, ch. iii, p. 74.)

Eutychus puts the following words in the mouth of Lamech, who, when dying, in the five hundred and fifty-ninth year of Noah, said unto him: "God, the mighty and glorious, will not leave thee on this mountain. When, therefore, thou shalt go down, take with thee the body of Adam, and bring with thee the three offerings, namely, the gold, the myrrh, and the incense. Then command thy son that after thy death he take the body of our father Adam, and lay it in the middle of the earth.

"Then appoint from among thy sons one man to minister there; a man devoted to God all the days of his life; without a wife; who shall shed no blood, and bring no offering, neither bird nor beast, but only bread and wine; for from thence shall come the salvation of Adam [or, of man]. His raiment shall be of the skin of wild beasts; he shall not shave his hair, neither pare his nails; but remain alone; for he shall be called priest of God, that is, Melchizedec." After giving these commandments to his son Noah, Lamech died on a Sunday, at sunset, the nineteenth of Adar, which is Barmahat; Noah then embalmed him, and laid him in the Cave of Treasures, and they mourned for him forty days. (Eutych. *Nazam al-j.*, p. 33.)

9 The apocryphal history of Melchizedec found among the writings of S. Athanasius (vol. ii, p. 7, sq.) tells us that "there was a queen of Salem whose son was called Salaad." This Salaad had a son called Melchi, and Melchi having married a wife called Salem, had by her two sons, Melchi and Melchizedec.

Melchizedec, who was an idolater, was brought to the knowledge of the true God, by beholding the starry heavens and the works of nature. He then renounced his idols; and, leaving his home to avoid the sacrifice of his brother to the seven planets, went up Mount Tabor, where he prayed God to destroy all those who had slain and sacrificed his brother to idols. Upon this the earth suddenly opened, and swallowed up the whole of Melchizedec's family. Therefore is he said to be ἀπάτωρ, ἀμήτωρ, ἀγινεαλόγητος. He then continued seven years to live in a thick forest on Mount Tabor, almost naked, until his back became ὡσεὶ δέρμα χελώνης, like the back of a tortoise.

Then Abraham went to fetch him; pared his nails, and clothed him in pontifical vestments. Melchizedec then blessed Abraham, and gave him ποτήριον ἄκρατον καὶ κλάσμα ἄρτου καὶ τῷ λαῷ αὐτοῦ τιη, a cup of pure wine and a morsel of bread, to him and to the three hundred and eighteen men who were with him. This is the figure of the holy Eucharist, and of the three hundred and eighteen fathers assembled at the Council of Nicæa. Melchizedec also is taken for the Son of God, but not εἰς τὴν χάριν, as to spiritual gifts.

Gregory of Dathev, a celebrated Armenian divine of the fourteenth century, seems to have known this tradition. In his book (*Kirk hartsmants*, c. xvii, p. 300, ed. Const.) he says: "Melchizedec's father was called Melchi, and his mother, Sala; and they dwelt at Salem. From his birth he was consecrated to idols; but he was carried away by an angel to Mount Tabor, and fed there, until he was grown up. One day a cloud descended upon the mountain, and a hand stretched out of the cloud, ordained him priest saying: "Melchizedec, without father, mother or kindred, and like unto the Son of God;" because having been taken from his parents when quite a child, he had grown unlike them, not knowing them, and unknown to them. His dwelling was on Mount Golgotha where he sowed wheat with his own hands and made his own wine. So that when Abraham met him, he brought out to him some unleavened bread still warm, and some wine; a figure of the Lord's Supper.

"But why does S. Ephrem in his writings, say that Melchizedec was Shem?" asks Gregory. And he answers: "He had not two names neither is he a different person. But Irinos (Irenæus?) gives the reason which is difficult to understand. Noah blessed Shem, but Shem had no son like himself to bless. Abraham, however, was of the family of Shem, and worthy of a blessing. But Shem was not then living, to bless him; and Terah could not bless. So Melchizedec took Shem's place and did what Shem would have done, he blessed Abraham, and was called Shem."

The passage in S. Ephræm (Opp. Syr., vol. i, c. xiii, p. 60) runs thus: "Melchizedec was Shem. He was king by reason of his power as the head of fourteen tribes. He was also priest, having received the priesthood in due order [or, course b'γυσσίο] from Noah. Not only was he living in the days of Abraham, but he also saw Jacob and Esau, and was consulted by Rebecca, as to the children she was then bearing. To this S. Chrysostom (*Hom.* xxxv in Gen.) says that Melchizedec was ἴσως αὐτοχειροτόνητος οὕτω γὰρ ἦσαν τότε οἱ ἱερεῖς, perhaps self-ordained as priests were in those days; or by reason of his old age; or, may be, he had practised the offering of sacrifices like Abel, Noah, Abraham, etc. Marcus Eremita (*Opusc.* x, de Melchizedec), borrows from S. Athanasius, and agrees with his account, of the three hundred and eighteen men who were with Abraham, that they were a figure of the three hundred and eighteen patriarchs, who on Christ's side, ἐν τῇ Νικαίων πόλει ἀποστολικῶς ὁπλισάμενοι ἐτροπώσαντο τὰς αἱρέσεις, and in apostolic armour, put to flight heresies, when assembled at Nicæa. And so also wrote S. Ambrose. (Comp. *de Fide* lib. i, prolog. and *de Patr. Abrahamo*, lib. i, c. 3.)

10 R. Meir O. Gabbai, in *Avod. haqqodesh* iii, fol. 80 (quoted in Eisenm. vol. i, p. 318) found in the Midrash that R. Jukhanan taught, that God took Shem the son of Noah, and וְהִפְרִישׁוֹ לְכֹהֵן עֶלְיוֹן לְשָׁרְתוֹ set him apart for Priest of the Most High, to minister before His Shekinah; and then changed his name to Melchizedec; and that his brother Japhet had learnt the law in his school. And R. Bekhai (*Biur.* fol. 24) says of Melchizedec, king of Salem,

זֶה שֵׁם בֶּן נֹחַ " he is Shem, the son of Noah."

Tradunt Hebræi hunc esse Sem, primum filium Noe, et eo tempore quo ortus est Abraham, habuisse antiquitatis annos ccxc. Nec esse novum si Melchizedech victori Abraham obviam processerit—et benedixerit ei quod ab nepote suo jure paternitatis dederit, etc. Salem etiam, Hierusalem esse plurimi arbitrantur, quod absurdum est. Non enim invia Abrahæ Hierusalem erat, sed oppidum in metropoli Sichem, dequa in Evangelio legimus. (S. Ambrose in *Epist. ad Hebr.*, c. vii.)

See *Apophthegmata Patrum*, c. viii, in *Eccles. Græc. Monumenta*, ed. Coteler, vol. i, p. 423, for an account of a monk of the desert who believed Melchizedec to have been the Son of God. The matter was referred to S. Cyril of Alex. who rebuked him for it. Meanwhile the monk had a revelation of all the patriarchs from Adam; when he saw that Melchizedec was indeed a man. (For the sect of the Melchizedekians, see S. Epiph. *Hæres.* xxxv, vol. i; and J. Damascen, *Hæres.* lv. in Cotel. *Eccl. Græc. Mon.* vol. i, p. 295.)

11 Then Noah went into the Cave of Treasures and embraced the body of Seth, of Enos, of Cainan, of Mahalaleel, of Jared, of Methuselah and of Lamech. Then he took the body of Adam, and also the offerings: Shem carried the gold, Ham the myrrh, and Japhet the incense. (Eutych. *Nazam al-j.*, p. 37.)

12 And as they came down the Holy mountain, they lifted up their eyes and wept, saying: "Farewell (lit. peace on thee) O thou sacred Paradise!" Then they kissed the stones and embraced the trees of the Holy mountain and came down. (Eutych. *Nazam al-j.*, p. 37.)

13 Then Noah went into the ark, he, his wife, his sons and their wives, and Noah carried the body of Adam and laid it in the middle of the ark, and the

offerings (of gold, incense and myrrh) upon it. Then he and his sons occupied the eastern side of the ark, and his wife and his sons' wives, the western side; lest they should come together. (Eutych. *Nazam al-j.*, p. 38.)

14 And God said unto Noah: "Fasten into the ark precious stones and pearls, to lighten you up as in mid-day." (Talmud Bab. *Sanhedr.*, p. 176.)

And God said to Noah: "Go to Phison, and choose from thence a precious stone [יוהרא, Pers. *juwar*, a 'gem,' also a 'pearl'] and fix it in the ark, in order to give you light." (Targ. *Jonathan* in Gen. vii.)

15 In *Bereshith Rabbah* (ad loc.) we are told that Mount Gerizim was not covered with the waters of the Flood; because it is but a small mountain; and only the highest mountains are said to have been covered! S. Eustathius Antiochenus, however, mentions in his *Hexaëmeron* (col. 752, ed. M.) that petrified shells and fishes were found on the top of Mount Lebanon, in proof that the waters of the flood had reached and covered the highest summits of that chain.

16 On the seventeenth day of Ilul, which is Thut, the seventh month (according to the reckoning of the Christians of Egypt), the ark rested on the mountains of Ararat, that is Djebel el-Djudi, near Mosul, in the country of Diarabia, near a town called Korda; but it is now called the land of Thamanim and Djezire Ben Omar. (Eutych. *Nazam al-j.*, p. 41.)

Quotations from the Assyrian accounts of the Flood, as well as from the Pehlevi Bundehesh [or, Creation] would be out of place here. But they are well worth the study of all who take interest in these matters.

The mountain on which the ark rested, is generally called Mount Ararat. But "Ararat" is the name of one of the provinces of Armenia, and is the Hebrew term for Armenia. The Armenians themselves, call that mountain Mount Masis. (See for a learned treatise on this subject, and for the many names of the mountain, Injidjean, *Armen. Geogr.*, vol. i, p. 54, sq.)

17 From the day this world was destroyed by fire, to the day it was destroyed by water, 100,000 years elapsed. Then 8000 years later, a voice came to me: "Build an ark." He then got builders, and cut cedars in Haran and in Lebanon, and was three hundred years building the ark, three hundred yards long, fifty broad, and thirty in height; wherein he gathered animals of all kinds, male and female. Then the fountains of heaven and earth broke forth—and the ark after floating on the waters eleven months, rested on the mountains of Kardun. [*Kardu*, Targ. *Onk. Carduæi M.* in Ararat.] Then Noah sent forth a raven, saying to it: "Go and see if the flood has abated." The raven went, found a carcase on which it began to feed, and forgot Noah's order. Then Noah sent forth a dove, saying to it: "Go and see if the flood is assuaged, and where the raven is I sent forth before thee." The dove went forth, found the raven feeding on a carcase; and then brought back a branch of olive to Noah, who then knew that the flood had abated. Then Noah cursed the raven, but blessed the dove. Thus was the race of his son Shem and of his wife Nuraito preserved; and by them was the earth peopled, etc. (*Cod. Nasar.* iii, p. 72.)

Bar. Hebræus *Syr.* (p. 7) says that the ark rested at Apamæa, chief city of Pisidia [of which there exists coins with the ark and the dove. Bryant. *Anc. Myth.*, vol. iii, p. 47, sq.]; but Bar. Hebræus *Arab.*, says, with the Targum, *Cod. Nasar.*, and the Coran, that it rested on Mount Kardu, or Juda [now called Dshudi] of Ararat or

Armenia. [This agrees with Scripture; and seems most likely, from the situation of those mountains as regards the plain at Shinar—Sinjar—where the first families settled after the Flood. The *Kufale* calls Lubar the mountain on which the ark rested ; and the Samaritan Pentateuch (Gen. viii, 4) says it rested in Serandib, or Ceylon.]

18 The dove is a figure of the Holy Ghost, says S. Ephrem (vol. i, p. 149.) Her finding no resting place for her foot, the first time, represents the wickedness of men's manners among which the Holy Ghost finds no resting place. The second time the dove went forth, figures the coming of Christ, and the shedding forth of the Holy Ghost ; while the olive branch is an emblem of our reconciliation with God the Father. The raven is of the devil. [See the original for a very fair explanation of the rainbow.]

19 Cedrenus alluding to the floods of Ogyges in Attica and of Deucalion in Thessaly says, that the Egyptians made mention of the flood of Deucalion, declaring that it had not reached them ; and rightly too, says Cedrenus τοπικὸς γὰρ γέγονεν οὗτος ὁ κατακλυσμός ·τὸν γὰρ πρότερον ἤτοι τὸν καθολικὸν κατακλυσμὸν οὐδὲ γινώσκουσιν· for that flood was local ; and they could have no knowledge of the universal deluge, for their ancestor was not yet born. For Ham, son of Noah, was father of Mitsraim, whence are the Egyptians. (*Hist. Comp.*, p. 26.)

One shows still on Mount Djudi the spot on which the ark rested, says Masudi [but so do Armenians the same, on Mount Masis, or Ararat]. Then the earth was commanded to absorb the waters; some portions of the earth were slow at obeying God, other portions did so at once. Those that obeyed, yield fresh water when dug ; the disobedient, were punished by God, by remaining salt. So that the seas are the remnant of the waters in which the families [of the earth] perished. (Masudi i, c. iii, p. 75.)

And on the seventh month, Nisan, the ark rested on the mountains of Kadron ; the name of one mountain is Kardania, and of the other, Armenia ; and there was the city of Armenia built, in the land of the east—so says Targ. *Jonathan* in Gen. viii.

So says also Abulfeda *Geogr. Arab.*, p. 69, and El-kaswini, '*Ajaib*, vol. i, p. 156, that remnants of the ark were still to be seen on Mount Djudi, whither people went on pilgrimage, and whence they brought wood of the ark.

20 S. Ephrem (vol. i, p. 54, 150) repeats this, which he rests on Gen. vii, 7, literally taken. But R. Jochanan says that three disobeyed Noah's order in this respect : the dog, the raven, and Ham, all of which were punished. The dog, by the leash ; the raven, by contempt ; and Ham, in his skin. (Talm. Bab. *Sanhedrin*, p. 216.)

21 And when they were come out of the ark, they built themselves a city and called it *Thamanin*, according to their number, for (said they) "we are eight." And the sons of Noah planted a vine, and gave of the wine to their father, etc. (Eutych. *Nazam al-j.*, p. 43.)

22 Νῶε ἐφύτευσεν ἀμπελῶνα ἐν ὄρει Λουβὰν τῆς 'Αρμενίας. (Cedrenus, *Hist. Comp.*, p. 21, A.M. 2251.) [Ararat, the name of a province of Armenia, and the Hebrew name for Armenia— bounded in the south by the Mountains Kardu, on which the ark most probably rested. They form the chain of mountains, north of the Plain of Shinar.] (See Injidjean *Geogr. of Armenia*, in Armenian, vol. i, p. 54.)

23 There are three, says *Midr. Tankhuma*, fol. 12, who, by their connection with the land, made it חולין common [or, unclean] Cain, Noah and Uzziah.

When Noah was planting the vine, Satan stood by him, and asked him what he was doing. "Planting the vine," answered Noah. "What is the good of it?" asked Satan. "The fruit thereof is soft and sweet, whether fresh or dry, and they make of it 'wine, that maketh glad the heart of man' as it is written." "Let me have a hand in it, and let us do it together," said Satan. And by and by, he brought a lamb under the vine and slew it there; likewise a lion, and also a swine. Thereby meaning that a man who was as meek as a lamb, is made furious by wine, or that he who drinks in moderation (as it becometh him) is made strong thereby, and he that drinks too much revels in filth like a swine.

In the third year after coming out of the ark, says S. Ephrem, did Noah sow vine, *men kamshūne daphkoshtō*, with stones of raisins [or, dried grapes] which he had stored up as provisions with him in the ark. It would then take the vine three or four years to bear fruit; so that Noah drank of the wine thereof, probably in the sixth or seventh year after the waters of the Flood were assuaged. (*Ibid.* vol. i, p. 56.)

According to the *Kufale* (c. vii, pp. 29, 30) Noah planted the vine first on Mount Lubar, on which the ark rested, one of the mountains of Ararat. Then Ham, after Noah's curse on him, severed himself from the rest and built a city, called after his wife, Nehelata-mek. Japhet, jealous of him, also built a city, called after his wife, Adatenases; and Shem did the same, and built a city which he called Sedukatelbab, also after his wife. These three cities are all near Mount Lubar, east, west and south. [Noah's city, "Semanan" is "Shamanin," "eight." It is mentioned by Abulfeda *Geogr. Arab.*, p. 69.]

Josephus (*Ant. Jud.*, lib. i, c. iii, p. 5) says, "that the place where the ark rested, and whence Noah descended, is called 'Ἀποβατήριον, and is shown by the inhabitants." And Mich. Tchamich in his *History of Armenia*, vol. i, p. 56, says, that the ark having rested on a mountain of Ararat [a province of Armenia, so called], that is on Mount Masis (τὸ Μάσιον, Strab. *Geogr.*, lib. xii, c. ii), Noah made *ar istchevan* his descent near it; there he settled his sons, and called the name of the city *Nakh-ist-chevan*, the "first descent," or according to others, *Nakh-tchwan*, "first departure," or migration. (See also Idjidjean, *Geogr. of Armenia*, vol. i, p. 54, sq.)

And Epiphan. *Hæres*, lib. i, c. 1, p. 4, speaking of the ark, says, it rested ἐν ὄρεσι τοῖς 'Αραράτ ἀνὰ μέσον 'Αρμενίων καὶ Καρδυέων ἐν τῷ Λουβὰρ ὄρει καλουμίνῳ—and that the settlement was there, πρόσω βαίνοντες ἀπὸ τοῦ Λουβὰρ ὄρους, καὶ ὀρέων τῆς 'Αρμενίας—γίνονται ἐν πεδίῳ Σενναάρ, ἐνθά που ἐπελέξαντο.

'Ηλίβατον τανύμηκες ὄρος, 'Αραράτ δὲ καλεῖται. (*Orac. Sibyll*, p. 152.)

And Berosus (ed. Richter, p. 56, sq.) telling how Xisuthrus having been divinely warned to build himself a ship —length five stadia—breadth two stadia —wherein to escape the Flood, he, his wife, children and all animals, etc., adds that the ship stood fast ἐν τῇ 'Αρμενίᾳ ἔτι μέρος τι (αὐτοῦ) ἐν τοῖς Κορδυαίων ὄρεσι· τῆς 'Αρμενίας διαμένειν—in Armenia, a portion of the ship still remained on the Cordyæan Mountains, whence people brought away some of the asphalte, or bitumen wherewith the ship was lined, etc. See also Josephus (*Ant. Jud.*, lib. i, c. iii, p. 6) who quotes a passage from Nicholas Damascenus, concerning Mount Baris [*i.e.*, βάρις, an ark or boat] in Armenia, whither many fled for safety at the time of the Flood, and where one landed in a ship, the wood of which remained there a long time. Perhaps it is the one mentioned by Moses. (See also Nicolas Dam. *Historiarum fragm.*, etc., ed. Jo. Conradus Orellius, Lips., p. 123.)

"We know," says Cedrenus (*Hist. Comp.*, p. 20), "that Mount Ararat ἐν τῇ Παρθίᾳ τῆς Ἀρμενίας εἶναι, is in the Parthian province of Armenia; some say in Κιλαίναις τῆς Φρυγίας in the Celænæ of Phrygia." [Legend of Apamæa Kibotos.]

24 According to the *Kufale* (c. vii, p. 31), in the twenty-eighth Jubilee, Noah began to give his laws and precepts to his children's children, with right and judgment, and adjured them to practise righteousness, to cover the shame of their bodies, to bless their Creator, to honour their father and mother, to love their neighbour, and to keep themselves from all adultery, defilement, and violence. For it was on account of this that God had overwhelmed the earth with the Flood. [These are the precepts which alone were binding on the proselytes of the Gate, or sojourners, among the Israelites. Maimonides, *Melakim*, c. xiv, vol. iv, p. 300, ed. fol. Amst.]

According to *Avodath haqqodesh* lii, fol. 80 (quoted in Eisenmenger, vol. i, p. 318), albeit the law was created before the world, yet it had so far been forgotten, and was likely to be forgotten still so much more through the wickedness and troubles that were before the Flood, that God decreed to give as few and as short commandments as possible; so as to be easily remembered. Noah had learnt these commandments at school under Seth, and handed them down to his sons.

25 When the death of Noah drew near he called secretly his son Shem and commanded him saying: "Take out of the ark, unknown to any one, the body of Adam; and take with thee bread and wine as provision by the way; then take with thee Melchizedec the son of Phalek, and go and lay the body of Adam where the angel of God shall show you. Then command Melchizedec to settle in that place; not to take him a wife; but to devote himself to the service of God all the days of his life; for God has chosen him to minister before Him. He shall not build for himself a house, neither shall he shed the blood of either beast, bird, or other living thing; neither shall he bring there any other offering to God than bread and wine. His raiment shall be skins of wild beasts [or, of a lion]; he shall not shave his hair, nor pare his nails; but he shall remain alone [or, single] as priest of the Most High. And the angel of God will go with you two (lit. between you two) until ye come to the place where ye shall bury the body of Adam. And know thou that that place is the middle of the earth. (Eutych, *Nasam al-j.*, p. 45.)

26 The *Kufale* makes Noah divide the earth by lot, among his sons. He rejoiced over the lot fallen to Shem, in fulfilment of his blessing on him, because his possession which was to be for ever, reached unto the River Gihon and the Garden of Eden, taking in the most holy places on earth, Mount Zion, Mount Sinai, and the Garden of Eden, where the Lord dwelt. (*Ibid.* c. viii, pp. 36, 73.)

And the three sons of Noah, divided the lot of their inheritance, among their children, in presence of Noah their father, who adjured them with a curse, not to seek another inheritance than that which had fallen by lot to them, and they all said, *laikun walaikun*, So be it, and so be it! (*Ibid.* c. ix, p. 40.)

Soon after wicked spirits, or devils, began to lead astray the children of Noah, that were born in the earth. He then prayed to God, who commanded us, said the Angel of the Face, to bind them for ever. But the Prince of the Spirits, Mastema, stood before the Lord, and prayed that He would leave him some spirits of his race whereby to deceive and harass the children of men. So the Lord granted him one-tenth part of his spirits; and the rest he sent to the place of judgment. Then we taught Noah the use of remedies and the art of healing; and he gave all his writings to his son Shem, whom he loved most. (*Kufale*, c. x, pp. 41, 42.)

But whereas Ham, Cush and Mitsraim, took possession of the land fallen to them by lot, Canaan took with violence possession of the land he coveted, along the sea-shore. His brothers remonstrated with him, and told him he would be accursed for having taken a lot that belonged to Shem and had not fallen to him. But he would not hearken to them; and dwelt in the land from Hamath to Egypt. (*Ibid.* pp. 44, 45.)

Bar. Hebr. *Syr.*, p. 9, attributes this to all the sons of Ham.

27 Noah died nine hundred and fifty years old. According to the reckoning of the LXX, there are two thousand two hundred and forty-two years from the Creation to the Flood; according to the Jews, sixteen hundred and six; and according to the Samaritans, thirteen hundred and seven, which reckoning is entirely wrong; in that it makes Noah to have lived two hundred and twenty-three years with Adam, whereof nothing is said, either by God or by His prophets. According to the reckoning of Abinanus [Anianus?] of Alexandria, however, from the creation of Adam and the night of the Friday on which the Flood began, there were two thousand two hundred and twenty-six years, one month, twenty-three days, and four hours. (Abulpharaj, *Dyn.* Arab., p. 14.)

28 It is commonly reported, says Abulpharaj (*Dyn.* Arab., p. 15), that Noah just before his death gave Shem a commandment saying: "When I am dead, bring the coffin of our father Adam out of the ark, and take with thee of thy children, Melchizedec, for he is priest of the Most High God, and go with him and the coffin to the place, whither the angel of the Lord will lead you." Those two did according to this commandment; and the angel brought them to the hill of Beth-el-Maqdes [or, Muqaddas] and Melchizedec laid the coffin on the hill, and settled there; but Shem went back to his people.

Melchizedec, however, did not go back, but built there the city of Jerusalem, which means the City of Peace (whence himself is also called Melek Salem, that is King of Peace); and he spent the rest of his days in devotion to the service of God; he never drew near a woman; never shed blood; and his offering [qorban] was of bread and wine only. But as Holy Scripture, speaking of his exalted state, mentions neither his birth nor his death, the holy Apostle Paul says of him that he had "neither beginning of days, nor end of life." He was made a type of Christ in David's prophecy. "Thou art a priest for ever, after the order of Melchizedec." On the very same hill on which our father Adam was buried, was Christ also crucified.

Melchizedec is called Lamech, Noah's grandson, by Masudi, who adds that those who believe the Scripture, think Lamech is still living; because God said to Shem that he to whom He should entrust the body of Adam, would live for ever. And Shem, after having laid Adam's body in the centre of the earth, left it in charge of Lamech. (*Masudi* i, ch. iii, pp. 80, 81.)

29 And Phalek begat Melchizedec the priest. Then Shem did according to what Noah had commanded him; he went into the ark by night, and brought out the body of Adam; no one being aware of it. He then called his brothers and said to them: "My father, indeed, did command me before his death, that I go forth until I arrive at the sea, and see how the land lies and the rivers and valleys thereof; then that I return to you. I will, therefore, leave with you my wife and children; and take care of them until my return."

Then Shem said to Phalek: "Give me thy son Melchizedec, to be a help to me on my journey." Then Shem took with him the body of Adam and Melchizedec, and departed. And the angel of God met them, and did not depart from between them until he had led them to the middle of the earth, and showed them the spot. When they alighted the body of Adam upon it, the earth opened itself; Shem and Melchizedec laid the body into the place that had thus opened itself; and it closed itself again. And the name of that is El-jaljala, that is, Cranium (Golgotha). (Eutych. Nasam al-j., p. 49.)

30 On this day—third of Epagumenæ —we commemorate the death of Melchizedec. This Melchizedec was the son of Cainan, son of Shem. And when he was fifteen years old, God commanded Noah to send Shem his son, with the body of our father Adam, and to lay it in the middle of the earth, which is Cranin [Cranium, Golgotha]; and told him how the Saviour of the world should come, be sacrificed there, and redeem Adam with His blood.

Then Shem took Melchizedec from his father's house, and hid (him), and brought him hither, whither the Angel of the Lord brought them; and Melchizedec was consecrated priest, and took twelve stones, and offered on them a sacrifice of bread and wine, that came down to him from heaven in his sight (lit. he seeing), the mystery of a new (covenant) law. Angels also brought him food; and his raiment was of skins with a leathern girdle. And he continued to minister before the body of our father Adam. And when Abraham returned from his victory over the kings, Melchizedec offered him bread and wine; and Abraham also gave him tithe of all. And he was called priest and king of Salem. (Melchizedec, in Dillmann's *Chrestom. Æthiop.*, p. 16.)

31 Our Rabbis of blessed memory, says R. Abarbanel (*Com. in Pent.*, fol. 46) and R. Abendana (in *Leqet Shecha*, fol. 6) are of opinion that Melchizedec is Shem, the son of Noah. He is called, Melchizedec, that is king of Jerusalem, for Jerusalem is Zedec (righteousness), because it makes righteous its inhabitants. *Beresh. Rabbah*, fol. 47, and *Yedei Moshe*, ad l. add that Melchizedec was born already circumcised.

See S. Epiphanius (*Adv. Hær.*, vol. i, p. 468, sq.) for his refutation of the sect of Melchizedechians, who worshipped Melchizedec instead of Christ. S. Epiphanius says he has crushed them ὥσπερ μυογαλλίδιον λίθῳ πεπαικότες, "like a young shrewmouse struck with a stone." (p. 476.)

32 Then Shem gave Melchizedec the commandment he had received from Noah, and said unto him: "Abide here, and be priest of God: for God has chosen thee to minister before Him. And His angel shall come down to thee at all times." Then Shem went back to his brothers; and when Phalek asked him what had become of the youth Melchizedec, Shem answered, that he was dead, and that he had buried him. And they were much grieved at it. (Eutych. *Nasam al-j.*, p. 50.)

34 Arphaxad took to wife Rasuya,

daughter of Susan, daughter of Elam, who bare him a son, Cainan. This Cainan, taught letters by his father, while looking for a place where to build a city [Haran], found an inscription on stone, the work of the Watchers, wherein was recorded the course of heavenly bodies, etc.; but he hid the discovery from Noah. (*Kufale*, c. viii, p. 34.) Abulpharaj (Dyn. *Syn.*, p. 7, 8; *Arab.*, p. 15) remarks that Cainan, who lived four hundred and thirty years, is not reckoned in the Hebrew, Samaritan, and Syriac texts. But he is reckoned [in the LXX, and also] by S. Luke [c. iii]. He is said to have invented astrology; and that his children raised a statue to him, and worshipped him as a god.

That inscription of the Watchers, or children of Seth, and discovered by Cainan, is alluded to by Josephus (*Ant. Jud.*, lib. i, c. ii, p. 3) when he says that: "the children of Seth, like their father, excellent men given to virtue and to the study of the heavenly bodies—and not wishing that their discoveries should perish altogether, with the world that was to be destroyed by fire and water—set up two pillars, one of brick and the other of stone, on which they wrote their astronomical observations. So that if the pillar of brick was destroyed by the waters, the one of stone should remain. And it subsists to this day κατὰ γῆν τὴν Σιριάδα, somewhere in the Sirian land.

35 Χώρῃ ἐν Ἀσσυρίῃ, ὁμόφωνοι
δ'ἦσαν ἅπαντες,
Καὶ βούλοντ' ἀναβῆν' εἰς οὐρανὸν
ἀστερόεντα,
— αὐτὰρ ἔπειτ' ἄνεμοι μέγαν ὑψόθι
πύργον
Ῥίψαν, καὶ θνητοῖσιν ἐπ' ἀλλήλοις
ἔριν ὦρσαν,
Αὐτὰρ ἐπεὶ πύργος τ'ἔπεσε, γλῶσσαί
τ'ἀνθρώπων
Παντοδαπαῖς φωναῖσι διέστρεφον·

(*Orac. Sibyll.*, p. 336, quoted in Joseph) *Ant. Jud.*, lib. i, c. iv, p. 3.)

36 After they had worked at it forty years, God sent a strong wind, that threw down the tower. (Bar. Hebr. *Syr.*, p. 9; and *Arab.*, p. 18.) The languages were then seventy-two and one—ὅθεν καὶ Μέροπες οὗτοι κέκληνται, διὰ τὴν μεμερισμένην φωνήν. καὶ τὸν πύργον ἀνέμων βολὴ κατέστρεψεν. (S. Epiph. *Hæres.*, lib. i, c. i, p. 5.)

37 S. Basil and Mar Ephrem say that the original tongue was Syriac; but S. James and John of Medin say it was Hebrew, spoken by Eber, who would not consent to the building of the tower of Babel; whose tongue, therefore, was not altered (Abulpharaj, *Syr.*, p. 9; *Arab.*. pp. 16, 18; Cedren. *Hist. Comp.*, p. 22), who thinks it is a proof that Hebrew was the primitive tongue spoken by Adam.

In those days the language and speech of men were one and the same. Some say it was the Syriac tongue; others say it was the Hebrew; others again say, that the tongue was Greek; and this approves itself to me. For the Greek language is wiser, clearer and broader than either the Hebrew or the Syriac.

Then seventy-two men from among the people gathered together and said: "Let us build a city, and fortify it with a wall; and let us build a tower that shall reach unto heaven; that if a flood betake us hereafter we may be saved from it." They were three years making bricks, every one of which was thirteen yards long, ten yards broad, and five yards thick, etc., and they were forty years building the city. Then an angel came down, and confounded their languages, so that one could not understand another; and the name of that city was called Babel, because the languages were confused there, and the people were dispersed. Of these seventy-two men, twenty-five were of the children of Shem, thirty-two of those of Ham, and fifteen of the children of Japhet. Every one of these spake a different tongue, that spread over the face of the earth with their families. (Eutych. *Nasam al-j.*, pp. 53, 54.)

38 Bar Hebræus relates a similar legend, and says that Nimrud's royal crown was made of woven material [*zaqiro*—filagree?] (*Dyn.* Syr., p. 9), but the Arabic copy adds that—some said the crown had been let down from heaven. (p. 18).

In the days of Ragu the queen of Saba reigned many years. She built the city of Saba; and after her queens reigned over that country until the days of Solomon son of David.

In those days also reigned Karon, and they say that he melted gold, and built the city of Ukinin with bricks made of gold. (Eutych. *Nasam al-j*, p. 61.)

39 In the beginning of the thirty-fifth Jubilee, Ragu took Ara, the daughter of Kesed's son, who bare him Serug, so called [שׂרג] because in his day men increased greatly in wickedness fought one against another, took captives, made idols and defiled the earth with blood, etc. Ur, the son of Kesed, built a city which he called Ara, where he set up the worship of the host of heaven and idols, and taught men to worship them. Then did prince Mastema exert himself to further all manner of idolatry and wickedness among men. Serug dwelt in Ur of the Chaldees, where his wife Melka brought forth Nahor, who in time took Iyosaka daughter of Kheber the Chaldee, to wife, who bare him Terah, Abraham's father. (*Kufale*, c. xi, pp. 45, 46.)

Abulpharaj (*Syn.*, p. 10; and *Arab.*, p. 18, 19) relates that Serug invented the coining of money; and that the art of spinning silk and of dyeing, was introduced in his day, by Samirus, king of Babylon.

In the days of Serug idolatry began. καὶ ὁ 'Ελληνισμὸς and Gentile worship and superstitions. For not until then, were there statues carved in wood, stone, gold or silver; before that man's imagination represented wickedness only in colours. Serug begat Nahor, and Nahor Terah, who was the first to make idols of clay; and for his sin—in thus setting himself as rival against God ἔξοτι ἀντίζηλον τῷ Θεῷ προϊστήσατο, διὰ τῆς ἰδίας πηλουργίας τεχνήσαμενος, by his making idols of clay, he was punished by seeing the death of his son. (S. Epiphan. *Hæres.*, lib. i, c. i, p. 6.) Masudi (vol. i, p. 82, sq.) repeats the same thing, partly borrowed from the *Coran*, sur. c. vi, p. 75, sq. etc.; c. xix, p. 38, sq.

Arad the Canaanite, says Abulpharaj (*Dyn.* Syr., p. 10), affirms that at this time the conflict of Job with Satan took place. He fought him seven times, and defeated him in every temptation.

And the Coptic calendar says that on the first day of the year, Job took a warm bath, that cured him of his leprosy.

40 In those days giants multiplied in the earth. Then was 'Ad born, son of Aram, son of Shem, son of Noah, in whose time measures and weights were invented. In his days there was also a great and violent earthquake, such as there had never been before; and this was, because the worship of idols had increased, and men sacrificed their sons and their daughters to devils; therefore did God send upon them a tempestuous wind, and a hurricane that broke down all the idols, and demolished their shrines; until the dust of them became heaps and mounds that subsist unto this day. (Eutych. *Nasam al-j.*, p. 61.)

41 After the Flood, in the days of Eber and Phaleg, when the first city and the tower were built, Nembroth

[Nimrud] was the first to gather people together and to exercise dominion over them. Νεμβρὼθ γὰρ βασιλεύει—ὃς πρόσω χωρήσας ἐπὶ τὰ ἀνατολικὰ μέρη, διειστὴς γίνεται Βάκτρων, ἐντεῦθεν τὰ κατὰ τὴν γῆν παράνομα διανενέμηται. (S. Epiphan. Hæres., lib. i, c. i, p. 6.)

NOTES TO BOOK IV.

1 " Things," says R. Maimonides, "went on from bad to worse, and the knowledge of God continued only among a few, such as Shem, Methuselah, Enoch, Noah and Eber, until the pillar of the world, our father Abraham, was born. No sooner was that valiant one weaned, than he began to wonder, or doubt, in his own mind, and small as he was, he began to think day and night, how it could be הגלגל הזה נוהג תמיד ולא יהיה לו מנהיג that this round world could go on so continually without a Ruler; or who makes it go round, since it could not go round of itself. And so he went on doubting, until he came to the knowledge of the only true God, at forty-eight years of age," etc. (Halakot 'avoda kok., Opp. vol. i, fol. p. 26.)

2 Astrologers [men of the stars] observed the rising of the year in which Abraham was born ; and they sent word to Nimrud that a child should be born who would set at naught their dreams and overturn their worship. Then Nimrud ordered all children to be put to death. But Abraham was hidden in a cave [shown as his birth-place at Ur, or Urfah]. (Masudí i, c. iii, p. 83.)

3 " It is well known," says R. M. Maimonides, "that our father Abraham, on whom be peace, was brought up in the faith of the Sabæans, and ודעתם

שאין אלוה רק הכוכבים in their teaching [or, knowledge, doctrine] that there was no other God than the stars. When Abraham objected to this, and opposed their worship, we read in העבודה הנבטיה the Book of the Agriculture of the Nabathæans, that the king of the place where Abraham lived, shut him up in prison ; but fearing lest his people should be turned from their faith, he confiscated all his property and banished him לקצה המזרח to the extreme east. (More Nevukim, iii, c. 29.)

In those days prince Mastema [Satan] sent ravens in great numbers, that devoured the seed sown, and the crops that were raised ; so that men gathered in the fruits of the earth with great difficulty. And about that time Terah took Edna, daughter of Abram, to wife, who bare him a son whom he called Abram, after his wife's father. This Abram, when fourteen years old, began to pray his Creator to save him from the wickedness around him, and to give him an inheritance with the righteous. Then came sowing time ; and Abram went with others to watch the fields sown with seed. A flight of ravens then came down, and when about to alight, Abram ran, and bade them go back to whence they came. He did so seven times that day. And all people came to entreat him to go with them when they sowed their seed, to keep off the ravens. He then contrived a plough whereby the seed fell into the earth and got covered at once; so that they no longer were afraid of the ravens. And Abram's name waxed great in Chaldæa. (*Kufale*, c. xi, pp. 47, 48.) This legend is variously told by eastern writers. Bar. Hebræus (*Chron. Syr.* Arab., p. 11) simply says Abram drove away ravens, when fourteen years old; but (in his *Hist. Dyn.* Arab., p. 19, 20) he adds, "God heard Abram's prayers when fifteen years old, about magpies that laid waste the land of Chaldæa. S. Ephrem (vol. i, p. 156) says, "that Abram when a child, having been sent by Terah to drive away ravens [wrongly rendered 'locusts' by the translator] sent to destroy the crops, as a punishment for the idolatry of the land, Abram—unable to drive them away—by a sudden impulse called upon God to order them off, who answered : 'Here am I,' and ordered the ravens away from Terah's field." [For the story of Abraham being cast into a burning furnace by the inhabitants of Ur, see *Coran*, sur. xxi; and *Kufale*, c. xii.]

Targ. *Jonathan*, in Gen. xii, says : "Abram was cast into the fiery furnace by order of Nimrud; because he would not worship the idol Nimrud had set up," etc.

4 Terah was a worshipper of idols. But Abraham turned him from them, and talked to him, and taught him Hebrew, his native tongue [lit. of his creation]; and showed him how God had commanded him to go out of Haran unto the land of Canaan, to look at it, and come back. To which Terah said : "Go in peace, God of the worlds prosper thy way, and the Lord keep thee safe from all evil, and show thee kindness and mercy, and give thee favour in the eyes of all those who see thee ; that no man do thee harm. Go in peace. And if thou seest the land is pleasant in thine eyes, to dwell there, then come and take me to be with thee. Take with thee Lot, the son of Haran thy brother, to be a son unto thee. But leave thy brother Nahor with me, until thy return in peace ; when all of us shall go together with thee." (*Kufale*, c. xii, pp. 51, 52.)

5 "In those days appeared Melchizedec, παρθένος ἱερεύς, an unmarried priest, son of king Sidus, son of Egyptus, who founded the town of Sidon. He is said to be without father and mother, and without kindred, διὰ τὸ μὴ ἐξ Ἰουδαϊκῆς γενεᾶς κατάγεσθαι, from his not being of the Jewish race, and because his parents being wicked, they were not reckoned among the good, and because being ruler or prince among the Canaanites, he reigned at Jerusalem. He met Abraham, and as priest, ἐν ἄρτῳ καὶ οἴνῳ προτυπῶν τὴν ἀναίμακτον θυσίαν Χριστοῦ τοῦ Θεοῦ ἡμῶν figuring with bread and wine, the bloodless sacrifice of Christ our God." (Cedrenus, *Hist. Comp.*, p. 49.)

Melchizedec, king of Jerusalem, and king of righteousness, מלך צדק he is Shem, Noah's son, priest of the Most High. (Targ. *Jonathan* and *Hieros*, in Gen. xiv.)

6 When Abraham came to Egypt, he shut up Sarah in a box. But at the custom-house the officers asked him to pay duty on his luggage. "What is it, wares ?" asked they. "I will pay duty on them," answered Abraham. "Is it gold ?" "Also on gold," said he. "Is it pearls, then ?" "I will pay duty also on pearls," answered Abraham. "This will never do," said the officers, "Open thy trunk !" As Abraham opened it the whole land of Egypt was חבהיקת מזיוה lighted up with Sarah's brilliancy. (*Bereshith Rabbah*, sect. xl, fol. 44.)

7 About the rising of the moon [new moon] of the fourth month, "We," says the Angel of the Face, "appeared unto Abraham, by the oak of Mamrim, and we conversed with him, and gave him to understand that a son would be given him of Sarah his wife. But Sarah laughed, when she heard us say these words to Abraham ; and we rebuked her ; but she was afraid and lied about having laughed at these [our] words." (*Kufale*, c. xvi, pp. 61, 62.)

About this time as our father Abraham sat at the door of his tent, three ministering angels were sent to him, on three errands : (1) to tell him of the birth of his son ; (2) to deliver Lot ; (3) to destroy Sodom and Gomorrah ; for it cannot be that a ministering angel be sent with ליתיר מן מילא חד more than one message at a time. (Targ. *Jonathan* and *Hieros*, in Gen. xvii.)

8 Isaac was thirty-seven years old, born when Sarah was ninety years of age. Hearing of God's order to Abraham to sacrifice Isaac, she sickened, from grief, and died of that sickness that same year, aged one hundred and twenty-seven. (Eutych. *Nazam al j.*, p. 77.)

For the conversation that took place between Abraham and Isaac on this occasion, *see* S. Eustathius Antioch. in *Hexaëmeron*, col. 764, éd. M.

9 And it happened about this time that words were spoken in heaven about Abraham, how faithful he was in all that the Lord told him, and how true in all temptations. Then prince Mastema came forward and said to God : "Behold, Abraham loves his son Isaac best of all, tell him to offer him in sacrifice upon an altar ; then shalt thou see if he will do it, and be true and faithful in all that Thou commandest him." Then follows the Scripture account, as far as "Abraham took a knife," etc., when I, the Angel of the Face, stood before God and Prince Mastema. And God said to me : " Go and tell him not to lay his hand on the child, and not to hurt him ; for I know now that he fears God," etc. Then Mastema felt ashamed of himself. (*Kufale*, c. xvii, xviii, pp. 67, 68, 69.)

Cedrenus (*Hist. Comp.*, p. 53) repeats this legend, but calls Mastema, Μαστιφάτ borrowed probably from the Greek original of the Ethiopic Kufale.

"It is well known," says R. M. Maimonides, "that the worshippers of idols always chose high places and mountains whereon to build their temples. Therefore did Abraham choose Mount Moriah, on which פרסם שם ביחוד ה״ he proclaimed the unity of God, as being one of the highest hills in that neighbourhood. But he consecrated the western side of it for the sanctuary ; so as to turn his back on the idolaters who always turn to the east, in worshipping the morning sun." (*More Nevukim*, sect. iii, ch. 45.)

10 After Abraham had done blessing all his children and grandchildren, he and Jacob, lay together on the same bed. Then Abraham in his anxiety [or care] embraced Jacob seven times, and rejoiced over him, and added yet more to all the blessings he had given him. He then lay two of Jacob's fingers on his own eyes ; he blessed the God of gods, covered his face, stretched his legs, and died. And when Jacob awoke from sleep, he knew not that Abraham was dead, but called to him : "Father, father !" But when he felt him cold, he ran and told Rebekah, his mother, who told Isaac ; and they both came with a light, and found Abraham laid out. Then they buried him, in the double-cave [Machpelah], and mourned over him forty days. (*Kufale*, c. xxii, xxiii, pp. 82, 83.)

Abraham lived upwards of three Jubilees and a half, because he was righteous; for after the Flood man's life was cut short. And from Abraham forth, it will be said that, whereas the patriarchs lived eighteen or nineteen Jubilees, and had peace, now men only live seventy or eighty years and all is trouble, because of the wickedness of the world, that will grow worse and worse. Men will be covetous, eager for wealth, in order to get themselves a name thereby; and defile the Most Holy with their evil deeds. They shall do evil—the young with the old, the old with the young; the poor with the rich, and rich with the poor; the mean with the judge, by reason of the law and judgment; because they shall have forgotten the commandments of God and right, feasts, moons, Sabbaths, jubilees, and all manner of judgment. (*Kufale*, c. xxiii, pp. 84, 85.)

11 Eutychus says Hiram was the first to clothe himself in purple, that was discovered thus: There was a shepherd with his dog one day tending his sheep on the sea-shore. The dog found a purple shell creeping on the shore and having eaten it, the shepherd wiped with some wool the dog's mouth that was full of purple colour. With the wool thus dyed the shepherd made himself a fillet or crown which he placed on his head. Every one who saw him walking in the sun thus arrayed, thought that a ray of light shone forth from his head. Hiram heard of it, sent for the shepherd, wondered at the beauty of the colour, and ordered his dyers of stuffs to dye a cloak for him of the same colour. (*Nasam al-j.*, pp. 173, 174.)

12 As with Abraham, so with Solomon there exists a whole literature about his wisdom and marvellous deeds, celebrated from his throne (Takht-i-Suleyman) on the Suleyman range of the Hindoo Koosh, to his dialogue with Saturn in the far north. The *Suleyman Nameh*, of which extracts are given by Baron Hammer-Purgstall, in *Rosen-öl*, vol. i, is said to consist of sixty volumes; but the stories of him in the Targum of Jerusalem on Esther, and in the Talmud (Gittin 68; see Fürst *Perlenschüre*, p. 121) are a thousand years older; so also the accounts of the Wise King found in Eusebius (*Præp. Ev.*), Josephus, the Coran, etc. For his psalms, see Fabric. *Cod. Apoc. V. T.*, vol. i, and Woide's Sahidic New T. pref. for the same in Sahidic.

"In the opinion of many Syrian authors," says Abr. Echellensis (*Catal. Lib. Hebed Jesu*, p. 238, sq.), "Solomon not only translated into Syriac the greater part of the Old Testament—the Pentateuch, Joshua, Judges, Ruth, Samuel, David, Proverbs, Ecclesiastes, Song of Songs, and Job—at Hiram's especial request, but he also invented the characters, according to Jesudad, who says that, 'Whereas Moses invented the Hebrew letters, Solomon invented all others, which he gave to the peoples by which he was honoured; but he first of all invented the Syriac letters which he gave to Hiram, king of Tyre.'"

13 After the death of Hezekiah, Manasseh forgot his father's commandments; and Samaël took possession of Manasseh, and clung to him. Then Manasseh forsook God, served Satan, his angels and his powers, and turned his heart to the worship of Berial [Belial]. Then all manner of wickedness, magic and sorcery increased in Jerusalem; Isaiah seeing this removed from Jerusalem, went and dwelt at Bethlehem. But as Bethlehem was equally corrupt, he and Michaiah, Joel, and Habakkuk and his son Josheb, and others who believed that the righteous would go up to heaven—resided on a hill, clothed in skins and living on roots and herbs of the mountains.

Then Isaiah had a vision of the

coming of the Beloved, for which Berial was angry with him, and took possession of the heart of Manasseh who sawed Isaiah with a saw to cut wood.

While he was being thus cut asunder, Belkira, Bankembeki and Berial stood opposite, deriding him. Manasseh also and Melkira and his false prophets, stood by looking on. But Isaiah while being thus sawn asunder neither cried nor wept; but his mouth conversed with the Holy Ghost.

Thus did Manasseh according to the will of Satan. (*Ascension of Isaiah*, c. 2-5.)

14 The Ethiopic translator omitted the story told in the Arabic original—that, when Isaiah was about to be sawn asunder, he wanted water to drink and prayed God to give him some, as He had done to Moses, when smiting the rock. Then God told him to stamp the rock under him with his foot, whence a spring of water at once burst forth, that has continued unto this day.

15 As for Jeremiah the prophet, they found him hidden and covered with mud in a land of waters (marsh). (Euseb. *De Stella*, p. 2, ed. W. Wright.) Jeremiah having fled into Egypt, was there stoned to death, and buried. But Alexander when he came into Egypt, brought the body of Jeremiah to Alexandria, and buried it there. (Eutych. *Nasam al-j.*, p. 252.)

16 Eutychus reckons thus:—

From the end of Cleopatra's reign to the birth of Christ	30 yrs.
From Alexander's reign	319 „
From the removal to Babylon	582 „
From David's reign	1059 „
From the Exodus	1665 „
From Abraham	2172 „
From Phaleg	2713 „
From the Flood	3244 „
From Adam	5500 „

17 In the year 309 of Alexander, the Lord Christ was born of the Virgin Mary, when Cyrenius was sent by Cæsar to Jerusalem. Joseph went up with Mary to Bethlehem to inscribe their names. Mary brought forth. And Magi in their journeyings came and offered unto Christ gold, incense and myrrh, who on their first interview with Herod, when asked by him their errand, said to him: "There was a great man among us who prophesied in a book he wrote, that in Palestine should be born a child of heavenly race, whom the greater part of the world would serve. And the sign thereof unto you will be a star that will guide you to the place where the child is; and when ye see it ye shall offer to Him gold, incense and myrrh. We saw the star and we are come to worship Him," etc. (Abulpharaj, *Dyn.* Arab., pp. 109, 110.)

This supposed prophecy is again mentioned by Abulpharaj (*id.*, p. 83). When speaking of Cyrus he says: "In those days came Zeradasht, chief of the Magian sect, by birth of Adjerbijan, or, as some say, of Assyria. It is reported that he was one of the prophet Elijah's disciples [as Confucius was of Daniel (?)], and he informed the Persians of the sign of the birth of Christ, and that they should bring Him gifts. And he told them that in after-time a virgin should be with child without having known man; and that about the time of her bringing forth a star brilliant by day would appear, in the midst of which would be seen the figure of a young virgin. You, then, my children, will be favoured before all other people with the Light of that Star; and when ye see it, go whither it leads you; worship the child, and offer Him gold, incense and myrrh."

It is needless to say that no such prophecy of Zeradasht or Zoroaster does exist. Neither does Abulpharaj allude to it in his Syriac work, which in many respects differs from the same in Arabic; done by him shortly before his death for his Arab friends at Mabug, some considerable time after his first work in Syriac.

The number of Magi—or, as some say, of kings with their armies—is variously stated. Eutychus (*Nasam al-j.*, p. 310) says that only three Magi came, who told Herod the star had appeared to them two years before their arrival at Jerusalem. τὸν ἀστέρα, ἐπιτίλλοντα ἤδη πρὸ δύο μάλιστα τῶν ἐνιαυτῶν, καὶ οὐχὶ μετὰ δύο τῆς γεννήσεως ἔτη, says Nicephorus Callixtus (*Eccles. Hist.*, lib. i., c. 13), who with Origen, S. Basil, S. Chrysostom, etc., refers the star to Balaam's prophecy. Nay, Eusebius probably wrote the small treatise on the star attributed to him, which exists only in Syriac, in order to show that Balaam's prophecy travelled eastward from Moab, and was handed down by Persian kings until the days of Augustus Cæsar; when the star did actually appear. Then were the king and the people greatly troubled at the light of the star that outshone all other celestial bodies by day as well as by night. The king therefore prepared offerings of myrrh and of incense, which he sent by Magi, worshippers of fire. But as the king did not know where Christ was born, he commanded those who carried the gifts, saying: "Follow the leading of the star as you go, by day and by night keep to the light of the star; for the brilliancy thereof will guide you even when the sun is risen." Then they went to Bethlehem, and returned and told the king what they had seen and heard, etc. (Pp. 16, 17, fol. 12 of MS., ed. W. Wright.)

Et factum est, cum natus esset Dominus Jesus Bethlehemi, ecce! Magi venerunt ex Oriente Hierosolymas quemadmodum prædixerat Zoradascht, erantque cum ipsis munera, aurum, thus et myrrha, et adoraverunt eum, suaque ipsi munera obtulerunt. Eadem hora apparuit illis angelus in forma stellæ [οὐκ ἦν οὗτος φύσει ἀστήρ, ἀλλ' ὄψει μόνον ἀστήρ, καὶ ὡς ἀληθῶς θεία τις δύναμις, S. Chrys. et Euthym., ad. loc.] illius, quæ antea dux itineris ipsis fuerat.

Aderant autem Reges and Principes illorum rogantes, ecquidnam vidissent aut egissent? Quomodo ivissent ac redivissent? Quos tandem itineris comites habuissent? Hi vero protulerunt illis fasciam istam, quam Diva Maria ipsis tradiderat, etc. (*Evangel. Infantiæ*, c. vii, viii, ed. Fabr.)

M. Tchamitch, in his *Badmuthyün Hayots* ("History of Armenia"), vol. i, p. 277, relates also that "the wonderful birth of Christ was made known by means of a star, *orits makuts thakavorats*, to three Magi-kings, who came to Judæa to find Him and to worship Him." (See note from the "History of Georgia," at Book I, ch. xx.)

"What sign then did you see," asked Herod of the wise men, "to tell you a king was born." They said unto him: "We saw a very large star, shining among the celestial bodies, and outshining them all, and we thus knew that a great king was born in Israel, and we came to worship Him." (*Proto-ev. Jacobi*, c. xxi.)

Fabricius thus quotes from his own edition of Chalcidius, p. 219, *ad Timæum* "Est quoque alia sanctior et venerabilior historia, quæ perhibet ortu stellæ cujusdam non morbos mortesque denunciatas, sed descensum Dei venerabilis ad humanæ conservationis verumque mortalium gratiam. Quam stellam cum nocturno itinere suspexissent Chaldæorum profecto sapientes viri—quæsisse dicuntur recentem ortum Dei, repertaque illa majestate puerili, veneratos esse," etc. (*Cod. Ap. N.T.*, vol. ii, p. 116.)

Solomon, Bp. of Botsra (or Bassora), says in his *Deburitho* (or Bee, as quoted by Assem. *Bibl. Or.*, vol. iii, p. 316), that the Magi were twelve Persian princes, whose names he gives at length. These occur also, with few changes, in other MSS., both Syriac and Arabic. Bar. Hebræus, or Abulpharaj, in his *Ozar rosé*, or "Store house of secrets," says that the Magi were only three princes who came with a thousand men (sent by Mahir-Shapur, king of Persia, to worship Christ). But James, the Bishop, says they were twelve princes, who having left seven thousand of their men at the Euphrates, came to Jerusalem with only one thousand. The Bp. of Botsra, however, does not quote the tradition received by other historians, that the presents brought by the Magi to Christ were those which Adam had laid up in the Cave of Treasures; which he made over to his son Seth, and which had been handed down unto the coming of Christ.

Of those twelve princes, four, namely, Zarvandad, Hormisdas, Guznasaph, and Arsaces brought gold; four, Zarvandad son of Varzud, Orthoes, Artaxerxes, and Estunabudanes brought myrrh; and four, Maruch, Assuerus, Sardalach and Merodach brought incense; according to the Bp. of Botsra.

INDEX.

		PAGE
Abel, his birth	. . .	93
,, his sacrifice	. . . . .	97—40
,, his death	. . . .	100
,, his burial	. . . .	101
Abraham, his call	. . . . .	179
,, meets Melchizedec	. . .	180
,, goes into Egypt	. . . .	181
,, sacrifices Isaac	. . . .	182
,, dies and is buried	. . . .	184
Aklemia, Abel's twin sister	. . . .	93
Adam and Eve in the Cave of Treasures	. . .	2
,, ,, receive the promise of a Saviour, after 5500 days	.	2, 3, 9
,, ,, meet the Serpent	. . . .	19
,, ,, their first offering	. . . .	23
,, ,, first apparition of Satan to them	. . .	27
,, ,, second apparition of Satan to them	. .	29
,, ,, third apparition of Satan to them	. . .	35
,, ,, fourth apparition of Satan to them	. .	45
,, ,, fifth apparition of Satan to them	. .	55
,, ,, sixth apparition of Satan to them	. . .	58
,, ,, seventh apparition of Satan to them	. . .	64
,, ,, eighth apparition of Satan to them	. .	66
,, ,, ninth apparition of Satan to them	. . .	67
,, ,, tenth apparition of Satan to them	. . .	72
,, ,, eleventh apparition of Satan to them	. . .	78
,, ,, twelfth apparition of Satan to them	. .	83
,, ,, thirteenth apparition of Satan to them	. . .	84
,, ,, fourteenth apparition of Satan to them	. .	87
,, ,, fifteenth apparition of Satan to them	. . .	106

INDEX.

	PAGE
Adam weds Eve	90
„ his advice to Cain and Abel	94
„ his last words to Seth	114
„ his death	116
Babel	173
Babylon; captivity there	199
Cain, his birth	92
„ is tempted of Satan	95
„ kills his brother Abel	101
„ marries his twin sister Luluwa	104
„ is killed by Lamech	122
Cainan	119
Christ, His birth at Bethlehem	203
Cyrus	197
Daniel, his birth	199
Enoch	137—141
Enos	113—123
Eve, her death	118
Ezra	198
Genealogies	199—201
Genun, his doings	133—138
Jared; increase of idolatry	124—140
Jeremiah dies in Egypt	197
Isaiah is sawn asunder	194
Lamech the blind	121
„ Noah's father	138—145
Luluwa, Cain's twin sister	92
Magi-kings, worship Christ	204—206
Mahalaleel	113
Melchizedec	149—172
Methuselah	138—150
Nimrud	173—178
Noah and the Ark	138—163
Phaleg, Ragu, Serug, &c.	172
Seth and his children on the Holy Mountain	105—121
Shem, Ham, and Japhet	145—163
„ goes with Melchizedec to the middle of the earth	164—172
The star and the Magi	204

www.ingramcontent.com/pod-product-compliance
Lightning Source LLC
Chambersburg PA
CBHW032141230426
43672CB00011B/2407